D1171097

COLERIDGE
among the Lakes & Mountains

Samuel Taylor Coleridge in 1795

COLERIDGE
among the Lakes & Mountains

From his Notebooks, Letters and Poems 1794–1804

Selected and edited by
ROGER HUDSON

The Folio Society   London   1991

© The Folio Society Ltd 1991

Material from the Notebooks is reprinted from *The Notebooks of Samuel Taylor Coleridge*, edited by Kathleen Coburn, Bollingen Series L, Vol. 1: 1794–1804, copyright © 1957 renewed 1985, by permission of Mrs A.H.B. Coleridge, Routledge and Princeton University Press.

The letter to Sara Hutchinson, 25 August 1802, and the extracts from letters to Francis Wrangham, 19 December 1800, and to Thomas Poole, 24 March 1801, are reprinted from *Collected Letters of Samuel Taylor Coleridge*, edited by E.L. Griggs, 1956–1971 by permission of Oxford University Press.

The maps were drawn by Denys Baker.

The painting reproduced on the binding is *Lake Windermere* by Francis Nicholson, c.1805 (Whitworth Art Gallery, University of Manchester).

Set in Baskerville and printed in England
by Jolly & Barber Ltd, Rugby,
on Fineblade Smooth Cartridge.
Bound at The Bath Press, Avon,
in full printed cloth.

Typography by Malcolm Harvey Young

Contents

Illustrations

Introduction

If asked that analyst's question, 'What do you think of when I say the word "Coleridge"?' most of us would reply '"Kubla Khan", *The Ancient Mariner*, *Christabel*.' We might add something uncomplimentary about opium addiction leading to a descent into plagiarism, and something imprecise about his role as transmitter of the best of German thought and literature, or about him as a philosopher and theologian in his own right.

The object of this book is to show Coleridge in yet another light, as one of the most alert, attuned and sensitive recorders of nature, landscape, and the elements. It is nature in a constant state of change, transition, movement and flux that particularly fascinates him: 'The sudden charm which accidents of light and shade, which moonlight or sunset diffused over a known and familiar landscape', as he puts it in a famous passage from the *Biographia Literaria* (1817). He is a connoisseur of water – reflections in it, the flicker of light on the surface of tarns and lakes, the motion of waterfalls, the squalls of rain and banks of mist on mountains, particularly in his beloved Lake Country. These are the attributes of the western fringe of Britain, familiar, some perhaps all too familiar, to anyone who has holidayed in the Highlands, Cumbria, Wales or the West Country. Like his contemporary, the painter J. M. W. Turner, Coleridge was trying to get down on paper, on a flat surface, that quintessential British concern, the weather. They were both bent on transforming a mere topic of conversation into art.

Coleridge constantly rails against his limited repertoire for tackling the job compared with a painter's: 'the Head of Glen Nevis, how simple for a painter, and in how many words and how laboriously, in what dim similitudes and slow and dragging circumlocutions must I give it' (September 1803). But he protests too much. He may say he is maddened 'that I am not a painter or that painters are not I', but he goes on to describe 'the chapped bark' of a birch tree near Loch Ness as 'like a rhinoceros rolled in mud and exposed to the tropic heat'. In addition to the humour, or the 'brooks in their anger' and the 'dark, misty, thunder-murmured scenes', there are moments in his Notebooks when his evocations of a particular view achieve a visionary quality. Then it is less Turner's paintings that come to mind than the clouds and cornfields of the young Samuel Palmer, from his Shoreham period of the late 1820s. In 1811 Coleridge wrote, 'Sometimes when I earnestly look at a beautiful object or landscape, it seems as if I were on the *brink* of a fruition still denied – as if a vision were an appetite. . .' One feels that, ten years earlier in the Notebooks, the full fruition was, in fact, often achieved.

To what degree were Coleridge and Wordsworth pioneering in their devotion to landscape and nature in its wilder manifestations? The move away from the picturesque idealizations of the Age of Reason, from viewing things through a Claude Glass or what Coleridge derided as 'the fixed immoveable telescope of Mr Locke's human understanding', had begun early in the century. Thomas Gray and Horace Walpole were able to frighten themselves agreeably when they were crossing the Alps in 1739. Thirty years later Gray was an early visitor to the Lake District and published the journal of his tour. Boswell and Johnson penetrated the Scottish Highlands, and the Derbyshire Peak District became a regular resort of those in search of a frisson from the Sublime. By the time Coleridge came to live in what he called 'the very pith and marrow of the Lakes' at Keswick in 1800, he said that for a third of the year that town 'swarms with tourists of all shapes, sizes and characters. It is the very place I would recommend to a novelist or farce writer.' Where he and Wordsworth differed from the crowd was in choosing to live in the Lakes permanently (though in Wordsworth's case it was a return to the area where he was born and brought up); in walking in preference to going by carriage (in Coleridge's case he also preferred to walk by himself); and in not being content simply to view the mountains, but actually climbing up them – this at a time when there were no large-scale maps worthy of the name. Coleridge was probably the first person to climb Scafell for pleasure or to rhapsodize over the precipices of Helvellyn.

Both Coleridge and Wordsworth, however, had something more fundamental that distinguished them from the ordinary tourist, and that was their high and holy seriousness in relation to their surroundings. Coleridge put it movingly in two letters. The first he wrote in 1797 to John Thelwall before he had even seen the Lakes.

'I can contemplate nothing but *parts*, and parts are all little! My mind feels as if it ached to behold and know something *great*, something *one* and *indivisible*. And it is only in the faith of that, that rocks or waterfalls, mountains or caverns, give me the sense of sublimity or majesty!'

The second he wrote to William Sotheby in 1802.

'Nature has her proper interest, and he will know what it is, who believes and feels that every thing has a life of its own, and that we are all *one life*. A poet's heart and intellect should be combined, intimately combined and unified, with the great appearances in Nature, and not merely held in solution and loose mixture with them, in the shape of formal similies.'

It is the freshness and immediacy of his writings brought together in this book, the total lack of 'formal similies', that gives such delight.

If the reader wants the bare outline of Coleridge's life before and during 1794 to 1804, I have given it in a series of linking passages within the main text. Here it is enough to say that the book begins with his undergraduate jaunt to Wales, before covering his early married life at Clevedon and Nether Stowey in Somerset from October 1795 to September 1798. Then comes an interlude in Germany, the highlight of which is his walking tour in the Hartz Mountains in May 1799. In October and November 1799 he makes his first trip to the Lakes with Wordsworth. He and his family move to Greta Hall at Keswick in July 1800 where he remains until he takes off for London from November 1801 to March 1802. There are gaps in the extracts in early 1801, the result of illness and opium, and more during the London sojourn (see pp. 78 and 120). In August 1802 he performs his famous Scafell excursion, before going to Wales with his patron and friend Tom Wedgwood in November. He returns to Keswick on Christmas Eve, but is off again with Wedgwood from late January to April 1803, occasioning another large gap. In August he goes to Scotland, accompanied by William and Dorothy Wordsworth, and is back at Greta Hall in mid-September for a last spell until mid-December, when he visits the Wordsworths at Grasmere before setting out abroad.

The German interlude and the Scafell excursion are covered by letters that he wrote, the former by ones to his wife and to Thomas Poole, the latter by ones to Sara Hutchinson, who had replaced Sara Coleridge in his affections (see pp. 56 and 120). There are many other letters throughout the book, as well as a few extracts from his *Biographia Literaria*, his *Table Talk* (published posthumously in 1835), and from his poems, where they are directly descriptive of scenery. But the bulk of the material is drawn from the extraordinary Notebooks which Coleridge kept for most of his life. Sixty of them survive and their content ranges from the odd laundry list, through symptoms of his ill-health, self-analysis, recordings of dreams, reports of his reading, plans for his writing, resolutions to reform his life, and much serious philosophical and theological speculation. Richard Holmes, in his biography *Coleridge: Early Visions* (1989), has argued convincingly that Wordsworth's refusal to include *Christabel* in the second edition of his and Coleridge's joint book of *Lyrical Ballads* in October 1800 effectively choked off Coleridge's ability to write poetry. Thereafter his main channel of expression for his most intense responses to nature became his Notebooks. Richard Holmes goes on to point out that Coleridge could not work up his prose descriptions of, for example, Scafell, Moss Force, or Lodore Falls into effective poetry because they were already so poetically charged. Thus, in one sense, we owe a debt of gratitude to Wordsworth for the snub that he administered, forcing Coleridge's genius into this new channel. In the same way, we perhaps benefit from the increasing antipathy which Coleridge felt for his wife and which helped to keep him restlessly on the move over the fells and mountains, or off to Germany, Scotland and Wales. His tragedy was that the other path he took to bypass his wife and Wordsworth was by way of the laudanum and brandy bottles.

Although the main theme of this book is Coleridge's observation of scenery and nature, whenever he remarks on local activity or the oddity or nobility displayed by passing humanity, his comments have been kept. For Coleridge to relish it, landscape had to have the salt of human habitation or cultivation somewhere in it. As he said in August 1803 of the west side of Loch Lomond, 'Everywhere we miss the statesmen's [small farmers'] houses and the sweet spots of Cumberland cultivation. Everywhere there is a distressing sense of unrememberableness.' Likewise some of his fascinated study of the behaviour of his sons Hartley and Derwent is included, since his close observation of them shows all the passion to record of the keen entomologist or botanist. To anyone inclined to charge him with political apostasy, his loathing of cotton mills – 'a Sodom and Gomorrah manufactory' – his attack on the poor money earned by women for spinning wool at home, and his praise for the enlightened provision of public facilities for those who wanted to set up as washerwomen in Glasgow, give the lie.

In the end, however, it is his 'nature' writing that is here most important. We delight in his *cognoscente*'s comparison of one 'force' or Lake Country waterfall with another and of the optical effects they give as they plunge and wheel: 'What a self-same thing [is] a waterfall if you like, [but] if you look at it steadfastly, what fits and starts and convulsive twitches of motion.' No waxing and waning moon has been dwelt on so lovingly as the one whose passage above the Lakes Coleridge recorded in the late October and early November of 1803. We soon spot his particular weakness for the sight of smoke rising in pillars from cottage chimneys, for thatched roofs gone green with parasitic vegetation, and for 'the ruined sheepfold in a desolate place . . . of all things the dearest to me'. In writing in this way, Coleridge earns his place in that small group of much-loved country observers that begins with Gilbert White of Selborne (1789) and has Dorothy Wordsworth and Francis Kilvert as its other obvious stars. Shining, gem-like observations alternate with setpiece *tours-de-force* of description. Boisterous exuberance and humour keep on breaking through to balance the solemnity of his elemental communings. The 'hills, rocks, and steep waters' take on a new significance and visual richness once we have accompanied Coleridge the fell walker.

Coleridge kept his Notebooks for himself, and the usual cavalier attitude of his times to spelling and punctuation; the liberal sprinkling of capital letters, dashes and oblique strokes; the lack of paragraphs – all are taken by him to new heights. He also leaves words out in his haste, or because he is the worse for drink or drugs. I have been emboldened to sort out the punctuation, remove most capital letters, dashes and strokes, break the text up into sentences and paragraphs, and add missing words where they seemed necessary (but putting them in square brackets). Much of his idiosyncratic spelling has, however, been retained. His ampersands and abbreviations like 'thro' ' have been spelled out. I found courage to edit in this way for two reasons. The first is that when his grandson E. H. Coleridge edited *Anima Poetae* (a selection from the Notebooks) and his two-volume edition of the *Letters* in 1895, and his great-grandson G. H. B. Coleridge prepared the Notebook entries for October and November 1799 in *Words-worth and Coleridge* (edited by E. L. Griggs) in 1939, it seems to me that they took similar liberties. The second is that the magisterial edition of his *Notebooks* edited by Kathleen Coburn, of which the first volume appeared in 1957, prints every last dash, stroke and crossing out. Anyone so inclined can revel in the full but rather overwhelming glory of these extraordinary documents, thanks to her great feat of scholarship and perseverance. There is much excitement to be got from the immediacy of one's contact with Coleridge as he pours his thoughts hot onto the page, but it is at the expense of constant distraction and interruption to the flow.

Where longer explanation is needed, there are conventional footnotes. Where only a word or two is called for, these have been put in the text in square brackets. Ellipses are used to indicate cuts within an extract from a Notebook or letter. They have not been used where an extract doesn't start at the beginning or stops before the end of a Notebook entry or letter. Sometimes Coleridge dated his entries down to the very minute when he wrote them. But often several entries follow each other with no dates at all and often he was using several notebooks at the same time. One of Kathleen Coburn's tasks was to impose a chronological order on the entries, but there are many where the dating can be only to the likely month, rather than a date within a month. This is reflected in the Notebook entry headings here.

I love fields and woods and mountains with almost a
visionary fondness – and because I have found benevolence
and quietness growing within me as that fondness
has increased, therefore I should wish to be the means
of implanting it in others.

Coleridge to his brother George, 16 October 1797

SAMUEL TAYLOR COLERIDGE WAS BORN ON 21 OCTOBER 1772, THE *youngest of ten children, at Ottery St Mary in Devon, where his father was the vicar. His father died in 1781 and from 1782 to 1791 Coleridge was a charity scholar at Christ's Hospital School in the City of London. He then went to Jesus College, Cambridge where his career was a mixture of brilliance and debauch. In December 1793, heavily in debt, he enlisted in the 15th Light Dragoons, only to be bought out a few months later by his brother George. He went back to Cambridge briefly before setting out on a walking tour of Wales with Joseph Hucks, a fellow undergraduate. On the way he stopped in Oxford where he met Robert Southey, the future Poet Laureate and biographer, and between them they had the idea for a rural commune in America – a pantisocracy.*

In August 1794 Southey introduced Coleridge to Sara, the sister of his fiancée, Edith Fricker. In the same month Coleridge met Thomas Poole of Nether Stowey in Somerset. Poole was the young owner of a tannery, well-known for his democratic views. Coleridge never took his degree and instead went to live in Bristol with Southey, until the two quarrelled in September 1795. Southey was irritated by Coleridge's dilatoriness while Coleridge felt Southey was falling away from the original high pantisocratic ideals under the strain of having to provide for a wife. In October Coleridge married Sara Fricker and went to live at Clevedon on the Bristol Channel. He had been giving a series of radical political and religious lectures in Bristol and he carried on the same trains of argument in a magazine entitled the Watchman, *which lasted from March to May 1796. His first volume of poetry appeared in April and his son Hartley was born in September.*

In December 1796 the Coleridges moved to Nether Stowey, to a house found for them by Thomas Poole, who also saw to the paying of their debts. Charles Lloyd, of the Birmingham banking family, came to stay as a paying guest, but he was unbalanced as well as epileptic and this was not a success. Coleridge was trying to write a verse play for Sheridan to put on in London, and a second volume of his poems appeared in May 1797. This, like the first, was published by Joseph Cottle of Bristol, who also published William Wordsworth. Coleridge and Wordsworth met in the spring of 1797 and in July Wordsworth and his sister Dorothy moved from Racedown in Dorset to Alfoxden, near Nether Stowey, to be close to the Coleridges.

Robert Southey in 1795

To Robert Southey   *Gloucester, 6 July 1794*

S. T. Coleridge to R. Southey, Health and Republicanism to be! . . . Our journeying has been intolerably fatiguing from the heat and whiteness of the roads, and the *unhedged* country presents nothing but *stone* fences, dreary to the eye and scorching to the touch. But we shall soon be in Wales.

Gloucester is a nothing-to-be-said-about town. The women have almost all of them sharp noses.

It is *wrong*, Southey! for a little girl with a half-famished sickly baby in her arms to put her head in at the window of an inn – 'Pray give me a bit of bread and meat!' from a party dining on lamb, green peas, and salad. Why? Because it is *impertinent* and *obtrusive*! 'I am a gentleman! and wherefore the clamorous voice of woe intrude upon mine ear?' My companion is a man of cultivated, though not vigorous understanding; his feelings are all on the side of humanity; yet such are the unfeeling remarks, which the lingering remains of aristocracy occasionally prompt.

To Robert Southey   *Denbigh, 15 July 1794*

And now to give you some little account of our journey. From Oxford to Gloucester, to Ross, to Hereford, to Leominster, to Bishop's Castle, to Welsh Pool, to Llanfyllin, nothing occurred worthy notice except that at the last place I preached pantisocracy and aspheterism* with so much success that two great huge fellows of butcher-like appearance danced about the room in enthusiastic agitation. And one of them of his own accord called for a large glass of brandy, and drank it off to this his own toast, 'God save the King! And may he be the last.' Southey! Such men may be of use. They would kill the golden calf *secundum artem*. From Llanfyllin we penetrated into the interior of the country to Llangunnog, a village most romantically situated. We dined there on hashed mutton, cucumber, bread and cheese, and beer, and had two pots of ale – the sum total of the expense being sixteen pence for both of us! From Llangunnog we walked over the mountains to Bala – most sublimely terrible! It was scorchingly hot. I applied my mouth ever and anon to the side of the rocks and sucked in draughts of water cold as ice, and clear as infant diamonds in their embryo dew! The rugged and stony clefts are stupendous, and in winter must form

*Communal living with all of equal status, and ownership of property in common.

cataracts most astonishing. At this time of the year there is just water enough dashed down over them to 'soothe, not disturb the pensive traveller's ear'. I slept by the side of one an hour or more. As we descended the mountain, the sun was reflected in the river, that winded through the valley with insufferable brightness; it rivalled the sky. At Bala is nothing remarkable except a lake of eleven miles in circumference. At the inn I was sore afraid that I had caught the itch from a Welsh democrat, who was charmed with my sentiments: he grasped my hand with flesh-bruising ardor, and I trembled lest some disappointed citizens of the *animalcular* republic should have emigrated.

Shortly after, into the same room, came a well-dressed clergyman and four others, among whom (the landlady whispers me) was a justice of the peace and the doctor of the parish. I was asked for a gentleman. I gave General Washington. The parson said in a low voice, 'Republicans!' After which, the medical man said, 'Damn toasts! I gives a sentiment: May all republicans be guillotined!' Up starts the Welsh democrat. 'May all fools be gulloteen'd – and then you will be the first.' Thereon rogue, villain, traitor flew thick in each other's faces as a hailstorm. This is nothing in Wales. They *make calling one another liars*, etc., necessary vent-holes to the superfluous fumes of the temper. At last I endeavoured to articulate by observing that, whatever might be our opinions in politics, the appearance of a clergyman in the company assured me we were all Christians; 'though', continued I, 'it is rather difficult to reconcile the last sentiment with the spirit of Christianity.' 'Pho!' quoth the parson, 'Christianity! Why, we are not at church now, are we? The gemman's sentiment was a very good one; it showed he was *sincere* in his principles.' Welsh politics could not prevail over Welsh hospitality. They all, except the parson, shook me by the hand, and said I was an open-hearted, honest-speaking fellow, though I was a bit of a democrat.

From Bala we travelled onward to Llangollen, a most beautiful village in a most beautiful situation. On the road we met two Cantabs of my college, Brookes and Berdmore. These rival *pedestrians* – perfect *Powells* – were vigorously pursuing their tour in a *post-chaise*! We laughed famously. Their only excuse was that Berdmore had been ill. From Llangollen to Wrexham, from Wrexham to Ruthin, to Denbigh. At Denbigh is a ruined castle; it surpasses everything I could have conceived. I wandered there an hour and a half last evening (this is Tuesday morning). Two well-dressed young men were walking there. 'Come,' says one, 'I'll play my flute; 't will be romantic.' 'Bless thee for the thought, man of genius and sensibility!' I exclaimed, and preattuned my heartstring to tremulous emotion. He sat adown (the moon just peering) amid the awful part of the ruins, and the romantic youth struck up the affecting tune of 'Mrs Carey'.* 'Tis fact, upon my honour.

To Henry Martin†   *Caernarvon, 22 July 1794*

Three miles from Denbigh, on the road to St Asaph, is a fine bridge with one arch of great grandeur. Stand at a little distance, and through it you see the woods waving on the hill-bank of the river in a most lovely point of view. A beautiful prospect is always more picturesque, when seen at some little distance through an arch. I have frequently thought of Mich. Taylor's [Michael Angelo Taylor, 1757–1834] way of viewing a landscape by putting his head between his thighs. Under the arch was the most perfect echo I ever heard. Hucks sung 'Sweet Echo' with great effect. At Holywell I bathed in the famous St Winifred's Well – it is an excellent cold bath. At Rudland is a fine ruined castle. Abergeley is a large village on the sea coast. Walking on the sea sands, I was surprized to see a number of fine women bathing promiscuously with men and boys – *perfectly* naked! Doubtless, the citadels of their chastity are so impregnably strong, that they need not the ornamental outworks of modesty. But seriously speaking, where sexual distinctions are least observed, men and women live together in the greatest purity. Concealment sets the imagination a working, and, as it were, *cantharidizes* our desires.

Just before I quitted Cambridge I met a countryman with a strange walking stick, 5 feet in length. I eagerly bought it, and a most faithful servant it has proved to me. My sudden affection for it has mellowed into settled friendship. On the morning of our leaving Abergeley just before our final departure I looked for my stick, in the place where I had left it over night. It was gone! I alarumed the house. No one knew anything of it. In the flurry of anxiety I sent for the cryer of the town and gave him the following to cry about the town and on the beach, which he did with a gravity for which I am indebted to his stupidity.

Missing from the Bee Inn, Abergeley – A curious Walking-Stick. On one side it displays the head of an eagle, the eyes of which represent rising suns, and the ears Turkish crescents. On the other side is the portrait of the owner in woodwork. Beneath the head of the eagle is a Welch wig – and around the neck of the stick is a Queen Elizabeth's ruff in tin. All adown it waves

*A bawdy song.
†A friend at Jesus College, Cambridge.

the Line of Beauty in very ugly carving. If any gentleman (or lady) has fallen in love with the above-described stick and secretly carried off the same, he (or she) is hereby earnestly admonished to conquer a passion, the continuance of which must prove fatal to his (or her) honesty; and if the said stick has slipped into such gentleman's (or lady's) hand through inadvertence, he (or she) is required to rectify the mistake with all convenient speed. God save the King.

Abergeley is a fashionable Welch watering place and so singular a proclamation excited no small crowd on the beach, among the rest a lame old gentleman, in whose hands was descried my dear stick. The old gent, who lodged at our inn, felt great confusion, and walked homewards, the solemn cryer before him, and a various cavalcade behind him. I kept the muscles of my face in tolerable subjection. He made his lameness an apology for borrowing my stick, supposed he should have returned before I had wanted it et.cetera. Thus it ended except that a very handsome young lady put her head out of a coach window, and begged my permission to have the bill, which I had delivered to the cryer. I acceded to the request with a compliment, that lighted up a blush on her cheek, and a smile on her lip.

To Thomas Poole   *Clevedon, 7 October 1795*

My dear Sir, – God bless you; or rather, God be praised for that he *has* blessed you!

On Sunday morning I was *married* at St Mary's Redcliff, poor Chatterton's church!* The thought gave a tinge of melancholy to the solemn joy which I felt, united to the woman whom I love best of all created beings. We are settled, nay, quite domesticated, at Clevedon, our comfortable cot!

Mrs Coleridge! I like to write the name. Well, as I was saying, Mrs Coleridge desires her affectionate regards to you. I talked of you on my wedding night. God bless you! I hope that some ten years hence you will believe and know of my affection towards you what I will not now profess.

The prospect around is perhaps more *various* than any in the kingdom. Mine eye gluttonizes the sea, the distant islands, the opposite coast! I shall assuredly write rhymes, let the nine Muses prevent it if they can.

---

*Thomas Chatterton, the precocious Bristol poet and Romantic forerunner, who killed himself, aged eighteen, in 1770.

Edith Southey (left) and her sister Sara Coleridge

To Rev. J. P. Estlin*   *Nether Stowey, early 1797*

We are all remarkably well, and the child grows fat and strong. Our house is better than we expected – there is a comfortable bedroom and sitting-room for C. Lloyd, and another for us, a room for Nanny, a kitchen, and outhouse. Before our door a clear brook runs of very soft water; and in the back yard is a nice well of fine spring water. We have a very pretty garden, and large enough to find us vegetables and employment, and I am already an expert gardener, and both my hands can exhibit a callum as testimonials of their industry. We have likewise a sweet orchard, and at the end of it T. Poole has made a gate, which leads into his garden, and from thence either through the tan yard into his house, or else through his orchard over a fine meadow into the garden of a Mrs Cruikshank, an old acquaintance, who married on the same day as I, and has got a little girl a little younger than David Hartley. Mrs Cruikshank is a sweet little woman, of the same size as my Sara, and they are extremely cordial. T. Poole's mother behaves to us as a kind and tender mother. She is very fond indeed of my wife, so that, you see, I ought to be happy, and, thank God, I am so.

From the Notebooks, 1796–1797

The swallows interweaving there mid the paired sea-mews, at distance wildly-wailing.

The brook runs over sea-weeds.

Sabbath Day: from the miller's mossy wheel the waterdrops dripped leisurely.

On the broad mountain-top the neighing wild-colt races with the wind over fern and heath-flowers.

A long deep lane so overshadowed, it might seem one bower – the damp clay banks were furred with mouldy moss.

Broad-breasted pollards with broad-branching heads.

The subtle snow in every breeze rose curling from the grove, like pillars of cottage smoke.

A dunghill at a distance sometimes smells like musk, and a dead dog like elder-flowers.

The flat pink-coloured stone painted over in jagged circles and strange parallelograms with the greenish black-spotted lichens.

*A Unitarian preacher in Bristol.

To Robert Southey   *Nether Stowey, 1797*

I had been on a visit to Wordsworth's at Racedown, near Crewkerne, and I brought him and his sister back with me, and here I have *settled them*. By a combination of curious circumstances a gentleman's seat [Alfoxden], with a park and woods, elegantly and completely furnished, with nine lodging rooms, three parlours, and a hall, in the most beautiful and romantic situation by the seaside, four miles from Stowey – this we have got for Wordsworth at the *rent of twenty-three pounds a year, taxes included*! The park and woods are *his* for all purposes *he* wants them, and the large gardens are altogether and entirely his. Wordsworth is a very great man, the only man to whom *at all times* and *in all modes of excellence* I feel myself inferior, the only one, I mean, whom *I have yet met with,* for the London *literati* appear to me to be very much like little potatoes, that is, *no great things*, a compost of nullity and dullity.

    Charles Lamb has been with me for a week.* He left me Friday morning. The second day after Wordsworth came to me, dear Sara accidentally emptied a skillet of boiling milk on my foot, which confined me during the whole time of C. Lamb's stay and still prevents me from all *walks* longer than a furlong. While Wordsworth, his sister, and Charles Lamb were out one evening, sitting in the arbour of T. Poole's garden which communicates with mine I wrote these lines, with which I am pleased . . .

> Well, they are gone, and here must I remain,
> Lam'd by the scathe of fire, lonely and faint,
> This lime-tree bower my prison! They, meantime
> My Friends, whom I may never meet again,
> On springy heath, along the hill-top edge
> Wander delighted, and look down, perchance,
> On that same rifted Dell, where many an ash
> Twists its wild limbs beside the ferny rock
> Whose plumy ferns forever nod and drip,
> Spray'd by the waterfall. But chiefly thou
> My gentle-hearted *Charles*! thou who had pin'd
> And hunger'd after Nature many a year,
> In the great City pent, winning thy way
> With sad yet bowed soul, through evil and pain
> And strange calamity! Ah! slowly sink

---

*The essayist and lifelong friend of Coleridge, with whom he had been a schoolboy at Christ's Hospital.

Charles Lamb by William Hazlitt

Behind the western ridge, thou glorious Sun!
Shine in the slant heaven of the sinking orb,
Ye purple heath-flowers! richlier burn, ye clouds
Live in the yellow Light, ye distant groves!
Struck with joy's deepest calm, and gazing round
On the wide view, may gaze till all doth seem
Less gross than bodily; a living thing
That acts upon the mind, and with such hues
As clothe the Almighty Spirit, when He makes
Spirits perceive His presence!
                                          A delight
Comes sudden on my heart, and I am glad
As I myself were there! nor in the bower
Want I sweet sounds or pleasing shapes. I watch'd
The sunshine of each broad transparent leaf
Broke by the shadows of the leaf or stem
Which hung above it: and that walnut-tree
Was richly ting'd, and a deep radiance lay
Full on the ancient ivy, which usurps
Those fronting elms, and now with blackest mass
Makes their dark foliage gleam a lighter hue
Through the late twilight: and though the rapid bat
Wheels silent by, and not a swallow titters,
Yet still the solitary humble bee
Sings in the bean-flower! Henceforth I shall know
That Nature ne'er deserts the wise and pure;
No scene so narrow, but may well employ
Each faculty of sense, and keep the heart
Awake to Love and Beauty! and sometimes
'Tis well to be bereav'd of promised good,
That we may lift the soul and contemplate
With lively joy the joys we cannot share.
My Sister and my Friends! when the last rook
Beat its straight path along the dusky air
Homewards, I bless'd it! deeming its black wing
Cross'd like a speck the blaze of setting day
While ye stood gazing; or when all was still,
Flew creaking o'er your heads, and had a charm
For you, my Sister and my Friends, to whom
No sound is dissonant which tells of Life.

Porlock on the north Somerset coast. Coleridge probably wrote 'Kubla Khan' at Ash Farm nearby, in October 1797.

I would make a shift by some means or other to visit you, if I thought that you and Edith Southey would return with me. I think – indeed, I am almost certain – that I could get a one-horse chaise free of all expense. I have driven back Miss Wordsworth over forty miles of execrable roads, and have been always very cautious, and am now no inexpert whip. And Wordsworth, at whose house I now am for change of air, has commissioned me to offer you a suite of rooms at this place, which is called 'All-foxen'; and so divine and wild is the country that I am sure it would increase your stock of images.

Twenty years later, in his extraordinary mixture of a book, the Biographia Literaria, *Coleridge recalled the large-scale poetical project he had on hand at this time.*

I sought for a subject, that should give equal room and freedom for description, incident, and impassioned reflections on men, nature, and society, yet supply in itself a natural connection to the parts, and unity to the whole. Such a subject I conceived myself to have found in a stream, traced from its source in the hills among the yellow-red moss and conical glass-shaped tufts of bent, to the first break or fall, where its drops become audible, and it begins to form a channel; thence to the peat and turf barn, itself built of the same dark squares as it sheltered; to the sheepfold; to the first cultivated plot of ground; to the lonely cottage and its bleak garden won from the heath; to the hamlet, the villages, the market-town, the manufactories, and the seaport. My walks therefore were almost daily on the top of Quantock, and among its sloping coombes. With my pencil and memorandum-book in my hand, I was *making studies*, as the artists call them, and often moulding my thoughts into verse, with the objects and imagery immediately before my senses. Many circumstances, evil and good, intervened to prevent the completion of the poem, which was to have been entitled *The Brook*.

FROM THE AUTUMN OF 1797 COLERIDGE ENTERED A PERIOD OF *particularly inspired poetical composition. It seems most likely that 'Kubla Khan' was written in October that year and he began the* Ancient Mariner *in November, working on it for the next five months. 'Frost at Midnight' and 'Fears in Solitude' came early in 1798, when he also wrote the first part of* Christabel. *In January 1798 he was saved from taking up the post of Unitarian minister at Shrewsbury by a counter offer from Tom and Josiah Wedgwood of a pension of £150 a year for life. He had met these sons of Josiah Wedgwood, the Staffordshire pottery manufacturer, a few months before. In March he and Wordsworth had the idea for a collaborative volume of* Lyrical Ballads. *His second son Berkeley was born in May. In June the young Hazlitt came to stay and to walk along the coast to Linton with Coleridge. Many years later he recalled: 'a thunder storm came on while we were at the inn, and Coleridge was running out bare-headed to enjoy the commotion of the elements . . . but as if in spite, the clouds only muttered a few angry sounds, and let fall a few refreshing drops.'*

In September 1798 Coleridge took ship for Germany with William and Dorothy Wordsworth; his aim, to use the independence afforded by the Wedgwood pension to complete his education at a university there. He meant to be away for three months, but it turned out to be ten. The first fortnight was spent in Hamburg; then the Wordsworths went to Goslar while Coleridge went thirty-five miles to the east of Hamburg, to the small resort of Ratzeburg. There he spent the winter, before moving south to the university town of Göttingen in February 1799. The news of the death of his son Berkeley reached him there in April. In May he embarked on a week's walking tour of the Hartz mountains along with five fellow-countrymen and one German. He eventually returned to Nether Stowey in July.

Excerpts from 'Frost At Midnight', written in February 1798:

> The Frost performs its secret ministry,
> Unhelped by any wind. The owlet's cry
> Came loud – and hark, again! loud as before.
> The inmates of my cottage, all at rest,
> Have left me to that solitude, which suits
> Abstruser musings: save that at my side
> My cradled infant slumbers peacefully.

'Tis calm indeed! so calm, that it disturbs
And vexes meditation with its strange
And extreme silentness. Sea, hill, and wood,
This populous village! Sea, and hill, and wood,
With all the numberless goings-on of life,
Inaudible as dreams! . . .

    Dear Babe, that sleepest cradled by my side,
Whose gentle breathings, heard in this deep calm,
Fill up the interspersèd vacancies
And momentary pauses of the thought!
My babe so beautiful! it thrills my heart
With tender gladness, thus to look at thee,
And think that thou shalt learn far other lore,
And in far other scenes! For I was reared
In the great city, pent 'mid cloisters dim,
And saw nought lovely but the sky and stars.
But *thou*, my babe! shalt wander like a breeze
By lakes and sandy shores, beneath the crags
Of ancient mountain, and beneath the clouds,
Which image in their bulk both lakes and shores
And mountain crags: so shalt thou see and hear
The lovely shapes and sounds intelligible
Of that eternal language, which thy God
Utters, who from eternity doth teach
Himself in all, and all things in himself.
Great universal Teacher! he shall mould
Thy spirit, and by giving make it ask.

    Therefore all seasons shall be sweet to thee,
Whether the summer clothe the general earth
With greenness, or the redbreast sit and sing
Betwixt the tufts of snow on the bare branch
Of mossy apple-tree, while the nigh thatch
Smokes in the sun-thaw; whether the eave-drops fall
Heard only in the trances of the blast,
Or if the secret ministry of frost
Shall hang them up in silent icicles,
Quietly shining to the quiet Moon.

Excerpts from 'Fears in Solitude' written in April 1798 'during the alarm of an invasion':

A green and silent spot, amid the hills,
A small and silent dell! O'er stiller place
No singing sky-lark ever poised himself.
The hills are heathy, save that swelling slope,
Which hath a gay and gorgeous covering on,
All golden with the never-bloomless furze,
Which now blooms most profusely: but the dell,
Bathed by the mist, is fresh and delicate
As vernal corn-field, or the unripe flax,
When, through its half-transparent stalks, at eve,
The level sunshine glimmers with green light.
Oh! 'tis a quiet spirit-healing nook!
Which all, methinks, would love; but chiefly he,
The humble man, who, in his youthful years,
Knew just so much of folly, as had made
His early manhood more securely wise!
Here he might lie on fern or withered heath,
While from the singing lark (that sings unseen
The minstrelsy that solitude loves best),
And from the sun, and from the breezy air,
Sweet influences trembled o'er his frame;
And he, with many feelings, many thoughts,
Made up a meditative joy, and found
Religious meanings in the forms of Nature!
And so, his senses gradually wrapt
In a half sleep, he dreams of better worlds,
And dreaming hears thee still, O singing lark,
That singest like an angel in the clouds! . . .

                              May my fears,
My filial fears, be vain! and may the vaunts
And menace of the vengeful enemy
Pass like the gust, that roared and died away
In the distant tree: which heard, and only heard
In this low dell, bowed not the delicate grass.

     But now the gentle dew-fall sends abroad
The fruit-like perfume of the golden furze:

The light has left the summit of the hill,
Though still a sunny gleam lies beautiful,
Aslant the ivied beacon. Now farewell,
Farewell, awhile, O soft and silent spot!
On the green sheep-track, up the heathy hill,
Homeward I wind my way; and lo! recalled
From bodings that have well-nigh wearied me,
I find myself upon the brow, and pause
Startled! And after lonely sojourning
In such a quiet and surrounded nook,
This burst of prospect, here the shadowy main,
Dim-tinted, there the mighty majesty
Of that huge amphitheatre of rich
And elmy fields, seems like society –
Conversing with the mind, and giving it
A livelier impulse and a dance of thought!
And now, beloved Stowey! I behold
Thy church-tower, and, methinks, the four huge elms
Clustering, which mark the mansion of my friend;
And close behind them, hidden from my view,
Is my own lowly cottage, where my babe
And my babe's mother dwell in peace! With light
And quickened footsteps thitherward I tend,
Remembering thee, O green and silent dell!
And grateful, that by nature's quietness
And solitary musings, all my heart
Is softened, and made worthy to indulge
Love, and the thoughts that yearn for human kind.

From the Biographia Literaria, *describing a Hamburg sunset in September 1798:*

From Klopstock's* house we walked to the ramparts, discoursing together
on the poet and his conversation, till our attention was diverted to the
beauty and singularity of the sunset and its effects on the objects around us.
There were woods in the distance. A rich sandy light, (nay, of a much
deeper colour than sandy,) lay over these woods that blackened in
the blaze. Over that part of the woods which lay immediately under the

---

*'The venerable father of German poetry' whom Coleridge and Wordsworth had just
visited.

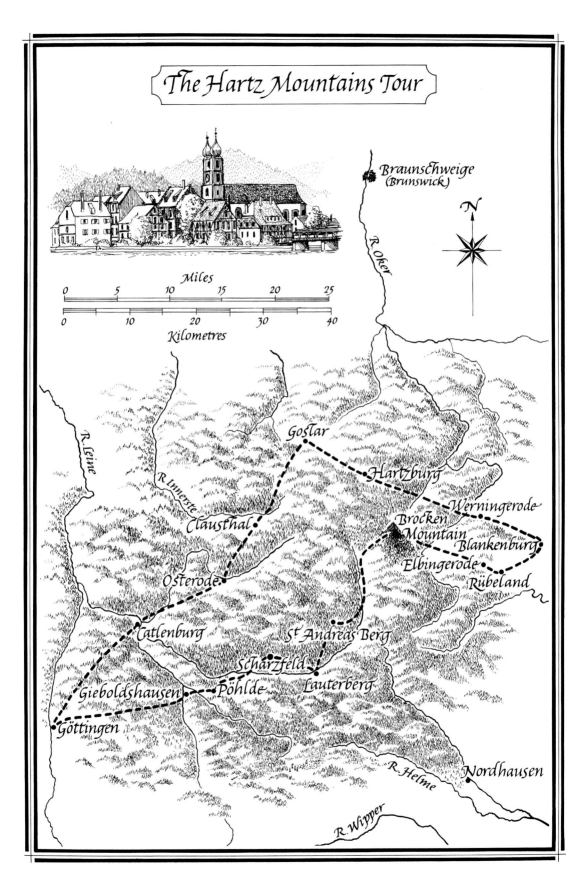

The Hartz Mountains Tour

Braunschweige
(Brunswick)

R. Oker

N

Miles

0   5   10   15   20   25

0   10   20   30   40

Kilometres

Goslar

Hartzburg

Werningerode

Clausthal

Brocken
Mountain

Blankenburg

R. Innerste

Elbingerode

Osterode

Rübeland

R. Leine

Catlenburg

St Andreas Berg

Scharzfeld

Gieboldshausen

Pöhlde

Lauterberg

Göttingen

R. Helme

Nordhausen

R. Wipper

intenser light, a brassy mist floated. The trees on the ramparts, and the people moving to and fro between them, were cut or divided into equal segments of deep shade and brassy light. Had the trees, and the bodies of the men and women, been divided into equal segments by a rule or pair of compasses, the portions could not have been more regular. All else was obscure. It was a fairy scene! – and to increase its romantic character, among the moving objects, thus divided into alternate shade and brightness, was a beautiful child, dressed with the elegant simplicity of an English child, riding on a stately goat, the saddle, bridle, and other accoutrements of which were in a high degree costly and splendid.

To Sara Coleridge   *Ratzeburg, 4 January 1799*

In October Ratzeburg used at sunset to appear completely beautiful. A deep red light spread over all, in complete harmony with the red town, the brown-red woods, and the yellow-red reeds on the skirts of the lake and on the slip of land. A few boats, paddled by single persons, used generally to be floating up and down in the rich light. But when first the ice fell on the lake, and the whole lake was frozen one large piece of thick transparent glass – O my God! what sublime scenery I have beheld. Of a morning I have seen the little lake covered with mist; when the sun peeped over the hills the mist broke in the middle, and at last stood as the waters of the Red Sea are said to have done when the Israelites passed; and between these two walls of mist the sunlight burst upon the ice in a straight road of golden fire, all across the lake, intolerably bright, and the walls of mist partaking of the light in a *multitude* of colours. About a month ago the vehemence of the wind had shattered the ice; part of it, quite shattered, was driven to shore and had frozen anew; this was of a deep blue, and represented an agitated sea – the water that ran up between the great islands of ice shone of a yellow-green (it was at sunset), and all the scattered islands of *smooth* ice were *blood*, intensely bright *blood*; on some of the largest islands the fishermen were pulling out their immense nets through the holes made in the ice for this purpose, and the fishermen, the net-poles, and the huge nets made a part of the glory! O my God! how I wished you to be with me!

In skating there are three pleasing circumstances – firstly, the infinitely subtle particles of ice which the skate cuts up, and which creep and run before the skater like a low mist, and in sunrise or sunset become coloured; second, the shadow of the skater in the water seen through the transparent ice; and thirdly, the melancholy undulating sound from the skate, not without variety; and, when very many are skating together, the sounds give an impulse to the icy trees, and the woods all round the lake *tinkle*. It is a pleasant amusement to sit in an ice stool (as they are called) and be driven along by two skaters, faster than most horses can gallop.

To Sara Coleridge   *Göttingen, 25 April 1799*

The graves in the little village churchyards are in square or parallelo-grammic wooden cases – they look like boxes without lids – and thorns and briars are woven over them, as is done in some parts of England. Perhaps you recollect that beautiful passage in Jeremy Taylor's *Holy Dying*, 'and the Summer brings briers to bud on our graves'. The shepherds with iron soled boots walk before the sheep, as in the East – you know our Saviour says – 'My Sheep follow me.' So it is here. The dog and the shepherd walk first, the shepherd with his romantic fur, and generally knitting a pair of white worsted gloves – he walks on and his dog by him, and then follow the sheep winding along the roads in a beautiful *stream*! In the fields I observed a multitude of poles with bands and trusses of straw tied round the higher part and the top – on enquiry we found that they were put there for the owls to perch upon. And the owls? They catch the field mice, who do amazing damage in the light soil all throughout the north of Germany.

The gallows near Göttingen, like that near Ratzeburg, is three great stone pillars, square, like huge tall chimneys, and connected with each other at the top by three iron bars with hooks to them – and near them is a wooden pillar with a wheel on the top of it on which the head is exposed, if the person instead of being hung is beheaded. I was frightened at first to see such a multitude of bones and skeletons of sheep, oxen, and horses, and bones as I imagined of men for many, many yards all round the gallows. I found that in Germany the hangman is by the laws of the Empire infamous – these hangmen form a caste, and their families marry with each other, etc. – and that all dead cattle, who have died, belong to them, and are carried by the owners to the gallows and left there. When their cattle are bewitched, or otherwise desperately sick, the peasants take them and tie them to the gallows – drowned dogs and kittens, etc., are thrown there – in short, the grass grows rank, and yet the bones overtop it (the fancy of *human* bones must, I suppose, have arisen in my ignorance of comparative anatomy). God bless you, my Love! I will write again speedily.

To Sara Coleridge   *Clausethal, 17 May 1799*

Saturday, May 11th, 10 o'clock, we left Göttingen, seven in party . . . We ascended a hill, N.E. of Göttingen, and passed through areas surrounded by woods, the areas now closing in upon us, now opening and retiring from us, till we came to Hessen Dreisch, which belongs to the Prince of Hesse Cassel. Here I observed a great wooden post with the French words, Pais Neutre (Neutral Country) on it – a precaution in case the French should march near . . . Here we dined on potatoes and pancakes – the pancakes throughout this part of the Country are excellent, but though pancakes in shape, in taste they more resemble good Yorkshire, or batter pudding. These and eggs you may almost always procure, when you can procure nothing else. They were brewing at the inn – I enquired and found that they put three bushels of malt and five large handfuls of hops to the hogshead. The beer as you may suppose, but indifferent stuff. Immediately from the inn we passed into a narrow road through a very lofty fir grove. These tall firs are branchless almost to the top, consequently no wood is so gloomy, yet none has so many spots and patches of sunshine. The soil consisted of great stones and rocks covered wholly and deeply with a bright-green moss, speckled with the sunshine, and only ornamented by the tender umbrella three-leaves and virgin white flower of the wood-sorrel – a most delightful acid to a thirsty foot-traveller.

Now we emerge from the fir-grove, and . . . journey on for a mile or two through coombes very much like those about Stowey and Holford, but still more like those at Porlock, on account of the great rocky fragments which jut out from the hills both here and at Porlock and which alas! we have not at dear Stowey! . . . We passed through Rudolphshausen, a village near which is the Amtman's house and farm-buildings. The Government give the Amtmen but moderate salaries; but then they let them great farms at a very very low rent – so the Amtmen throughout the Hanoverian Country are the great agriculturists, and form the only class that corresponds to our gentlemen-farmers. From them and in them originate all the innovations in the systems of agriculture here. I have never seen in England farm-buildings so large, compact, and commodious for all the purposes of storing, and stall-feeding as those of these Amtmen generally are. They have commonly from 1000 to 1500 English acres. From Rudolph's Hausen (i.e. Houses) we came to Womar's Hausen, a Catholic village belonging to the Elector of Mayence, and the first Catholic village I had seen – a crucifix, i.e. a wooden image of Christ on the Cross, at the end of the town and two others in the road at a little distance from the town. The greater part of the children here were

In the Hartz mountains: 'a grand plain,
mountains in the distance' (p.40)

naked all but the shirt, or rather the *relique* of a ci-devant shirt: but they were fat, healthy, and playful. The woman at the end wore a piece of silver round her neck, having the figure of St Andrew on it. She gravely informed us, that St Andrew had been a Man of the Forest and born near this village, and that he was remarkably good to people with sore eyes.

Here we met some students from the University of Halle, most adventurous figures, with leather jackets, long sabres, and great three cornered hats, with small iron chains dangling from them – and huge pipes in the mouth, the boles of which absolutely mounted above the forehead. Poole would have called them Knights of the Times. I asked young Blumenbach, if it was a uniform. He said No! – but that it was a student's *instinct* to play a character, in some way or other, and that therefore in the universities of Germany whim and caprice were exhausted in planning and executing blackguardisms of dress. I have seen much of this at Göttingen; but beyond doubt Göttingen is a gentlemanly and rational place compared with the other universities.

Through roads no way rememb'rable we came to Gieboldshausen, over a bridge, on which was a mitred statue with a great crucifix in its arms. The village long and ugly, but the church, like most Catholic churches, interesting – and this being Whitsun Eve, all were crowding to it with their mass-books and rosaries – the little babies commonly with coral crosses hanging on the breast. Here we took a guide, left the village, ascended a hill – and now the woods rose up before us in a verdure which surprized us like a sorcery! The Spring has burst forth with the suddenness of a Russian Summer. As we left Göttingen there were buds and here and there a tree half-green; but here were woods in full foliage, distinguished from summer only by the exquisite freshness of their tender green. We entered the wood through a beautiful mossy path, the moon above us blending with the evening lights; and every now and then a nightingale would invite the others to sing, and some *one* other commonly answered, and said, as we supposed, 'It is yet somewhat too early!' For the song was not continued. We came to a square piece of greenery compleatly *walled* on all four sides by the beeches – again entered the wood and having travelled about a mile emerged from it into a grand plain, mountains in the distance, but ever by our road the skirts of the green-wood. A very rapid river ran by our side. And now the nightingales were all singing and the tender verdure grew paler in the moonlight. Only the smooth parts of the river were still deeply purpled with the reflections from the fiery red lights in the West. So surrounded and so impressed, we arrived at Poele [Pöhlde], a dear little cluster of houses in the middle of a semicircle of woody hills, the area of the semicircle scarcely broader than the breadth of the village, the trees still for the most part beech. We left it, and now the country ceased to be interesting, and we came to the town of Schlachtfeld [Scharzfeld] belonging to Hanover. Here we had coffee and supper, and with many a patriotic song (for all of my companions sing very sweetly, and are thorough Englishmen) we closed the evening and went to sleep in our cloaths on the straw laid for us in the room. This is the only bed which is procurable at the village inns in Germany.

At half past seven, Whitsunday Morning, we left Schlachtfeld, passed through a broad coomb, turned up a smooth hill on the right, and entered a beech wood, and after a few hundred yards we came to the brink of an enormous cavern, which we descended. It went underground 800 feet, consisted of various apartments, dripping, stalactitious, and with mock chimnies; but I saw nothing unusual, except in the first apartment, or, as it were, antechamber. You descend from the wood by steps cut into the rock, pass under a most majestic natural arch of rock, and then you come into the light – for this antechamber is open at the top for a space of twenty yards in length, and eight in breadth. The open space is of an oval form and on the edges the beeches grow and stretch their arms over the cavern, but do not wholly form a ceiling. Their verdure contrasted most strikingly with the huge heap of snow which lay piled in this antechamber of the cavern into a white hill, imperfectly covered with withered leaves. The sides of this antechamber were wet stones in various angles, all green with dripping moss. Reascended – journeyed through the wood with various ascents and descents . . . We ascended a smooth green hill, on the top of which stood the ruined castle. When we had nearly reached the top, I layed down by a black and blasted trunk, the remains of a huge hollow tree, surrounded by wild gooseberry bushes, and looked back on the country we had passed. . . In all the ruins I have seen in Germany, and this is no small number, I have never discovered the least vestige of ivy. The guide informed us that the castle had been besieged in the year 1760 by a French army of 11,000 men under General Beaubecour, who had pitched camp on the opposite hills – and was defended for eleven days by eighty invalids under Prince Ysenburg, and at last taken by treachery, and then dismantled et cetera. . .

Almost at the end of the valley, or rather of its first turning, we found the village of Lauterberg. Just at the entrance of the village two streams come out from two deep and woody coombes close by each other, meet and run into a third deep woody coomb opposite; before you a wild hill which seems the end and the barrier of the valley; on the right hand low hills now green with corn, and now wooded; and on the left a most majestic hill indeed! the effect of whose simple outline *Painting* could not give, and how poor a Thing are *Words*? We pass through this neat little town, the majestic hill on the left hand soaring over the houses, and at every interspace you see the whole of it, its beeches, its firs, its rocks, its scattered cottages, and the one neat little Pastor's house at the foot embosomed in fruit-trees, all in blossom, the noisy coomb-brook dashing close by it. We leave the valley or rather the first turning on the left, following a stream – and so the vale winds on, the river still at the foot of woody hills, with every now and then other smaller valleys on right and left crossing our vale, and ever before you the woody hills running, like grooves one into the other. Sometimes I thought myself in the coombes about Stowey, sometimes about Porlock, sometimes between Por-lock and Linton, only the stream was somewhat larger. Sometimes the scenery resembled parts in the River Wye almost to identity, except that the river was not quite so large.

We turn'd, and turned and entering the fourth curve of the vale we perceived all at once that we had been ascending – the verdure vanished! All the beech trees were leafless and so were the silver birches, whose boughs always, winter and summer, hang so elegantly! But low down in the valley, and in little companies on each bank of the river, a multitude of black-green conical fir trees, with herds of cattle wandering about, almost every one with a cylindrical bell around its neck of no inconsiderable size. And as they moved, scattered over the narrow vale and up among the trees on the hill, the noise was like that of a large city in the stillness of the Sabbath morning, when all the steeples all at once are ringing for church. The whole was a melancholy and romantic scene that was quite new to me.

Again we turned, passed three smelting houses which we visited. A scene of terrible beauty is a furnace of boiling metal, darting out every moment blue, green, and scarlet lightning, like serpents' tongues! And now we ascended a steep hill on the top of which was St Andreas Burg, a town built wholly of wood. . . Here we supped and slept, and I not being quite well procured a bed – the others slept on straw. We left St Andreas Burg, May 13th, 8 o'clock, ascended still, the hill unwooded except here and there with a few stubby fir trees. We descended again to ascend far higher; and now we came to a most beautiful road that winded on the breast of the hill, from whence we looked down into a deep deep valley or huge bason full of pines and firs, the opposite hills full of pines and firs, and the hill above us on whose breast we were winding, likewise full of pines and firs. The valley or bason on our right hand into which we looked down is called the Vale of Rauschenbach, that is, the Valley of the Roaring Brook – and *roar* it did, indeed, most solemnly! The road on which we walked was weedy with infant fir-trees, an inch or two high.

'An enormous cavern . . . it went underground 800 feet' (p.41)

On our left hand came before us a most tremendous precipice of yellow and black rock, called the Rehburg, that is, the Mountain of the Roe. A deer-stealer once was, as is customary in these cases throughout all Germany, fastened to a roe-buck, his feet to the horns, and his head towards the tail, and then the roe let loose. The frighted animal came at length to the brink of this precipice, leaped down it, and dashed both himself and the man to atoms. Now again is nothing but pines and firs, above, below, around us! How awful is the deep unison of their undividable murmur. What a *one* thing it is – it is a sound that impresses the dim notion of the Omnipresent!

In various parts of the deep vale below us we beheld little dancing waterfalls gleaming through the branches; and now on our left hand from the very summit of the hill above us a powerful stream flung itself down, leaping and foaming, and now concealed, and now not concealed, and now half-concealed by the fir trees, till towards the road it became a visible sheet of water, within whose immediate neighbourhood no pine could have permanent abiding-place! The snow lay everywhere on the sides of the roads, and glimmered in company with the waterfall-foam – snow-patches and water breaks glimmering through the branches in the hill above, the deep bason below and the hill opposite. Over the high opposite hills, so dark in their pine forests, a far higher round barren stony mountain looked in upon the prospect from a distant country.

Through this scenery we passed on, till our road was crossed by a second waterfall or rather aggregation of little dancing waterfalls, one by the side of the other, for a considerable breadth – and all came at once out of the dark wood above, and rolled over the mossy rock-fragments, little firs growing in islets scattered among them. The same scenery continued till we came to the Oder Teich, a lake half made by man and half by nature. It is two miles in length, and but a few hundred yards in breadth, and winds between banks or rather, through *high walls* of pine trees. It has the appearance of a most calm and majestic river, it crosses the road, goes into a wood, and there at once plunges itself down into a most magnificent cascade, and runs into the vale, to which it gives the name of 'the Vale of the Roaring Brook'. We clomb down into the vale, and stood at the bottom of the cascade, and climbed up again by its side. The rocks over which it plunged were unusually wild in their shape, giving fantastic resemblances of men and animals, and the fir-boughs by the side were kept almost in a *swing*, which unruly motion contrasted well with the stern quietness of the huge forest-sea everywhere else. Here and elsewhere we found large rocks of violet stone which when rubbed or when the Sun shines strong on them, emit a scent which I could not have distinguished from violet. It is yellow-red in colour.

My dear dear Love! and my Hartley! My blessed Hartley! – By hill and wood and stream, I close my eyes and dream of you!

If possible, I will this evening continue my little tour in a second letter.

To Sara Coleridge   *Clausethal, 17 May 1799*

Now the snow met us in large masses, and we walked for two miles knee deep in it, with an inexpressible fatigue, till we came to the mount called Little Brocken. Here even the firs deserted us, or only now and then, a patch of them, wind-shorn, no higher than one's knee, matted and cowering to the ground like the thorn bushes on our highest sea-hills. The soil was plashy and boggy. We descended and came to the foot of the Great Brocken, without a rival the highest mountain in all the north of Germany, and the seat of innumerable superstitions. On the first day of May all the witches dance here at midnight, and those who go may see their own ghosts walking up and down with a little billet on the back, giving the names of those who had wished them there: for 'I wish you on the top of the Brocken' is a common curse throughout the whole Empire. Well, we ascended, the soil boggy, and at last reached the height, which is 573 toises above the level of the sea. We visited the Blocksberg, a sort of bowling green inclosed by huge stones, something like those at Stonehenge; and this is the Witches' Ball-room. Thence proceeded to the house on the hill where we dined, and now we descended. My toe was shockingly swoln, my feet bladdered, and my whole frame seemed going to pieces with fatigue. However, I went on, my key-note pain, except when, as not unseldom happened, I struck my toe against a stone or stub. This of course produced a *bravura* of torture. In the evening, about 7, we arrived at Elbinrode [Elbingerode]. I was really unwell. The transition from my late habit of sitting and writing for so many hours in the day to such intense bodily exercise had been too rapid and violent. I went to bed with chattering teeth, became feverish-hot, and remained tossing about and unable to sleep till two in the morning, when a perspiration burst out on me, I fell asleep, and got up in the morning quite well...

We left Elbinrode, May the 14th ... We travelled for half a mile through a wild country of bleak stony hills by our side with several caverns, or rather mouths of caverns, visible in their breasts, and now we came to Rubelland – O it was a lovely scene. Our road was at the foot of low hills and here were a few neat cottages. Behind us were high hills with a few scattered firs, and flocks of goats visible on the topmost crags. On our right hand, a fine shallow river of about thirty yards broad and beyond the river a crescent hill clothed with firs that rise one above the other, like spectators in an amphitheatre . . . The firs were so beautiful, and the masses of rocks, walls, and obelisks of rocks, started up among them, in the very places where if they had not been, a painter with the poet's feeling, would have imagined them!

We crossed the river (its name Bode), entered the sweet wood, and came to the mouth of the cavern with the man who shews it. It was a huge place, 800 feet in length and more in depth; of many different apartments, the only thing that distinguished it from other caverns was that the guide, who was really a character, had the talent of finding out and seeing uncommon likenesses in the different forms of the stalactite. Here was a nun – this was Solomon's Temple – that was a Roman Catholic chapel – here was a lion's claw (nothing but flesh and blood wanting to make it completely a claw!) – this was an organ and had all the notes of the organ, et cetera and et cetera. But alas! with all possible straining my eyes, ears, and my imagination I could see nothing but common stalactite, and hear nothing but the dull *ding* of common cavern stones. One thing was really striking – a huge cone of stalactite hung from the roof of the largest apartment, and on being struck gave perfectly the sound of a death bell. I was behind, and heard it repeatedly at some distance, and the effect was very much in the fairy kind – Gnomes and Things unseen, that toll mock death bells for mock funerals! After this a little clear well, and a black stream pleased me the most; and multiplied by fifty and coloured ad libitum, might be well enough to *read of* in a novel or poem.

We returned and now before the inn on the green plat around the Maypole the villagers were celebrating Whit Tuesday. This Maypole is hung as usual with garlands on the top; and in these garlands spoons and other little valuables are placed – the high smooth round pole is then well greased – and now he who can climb up to the top may have what he can get. A very laughable scene, as you may suppose, of awkwardness and agility, and failures on the very brink of success. Now began a dance. The women danced very well, and in general I have observed throughout Germany that the women in the lower ranks degenerate far less from the ideal of a woman than the men from that of man. The dances were reels and the walzen; but chiefly the latter. This dance is in the *highest* circles sufficiently voluptuous; but here, the motions etc. were far *more* faithful interpreters of the passion or rather appetite, which doubtless the dance was intended to shadow out. Yet even after that giddy round and round is over, the walking to music, the woman laying her arm with confident affection on the man's shoulders, or (among the rustics) round his neck, has something inexpressibly charming in it. The first couple at the walzen was a very fine tall girl of two or three and twenty, in the full bloom and growth of limb and feature, and a fellow with huge whiskers, a long tail, and a woollen night-cap on. He was a soldier, and from the more than usual glances of the girl, I presumed, was her lover. He was beyond compare the gallant and the dancer of the party. Next came two Bauern, one of whom in the whole contour of his face and person, and above all in the laughably would-be-frolicsome fling-out of his heel irresistibly reminded me of Shakespear's Slender, and the other of his Dogberry. O two such faces, and two such postures! O that I were an Hogarth! What an enviable talent it is to have a genius in painting! Their partners were pretty lasses not so tall as the former, and danced uncommonly light and airy. The fourth couple was a sweet girl of about 17, delicately slender and very prettily dressed, with a full blown rose in the white ribbon that went round her head and confined her reddish-brown hair. Her partner waltsed – with a pipe in his mouth! smoking all the while! During the whole of this voluptuous dance the whole of his face was a fair personification of *true German Phlegm*.

After these, but I suppose, not actually belonging to the party, a little ragged girl and a ragged boy with his stockings about his heels waltsed and danced in the rear most entertainingly. But what most pleased me was a little girl of about three or four years old, certainly not more than four, who had been put to watch a little babe of exactly a year old (for one of our party had asked) and who was just beginning to run away. The girl teaching him to walk was so animated by the music that she began to waltse with him, and the two babes whirled round and round hugging and kissing each other, as if the music had made them mad. I am no judge of music – it pleased me! and Mr Parry who plays himself, assured me it was uncommonly good. There were two fiddles and a bass viol, the fiddlers, but above all, the bass violist, most Hogarthian phizzes! – God love them! – I felt far more affection for them than towards any other set of human beings whom I have met with in Germany, I suppose, because they looked so happy!

We left them – as we go out of the village the crescent shaped hill of firs sinks, and forms an irregular wood, but the opposite hill rises, and becomes in its turn a perfect crescent, but of a far other character – higher and more abrupt and ornamented not clothed with firs, the larger part of the hill being masses and variously jutting precipices of rocks, grey, sulphur-yellow, or mossy.

Shortly after we met with huge marble rocks – and about a mile from

Rubelland we arrived at a manufactory where the marble is polished. The veins of the Blankenburg marble have an exquisite beauty; a foot square is valued at half a crown. Young Blumenbach informed us that marble was a marine substance – that the veins, at least the brown and the red veins were true *corals*, and the white was the accidental cement. Here a huge angle of rock comes out and divides the road. Our path went on the left one way, and the river the other. We left the river Bode unwillingly – for it went immediately into a deep deep pine wood, where we saw high pillars of rock that, I don't know why, seemed to *live* among the black fir trees, and I wished to be its companion. But one always quits a dashing river unwillingly . . . I look back and see the snow on the Brocken, and all between the black *mineral* green of pine-groves, wintry, endlessly wintry, and the beech and the birch, and the wild ash all leafless. But lo! before us – a sweet spring! not indeed in the full youthful verdure as on our first day's journey, but timidly soft, half-wintry – and with here and there spots and patches of iron brown. Interesting in the highest degree is it to have seen in the course of two or three days so many different climates with all their different phaenomena!

The vast plain was before us, rocks on the right hand (a huge wall of rocks!), on the left and curving round into the front view, hills of beeches, soft surges of woody hills. At the feet of the hill lay the castle and town of Blankenburg, with all its orchards of blossoming fruit trees. Blankenburg is a considerable town, containing 500 houses and 3000 inhabitants; and belongs to the Duke of Brunswick. Immediately opposite to our inn is the house in which the unfortunate Louis the 18th lived during twenty-one months . . . He kept a regular mistress, a large fine tall woman of a fair complexion, a French woman, whose husband at the same time lived in the house, observing the most distant civilities and respect toward his wife. A washerwoman's daughter however of Blankenburg, by the name of Hase, had struck his Majesty's eye – a young girl of no unimpregnable chastity – and once or twice a week his Majesty was graciously accustomed to send one of his nobles for her . . .

Twice a week his Majesty bathed in gravy-soup, for which purpose eighty pounds of beef were constantly used – which soup with the meat was after given to the poor. He ordered his surgeons and physicians to attend the poor gratis, and wept when he quitted the place. We went and visited the castle which was shewn us by a young woman. Such an immense number of ugly rooms with such an immense number of pictures, not *one* of which possessed the least merit, or rather not *one* of which was not a despicable daub! – And almost all obscene! – So false is it that our ancestors were more innocent than we . . .

We returned, and spent the evening with a round of old English songs, of which God Save the King and Rule Britannia were, as you may suppose, repeated no small number of times – for being abroad makes every man a patriot and a loyalist – almost a Pittite!

God bless you, my Love and S.T. Coleridge
and good night!

To Thomas Poole   *Göttingen, 19 May 1799*

In my second letter to Sara I was still at Blankenburg – We left it on Wednesday morning, May 15th, taking first one survey more of the noble view which it commanded . . . On the left and curving round till they formed the front view, hills here green with leafy trees, here still iron-brown, dappled as it were with coming Spring and lingering Winter; not of abrupt and grand outlines, but rising and sinking yet on the whole still rising, in a *frolic surginess*. In the plain (or area of the view) young corn, herds of cattle, troops of goats, and shepherds at the head of *streams* of sheep. . . A mile from Blankenburg we came to a small lake quite surrounded with beech-trees, the margins of the lake solid marble rock. Two or three stone-thrushes were flitting about those rocky margins. Our road itself was, for a few strides, occupied by a pretty little one-arched bridge, under which the lake emptied itself, and at the distance of ten yards from the bridge, on our right hand, plunged itself down (its stream only once broken by a jutting rock nearly in the midst of the fall) into a chasm of thirty feet in depth and somewhat more in length (a chasm of black or mossy rocks) and then ran under ground. We now entered the woods, the morning thick and misty. We saw a number of wild deer, and at least fifty salamanders. The salamander is a beautiful lizard, perfectly harmless (I examined several in my naked hand), its length from six to seven inches, with a *nightingale's* eye, and just 22 yellow streaks on its glossy-black skin. That it can live in the fire, is a fable; but it is true, that if put on burning coals, for the first, or even the second time, it emits a liquid so copiously as to extinguish the coals. So we went, up hill and down dale, but all through woods, for four miles, when we came to a sort of heath stubby with low trunks of old fir-trees. Here were women in various groups sowing the fir-seed: a few ceasing from their work to look at us. Never did I behold aught so impressively picturesque, or rather *statue*-esque, as these groups of women in all their various attitudes. The thick mist, through which their figures came to my eye, gave such a soft *unreality* to them! These lines, my dear Poole, I have written rather for my own pleasure than yours – for it is impossible that this misery of words can give to you, that which it

'In the plain . . . shepherds at the head of *streams* of
sheep' (p.49)

may yet perhaps be able to recall to me. What can be the cause that I am so miserable a describer? Is it that I understand neither the practice nor the principles of painting? – or is it not true, that others have really succeeded? – I could half suspect that what are deemed fine descriptions, produce their effects almost purely by a charm of words, with which and with whose combinations, we associate *feelings* indeed, but no distinct *images*.

From these women we discovered that we had gone out of our way precisely four miles, so we laughed, and trudged back again, and contrived to arrive at Werningerode about 12 o'clock. This belongs to the Princely Count Stolberg, a cousin of the two brothers, the Princely Counts Stolberg of Stolberg, who both of them are poets and Christians – good poets, real Christians, and most kind-hearted princes – what a combination of rarities for Germany! The Prince-Count Stolberg at Werningerode gave on this day a feast to his People, and almost all the family of the Stolbergs were assembled. The nobles and people were shooting for a prize at a stuffed bird placed on the top of a high May-pole. A nobleman of the family, who had been lately at Göttingen, recognized Parry, and was about to have introduced us; but neither our dress or time permitting it, we declined the honour. In this little town there is a school with about twelve or thirteen poor scholars in it, who are maintained by the tenants and citizens – they breakfast with one, dine with another, and sup with a third, managing their visits so as to divide the burthen of their maintenance according to the capabilities of the people, to whose tables they solicit admission.*

... We entered the wood, passed woods and woods, every now and then coming to little spots of greenery of various sizes and shapes, but always walled by trees; and always as we entered, the first object which met us was a mount of wild outline, black with firs soaring huge above the woods. One of these greeneries was in shape a parallelogram, walled on three sides by the silver-barked weeping birches, on the fourth by conical firs. A rock on the fir-side rose above the trees just within the wood, and before us the huge fir-mount. It was a most impressive scene! perhaps, not the less so from the mistiness of the wet air. We travelled on and on, O what a weary way! now up, now down, now with path, now without it, having no other guides than a map, a compass, and the foot-paces of the pigs, which had been the day before driven from Hartzburg [Bad Harzburg] to Dribbock [Drübeck] where there had been a pig-fair. This intelligence was of more service to us than map or compass.

At length we came to the foot of the huge fir-mount roaring with woods,

*See the undated Notebook entry in August 1800, p.85.

and winds, and waters! And now the sky cleared up, and masses of crimson light fell around us from the fiery west, and from the clouds over our heads that *reflected* the western fires. We wound along by the feet of the mount, and left it behind us; close before us a high hill, a high hill close on our right, and close on our left a hill – we were in a circular prison of hills and many a mass of light, moving and stationary, gave life and wildness to the rocks and woods that rose out of them . . . On our right hand was a huge valley with rocks in the distance and a steady mass of clouds that afforded no mean substitute for a sea. On each side, as ever, high woody hills, but majestic river, or huge lake – O that was wanting, here and everywhere! – And now we arrived at Hartsburg, hills ever by our sides, in all conceivable variety of forms and garniture. It were idle in me to attempt by words to give their projections and their retirings and how they were now in cones, now in roundnesses, now in tonguelike lengths, now pyramidal, now a huge bow, and all at every step varying the forms of their outlines; or how they now stood abreast, now ran aslant, now rose up behind each other or now, as at Harzburg, presented almost a sea of huge motionless waves, too multiform for painting, too multiform even for the imagination to remember them. Yea, my very sight seemed *incapacitated* by the novelty and complexity of the scene. Ye red lights from the rain clouds! Ye gave the whole the last magic touch! I had now walked five and thirty miles over roughest roads and had been sinking with fatigue, but so strong was the stimulus of this scene, that my frame seemed to have drank in a new vitality; for I now walked on to Goslar almost as if I had risen from healthy sleep on a fine spring morning: so light and lively were my faculties.

On our road to Goslar we passed by several smelting houses and wire manufactures, and one particularly noticeable where they separate the sulphur from the ores. The night was now upon us and the white and blue flares from this building formed a grand and beautiful object, and so white was the flame, that in the manufactury itself all appeared quite like a natural day light. (It is strange, that we do not adopt some means to render our artificial lights more white.) As the clock struck ten we entered the silent city of Goslar and through some few narrow passages, called streets by courtesy, we arrived at our Inn, my companions scarcely able to speak, too tired even to be glad that the journey was over – a journey of forty miles, including the way which we lost.

. . . We left this ugly silent old desert of a city, and strolled on through hill and dale of pines, up which the little mists crept like smoke from cottage chimneys, till we came to Clausthal. . . We were such a hospital of bruised toes, swelled ancles, bladdered soles, and excoriated heels, that we stayed in this town till Saturday morning, May 18th. We passed up and down over little hills through a pine-covered country, still looking down into deep and wild coombes of pine and fir trees (I scarcely know the difference between pine and fir) till we came to . . . Osterode, a large and very ugly town, the people looking dirtier and poorer than is common in Germany. Over the Town Hall is the Rib of a Giant – these are common in the inland towns of Germany. They are generally Whales' Ribs . . . From Osterode we proceeded to Catlenburg . . . From henceforwards the views became quite English, except that in England we have water ever in our views, either sea or lake or river – and we have elmy hedges – and single cottages – and gentlemen's seats – and many a house, the dwelling of knowledge and virtue, between the cottage and the gentleman's seat. Our fields and meadows too are so green, that it is common here for novellists and describers to say when they praise a prospect 'It had a British greenness'. All this and more is wanting in Germany, but their woods are far finer, and their hills more diversified, and their little villages far more interesting, every house being separate with its little garden and orchard. This answers to my notion of human nature; which distinguishes itself equally from the tyger and the sheep, and is neither solitary or gregarious, but *neighbourly*. Add to this too, that the extreme misery and the earth and heaven-alarming wickedness and profanity of our English villagers is a thing wholly unknown in Germany. The women too, who are working in the fields, always behave respectfully, modestly, and with courtesy . . . I ought to say that in the church yard at Catlenburg I was pleased with the following Epitaph. Johann Reimbold of Catlenburg.

Ach! sie haben	Ah! they have
Einen braven	Put a brave
Man begraben:	Man in Grave!
Vielen war er mehr.	He was more than Many!

This is word for word.

About a mile and a half from Catlenburg we came to a lovely scene, hillocks, and scattered oaks, and beeches, a sweet though very small lake, a green meadow, and one white cottage, and this spot exactly so filled was completely encircled by the grandest swell of woods, that I ever beheld. The hills were clothed as with grass, so rich was the verdure. So complete was the circle that I stood and looked around me, in what part the wood opened to admit our road. We entered the wood, and walked for two miles under a complete bower, and as we emerged from it – O I shall never forget that glorious prospect. Behind me the Hartz Mountains with the snow-spots shining on them, close around us woods upon little hills, little hills of an hundred shapes, a *dance* of hills, whose variety of position supplied the *effect* of, and almost imitated, *motion*. Two higher than the rest of a conical form were bare and stony; the rest were all hid with *leafage*, I cannot say, trees, for the foliage concealed the boughs that sustained it. And all these hills in all their forms and *bearings*, which it were such a chaos to describe, were yet in all so pure a harmony! Before us green corn-fields that fill'd the plain and crept up the opposite hills in the far-off distance and, closing our view in the angle at the left, that high woody hill on which stands the Monarch Ruin of the Plesse. Close by me in a deep dell was a sweet neighbourhood of houses with their orchards in blossom. O wherefore was there no water! We were now only seven miles from Göttingen.

III ❧ June 1799–November 1799

ON HIS WAY BACK TO ENGLAND COLERIDGE MADE ANOTHER VISIT TO *the Brocken: '. . . Greenough and I lost our way and after much hallowing in which we were mocked by some fine echoes, we recovered our party. We were however amply repaid by the sight of a wild boar with an immense cluster of glow-worms round his tail and rump.' (From a letter of 26 June 1799.)*

Coleridge and Southey patched up their quarrel in August 1799. Coleridge was still restless and in October went to Bristol, where he was introduced to laughing gas by the young Cornish chemist, Humphry Davy, soon to make his name at the Royal Institution in London. While in Bristol, a report that Wordsworth was ill gave Coleridge the excuse to travel north with Cottle to see him, but without telling Sara. They set out on October 22nd for Sockburn-on-Tees in County Durham where William and Dorothy were staying with their old friends Tom Hutchinson and his three sisters. Mary Hutchinson was to marry Wordsworth a few years later. A tour of the Lake District was proposed. Cottle fell out at Greta Bridge and his place was taken by John Wordsworth, William's sailor brother. Coleridge eventually returned to London via Sockburn in late November. It was now that he fell in love with Sara Hutchinson.

25 October 1799

At Tadcaster saw a most interesting picture on the road. A flock of sheep and, perhaps 200 yards behind, a sick sheep with its head on the ground; a dog looking up at a little boy's face, and the poor little sheep boy standing close by the sick sheep, anxiously looking forward to the flock, not knowing what to do! I never saw distressful doubt so strongly painted. Saw, that day, some sheep passing a bank and leaping off it with their heads turned to the quarter from whence they leapt on the bank, repeatedly came to it again. A true *argumentum in circulo*!

Aspens, one a lovely light yellow, the other red, or rather *poppy*-coloured.

Easingwold, opposite the Crown, a thatched house, the thatch so completely covered with weeds of every description as to look like a hill bank.

26 October

Mr Ward, a good man, passionately fond of Nature and drawing, has a house on Neasham Bank, the most lovely scene on the Tees, and now he is almost stone-blind. Yet still he draws, using the eyes of his brother who lives with him. How affecting! Here too is a most delicious ferry, a smooth black glassy water, with a green hue from the broad branching trees on each bank. The Parish pays so much per annum for all to be ferried over to church. Well may one call this river the peninsulating Tees. This character continues through its whole course, almost to the very sea. In ascending the hill on leaving Stockton upon Tees, for Yorkshire etc., I saw a noble vessel with all its canvas spread, sailing like an arrow through a rich meadow field! For there was no suspicion of a river, which flowed beneath you clear and broad and again in the distance. The place where the ship was, you would have sworn must have been half a mile from the course of the river, at least.

27 October
Myself and Wordsworth on foot, and Cottle, his legs hugely muffled up, mounted on Lily – down that miry lane, by Neasham Bank, and so to Hurworth, the village where Emerson, the great mathematician, lived. And truly I never before or since saw a village so *bedialled*! A dial on every house. In the churchyard much Hebrew on the tombs. Here I found a fragment of a tombstone with these words on it: 'To the Memory of ——'. These were all. It more than amused, it affected me.

One mile from Hurworth, the village of Croft, where we discussed the question of polytheism and monotheism, of tombs by the roadside and tombs in churchyards. Thought of translating Schiller's *Götter des Griechenlandes* and of writing an antiphony to it. Better write both myself in the manner and metre of [Milton's] 'Penseroso' and 'Allegro'.

28 October
We all ascended the bank of the Tees, the high sylvan cottaged bank. Lord Darlington's estate [Raby Castle] begins, of farm houses built not by and for the tenant, but by and for the lord – gaudy red, white, and black.

Gainford, a sweet village with a mirror-smooth green before the parsonage house, behind which is the church whose low tower just looks over it. On the front of the green, neat houses. As we enter this green we find that the village is an irregular circus and by an opening near the parsonage we glance the Tees . . . The other side [of the Tees] rises at once, a hill bank shattered, with scattered rockery and sylva. The curve of the river, not indeed the line of exquisite beauty as at Croft, but wild and more playful, in true keeping with this lively scene. The rocky sylvan bank is a single hill, the water deep and smooth in its shadow, then rushes down at once in a rapid . . . Epitaph here, the letters all filled up with moss, and moss nowhere else,

A distant view of Barnard Castle

A shady pool where the River Greta meets the Tees

Arabic and Hebrew. About a mile from Gainford in that delicious country, on a board against a tree, 'Welcome to the Nuts, but Spare the boughs'.

Half past four – we arrive at the [Egglestone] Abbey, a grey ruin on a slope, the river in wild turns below it and the grey church tower and houses of Castle Barnard in the distance, rich woods in the vicinity of the Abbey. We pass on and come to a bridge built like castle walls with battlements. Here I am struck and astonished with the *rush* of sound which came upon the ear at each opening, 'till at last we look up the river and behold it pouring itself down through a steep bed of rocks, with a wall of woods on each side. Again, over the other wall of the bridge, the same scene in a long visto except that here, instead of a rapid, a deep-solemn pool of still water, which ends in a rapid only in the far distance. The grey ruin [of Barnard Castle] faces you on one side. Over the other, in contrast of this, the still pool with the soft murmur of the distant rapid and a handsome gentleman's house in the distance. . .

Star (at Barnard Castle) bright, large, the only one, right over the tower – now absolutely cresting it – and now as we come nearer, twinkling behind the motionless fragment, a high wall *ruined* into a rude obelisk.

River Greta near its fall into the Tees: shootings of water threads down the slope of the huge green stone. The *white rose* of eddy-foam, where the stream ran into a scooped or scolloped hollow of the rock in its channel – this shape, an exact white rose, was forever over-powered by the stream rushing down in upon it and, still obstinate in resurrection, it spread up into the scollop by fits and starts, *blossoming* in a moment into full flower. It *is the life* that we live. I hung over the bridge and, musing, considered how much of this scene of endless variety-in-identity was Nature's, how much the living organ's! What would it be if I had the eyes of a fly! What if the blunt eye of a Brobdingnag!*

Black round ink-spots, from five to eighteen, in the decaying leaf of a sycamore.

29 October
Huge dry root snapped or rather cracked in half, bent over the road for a Gothic arch, somewhat perilous to forehead of musing – NB a Vandal arch.

31 October
Maybrough [Maryborough near Penrith] – a stone fence. Inside the stone fence, which is circular, an irregular circle of trees. In the centre of the circle-plot thus inclosed, an upright stone ten foot high, with an ash close by its side umbrella-ing it. A scene of religion and seclusion.

*The region of the giants in *Gulliver's Travels*, a favourite reference of Coleridge's.

Haweswater

1 November

About two miles from Bampton, our road was walled by the mountains. That on our left Walla [Wallow] Crag – a mountain whose constituent lines [run] with infinite variety yet all in segments of circles, the whole crag a rude semicircle. The other hills are bare, save at their feet enclosed fields. The Walla's *toes* run into the lake [Haweswater] in *lingulis* [little tongues of land] . . . There the enclosures too from the opposite mountains run into it. These form that narrow part of the lake, which as you first approach appears the termination, but standing a hundred yards high you behold a second reach where no enclosures are seen, but the bare mountain on the right. . . It forms a bay, a beautiful crescent.

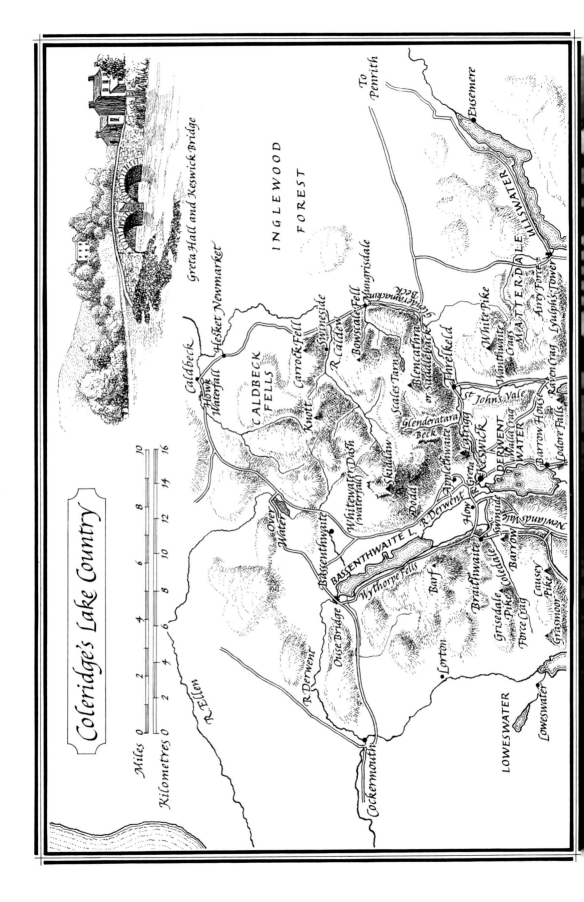

Coleridge's Lake Country

Miles 0   2   4   6   8   10

Kilometres 0   2   4   6   8   10   12   14   16

R. Ellen

Cockermouth

LOWESWATER

Loweswater

R. Derwent

Ouse Bridge

Lorton

Over Water

Bassenthwaite

Whitewater Dash (waterfall)

CALDBECK FELLS

Caldbeck

Howk Waterfall

Hesket Newmarket

Carrock Fell

Knott

Swineside

R. Caldew

Bowscale Fell

Mungrisdale

Glenderamackin Beck

I N G L E W O O D   F O R E S T

To Penrith

Eusemere

Scales Tarn

Skiddaw

Glenderatara Beck

Blencathra or Saddleback

Threlkeld

St. John's Vale

White Pike

Matterdale

ULLSWATER

Watthwaite

Raven Crag

Airey Force

Lyulph's Tower

LEA-

Dodd

Applethwaite

Keswick

Greta

R. Greta

R. Derwent

How

Walla Crag

Barrow House

DERWENT WATER

Lodore Falls

BASSENTHWAITE L.

Wythorpe Fells

Barf

Braithwaite

Swinside

Newlands Vale

Griesdale Pike

Coledale

Force Crag

Barrow

Causey Pike

Grismoor

Grasmoor

Greta Hall and Keswick Bridge

HAWES WATER

Miles

0 · 2 · 4 · 6 · 8 · 10

Kilometres

0 · 2 · 4 · 6 · 8 · 10 · 12 · 14 · 16

Place Fell

ULLSWATER

Sticks Pass
Glenruddin Screes
White Side
Patterdale
Helvellyn

Kirkstone Pass

Grisedale Tarn
Fairfield
Seat Sandal

Windermere

THIRLMERE
Raven Crag
Wythburn

Greenhead
Gill
Dove Cottage
RYDAL WATER
Ambleside

High Harrop Tarn
Watendlath Tarn

Wyth Burn
Waterfall

Lanrigg
Sour Milk Gill
Easedale
Stickle Tarn
GRASMERE
Silver Howe

Blelham Tarn

WINDERMERE

Barrow House
Grange
Bowder Stone
Castle Crag

DERWENT WATER
Borrowdale

Buttermere
Robinson

Pike o'stickle
Langdale
Gladramara
Harrison Stickle

Dungeon Gill Force

Coniston

CONISTON WATER

Crummock Water
Moss Force
Haskadale

BUTTERMERE

Sour Milk Force
Great Gable

Scafell

Coniston Old Man

R. Duddon

Ulpha

CRUMMOCK WATER

Raven Crag
Kirk Fell

Wastdale Head

Pillar

ENNERDALE WATER

WASTWATER

R. Esk
R. Mite
R. White

Rydal

Ravenglass

Walla Crag . . . is wooded up to the top. The wall by the road side roofed with moss running like a serpent in its firm lines. The solemn murmur of the unseen river far in the distance behind us and the silence of the lake. In the first and second views the only object of life is a flat roofed grey cottage, a little patch of clustered trees running above it, and above this *sylvula* [coppice], a silvery steep watercourse . . . Gleams of the white cows streaming behind the trees of the Walla on the marge of the lake.

3 November
Leave Esthwaite on the road.* Survey the whole of the lake on my right, straight before me a peep of Wynandermere, and over a gate on my left five huge ragged mountains, rising one above the other in wild relations of posture. Our road turns, we pass by Blelham Tarn, the five mountains now facing us.

Mr Law amid the awful mountains with his twenty cropped trees, four stumps standing upend on the trunk of each, all looking thus like strange devils with perpendicular horns. Head of the Lake of Wyandermere: Mr Law's white palace [Brathay Hall] – a bitch! Matthew Harrison's house where Llandaff† lived – these and more among the mountains! Mrs Taylor's house! The damned scoundrel on the right hand with his house and a barn built to represent a chapel: his name is Partridge from London and 'tis his Brother's cow-pen. This *fowl* is a stocking weaver by trade, have mercy on his five wits.

While at Sir [Michael Le] Fleming's a servant, red-eyed etc., came to us to the road before the waterfall, to reprove us for having passed before the front of the house [Rydal Hall]. Equalling by our trespass of feet with the trespass on the eye by his damned whitewashing!‡

5 November
A host of little winged flies on the snow mangled by the hail storm, near the top of Helvellyn.

---

*After leaving Haweswater they had gone via Kentmere to Troutbeck and then Bowness, before taking the ferry across Windermere to Esthwaite Water.
†The Bishop of Llandaff, Richard Watson (1737–1816), to whom Wordsworth had addressed an open letter in support of republicanism and justifying revolutionary violence in 1793. See also p. 121.
‡The whitewashing of buildings was a new fashion of which Wordsworth and Coleridge disapproved, though Coleridge later admitted that it had the advantage of making them stand out in moonlight.

November

Churnmilk Force [Sour Milk Ghyll in Easedale, near Grasmere] appearing over the copse, the steaming air rising above it. The rock that stands up and intercepts all but the marges and rims of the lower half. The copse whose trees, sometimes yielding and parting in the wind, make the waterfall beneath the rock visible. The first bridge from the waterfall, one-arched, ferny, its parapet or ledge of single stones not unmortared yet cemented more by moss and mould.

Exquisite network of film so instinct with gentle motion which, now the shower only steadies, and now it melts it into such a mistiness as the breath leaves on a mirror.

Ghost of a mountain, the forms seizing my body as I passed and became realities – I, a ghost, till I had reconquered my substance.

The sunny mist, the luminous gloom of Plato.

Mist as from volcano; waterfall rolled, after long looking at, like a segment of a wheel. The rock gleaming through it. Amid the roar, a noise as of innumerable grasshoppers or of spinning wheels. Distance, removing all sense of motion or sound, painted the waterfalls on the distant crags.

That rude wrinkled beetling forehead of rock, all between on both sides savage and helpless, obstinate sansculottism.

To Dorothy Wordsworth   *Keswick, 10 November 1799*

William has received your two letters. At Temple Sowerby we met your Brother John who accompanied us to Hawes Water, Windermere, Ambleside and the divine Sisters, Rydal and Grasmere – here we [he] stayed two days, and left on Tuesday [5 November]. We accompanied John over the fork of Helvellyn on a day when light and darkness coexisted in contiguous masses, and the earth and sky were but *one*! Nature lived for us in all her grandest accidents. We quitted him by a wild tarn just as we caught a view of the gloomy Ullswater. Your Brother John is one of you; a man who hath solitary usings of his own intellect, deep in feeling, with a subtle tact, a swift instinct of Truth and Beauty. He interests me much. . .

You can feel what I cannot express for myself – how deeply I have been impressed by a world of scenery absolutely new to me. At Rydal and Grasmere I received I think the deepest delight, yet Hawes Water through

Brathay Hall: 'Mr Law's white palace – a bitch!' (p.64)

many a varying view kept my eyes dim with tears, and this evening, approaching Derwentwater in diversity of harmonious features, in the majesty of its beauties and in the beauty of its majesty – O my God! and the black crags close under the snowy mountains, whose snows were pinkish with the setting sun and the reflections from the sandy rich clouds that floated over some and rested upon others! It was to me a vision of a fair country. Why were you not with us Dorothy? Why were not you, Mary [Hutchinson], with us?

11 November 1799

From Ouse Bridge, from the inn window, the whole length of Bassenthwaite, a simple majesty of water and mountains. In the distance the Bank [Skiddaw Dodd] rising like a wedge and in the second distance the crags of Derwentwater. What an effect of the shadows on the water! On the left the conical

Grasmere, 'that lovely lake' (p.81)

shadow, on the right a square of splendid black, all the area intermediate a mirror reflecting dark and sunny cloud. But in the distance the black promontory with a circle of melted silver and a path of silver running from it, like a flat cape in the lake. The snowy Borrowdale in the far distance and a ridge, nearer mountains sloping down as it were to the faint bank of the Bassenthwaite.

The unseen river Cocker roaring, passed through Lorton. Just over the bridge (there the brook flings itself down a small chasm of rock), in a field on the right hand a yew prodigious in size and complexity of numberless branches flings itself on one side entirely over the river, the branches all verging waterwards. Over the field it spreads seventeen strides. On its branches names numberless carved, some of the names being grown up, appear in *alto relievo*. . .

Beyond Lorton, Grasmere [Grasmoor] is a most sublime crag, of a violet colour, patched here and there with islands of heath plant, and wrinkled and guttered most picturesquely. Contrasts with the hills on my right, which though in form ridgy and precipitous, are yet smooth and green. We pass the inn at Scale Hill, leaving it to our right. And to our right is Lowes Water. 'Tis a sweet country that we see before us, Somersetshire hills and many a neat scattered house with trees round of the Estates Men.*

12 November

Scale Force – the first fall a thin broad white ribbon from a stupendous height, uninterrupted, though not unimpinged, by the perpendicular rock down which it falls, or rather parallel with. There is no pool at the bottom, but a common shallow brook over small flattish pebbles. But the chasm through which it flows is stupendous, so wildly wooded that the mosses and wet weeds and perilous tree increase the horror of the rocks which ledge only enough to interrupt, not stop, your fall. And the tree – O God! to think of a poor wretch hanging with one arm from it.

The lower fall, i.e. from the brook, is broader; but very low in comparison and only markworthy as combining admirably. Beyond the great fall there are six falls, each higher than the other, the chasm still gradually deepening, till the great fall, of which the height and depth is sudden and out of all comparison. I never saw trees on rock zigzag in their lines more beautifully, trees white in bark and more than overpatched with blackish moss. Then the green moss upon the rocks mingled with flats and little precipices of the grey rock, and trees again.

We climb up the hill and now have entered, entirely enclosed by hills, a plashy plain. Leeza [Lisa] River pours into the water of Ennerdale, the Enn flows out of it. On the island of rock in the lake the blackheaded seamews build in May, follow the ploughman in sowing time and pick up the worms, being quite harmless. Mr Syms won't let them be destroyed. Two years ago one friendly farmer saw eagles. One took off a full-fed harvest goose, bore it away, whelped when weary, and a second came and relieved it.

A little beyond Scale Force a man, named Jerome Bowman, slipped, broke his leg, and crawled on his hands and knees up and down hill three miles, to that cottage in sycamores where we met the dirty old woman with the two teeth – all this is in the night. He died soon after, his wounds festering. This man's son broke his neck before this by falling off a crag. Supposed to have layed down and slept, but walked in his sleep and so came to this crag. This was at Proud Knot on the mountain called Pillar

*Hereditary tenant farmers in Cumberland, of considerable independence. See p.114.

up Ennerdale. His pike staff stuck midway and stayed there till it rotted away.

The lake is so full of springs that it scarcely ever freezes.

The lower end of Ennerdale a circular bay, like the head of a battledore, and supposing the handle clumsily broad, the remaining part is the handle exactly. No house, no tree, and the unbroken line of the steep crag is tremendous. But on the left hand of the lake, as you ascend it, the rubbishy crag with sheep picturesque as goats, and as perilous, feeding. On the very summit, two large yews or hollies.

15 November
We left T. Tyson's [Wastdale Head] on Thursday morning [14 November] for Borrowdale. Brooks in their anger: all the gullies full and white, and the chasms now black, now half hid by the mist, and the waterfalls in them flashing through the mists. On the hill I counted seven huge gullies. A dark, misty, thunder-murmured scene. (Remember all about the sheep and larches.) Seven gullies but numberless tapes, white tiny streams to which mountains owe their colouring, in conjunction with the breaking and frost chasms of stone: the stone-cataract, the largest stones still at the bottom of this solid stream.

Tarn Force, Sour Milk Force, Raven Crag over it. The huge yew tree spreads its branches over a ruined cottage – the gavel [gable] end, part of the tiles and the woodwork remaining in the midst. Over the Yew Tree rocks, then the top of this single hill, above which is High Crag with all its waters.

Pocklington – Colonel* – had taken off the steeple of the mock church. Ey! Ey! Turned my church to a Presbyterian meeting. Derwentwater – they wished to have opened it at the foot, by which means the meadows would be less overflowed. Pocklington dissented: it would join his kingdom to England. Pocklington shaved off the branches of an oak, whitewashed and shaped it into an obelisk. Art beats Nature . . . Commonplace cascade at King Pocky's – whale's jaws, battlements at the top of the cascade . . .

Mile and a half from Keswick, a druidical circle. On the right hand the road and Saddleback on the left. A fine but unwatered vale walled by quarry hills and a fine black crag standing single at the termination. Ascending before me, towards Keswick, the mountains stand one behind the other in orderly array, as if evoked by and attentive to the assembly of white-vested wizards. NB The Keswickians have been playing tricks with the stones.

*He lived at Barrow House on an island on the east of Derwentwater. See p.112.

Lake Windermere from Ambleside

Sheep will not eat larches. Eat everything else. Only two funerals in the whole year at Wastdale. Something affecting may be made of it.

16 November
Friday night [15 November] we sleep at Threlkeld. Saturday morning proceed over the hills, a barren moss-peat, to Matterdale. The whole huge tract treeless, yet admirably adapted for wood, but under such tenure* who would plant it?

*The exact nature of this tenancy is unknown, but was presumably of only short-term security.

Arrive at Matterdale and are struck as by a flash with its similarity to the Devonshire cleaves: bare green hills, the knobs of them black moss, so cleft, so slop'd, so coomb'd, so cottag'd – and the cottages so the sole tree-possessors – all as between Maniton and Ashburton. The stream is quite a Devonshire brawling brook. One cottage we noticed more particularly. It stood two or three hundred yards above a cascade, in a small but sweet curve of the brook, its front to the hill, the gable end which faced with two windows so wildly placed, the other gavel end overbranch'd by the stately trees there, and the whole roof greener than the grass field on which it stood. As we proceeded, we came to a lovely delve, the Wye in miniature, but the brook brawled and foamed unsteadily. The scene, as we turn, still Devonshire.

We noticed on our right one field – the background a hill enclosed in part with stone fences knobbly with bare stones; the interspaces black, yellow, brown-red, yea all colours with the mosses and withered [growth] – the field itself a small enclosure of about an acre. [In the field were:] a stick with a rimless hat on it looking like a bell; another [stick with] the hat sunk down to the bottom, a bit of the crown remaining on the top; a single ram.

I have come suddenly upon Ullswater, running straight on the opposite bank, till the Placefell, that noble promontory, runs into it and gives it the winding of a majestic river. A little below Placefell, a large slice of calm silver; above this a bright ruffledness or atomic sportiveness – motes of the sun? Vortices of flies? How shall I express the banks [and] waters all fused silver? That house too, its slates rain-wet silver in the sun, and its shadows running down in the water like a column? The woods on the right shadowy with sunshine, and in front of me the sloping hollow of sunpatched fields, sloping up into hills so playful, the playful hills so going away in[to] snow-streaked savage black mountain[s]. But I have omitted the two island rocks in the lake (and the colours of the lake all changed!), the one scarce visible in the shadow-coloured slip now bordered by melted silver, the other nearer to me likewise in the glossy shadow, but far removed from the dazzle and quite conspicuous. The sun, it being just past noon, hangs over the lake, clouded so that any but a weak eye might gaze upon it, the clouds being in part bright white, part dusky rain-clouds, with islets of blue sky. How the scene changes, what tongues of light shoot out from the banks!

We visited the waterfall [Airey Force]; too much water and nowhere ground low enough to view it from. The chasm is very fine, and violet-coloured beeches and hawthorns quite trees, red and purple with fruits, as if the berries were flowers. The higher part of the water, the two streams running athwart each other, is original, but where the wheel-part is broken, it spreads into a muslin apron and the whole waterfall looks like a long-waisted lady-giantess slipping down on her back. But on the bridge where you see only the wheel, it is very fine. It circumvolves, with a complete half-wheel.

17 November
Sunday morning left our bad inn and went down the lake [Ullswater] by the opposite shore. The hoar-frost on the ground, the lake calm and would have been mirrorlike but that it had been *breathed* on by the mist, and that

Lyulph's Tower on Ullswater

shapely white cloud, the day-moon, hung over the snowy mountain opposite to us.

We passed the first great promontory, and what a scene! Where I stand on the shore is a triangular bay, taking in the whole of the water view. On the other shore is a straight deep wall of mist and one third of the bare mountains stands out from behind it, the top of the wall only in the sun, the rest black.

Now it is all one deep wall of white vapour, save that black streaks shaped like strange creatures seem to move in it and down it, in opposite direction to the motion of the great body! Over the fork of the cliff behind, in shape so like a cloud, the sun sent, cutting it, his thousand silky hairs of amber and green light. I step two paces and have lost the glory, but the

Raven Crag 'with its naked precipice and crowned head' (*Notebook*, 29 November 1803)

edge has exactly the soft richness of the silver edge of a cloud behind which the sun is travelling!

The fog has now closed over the lake, and we wander in darkness, save that the mist is here and there prettily coloured by the withered fern, over which it hovers.

Visit Clark's Niagara – one of Nature's occasionals, horse-shoe in shape but with none but two locum-tenentes of a petty order.

Now as we return the fog begins to clear off from the lake, still however leaving straggling detachments on it, and clings viscously to the hill. All the objects on the opposite coast are hidden, and all those hidden are reflected in the lake – trees, and the Castle (Lyulph's Tower),* and the huge cliff

*A pleasure house built by the Duke of Norfolk, one of whose homes was Greystoke Castle nearby.

F.Towne del 1786

Ullswater

that dwarfs it – Divine! The reflection of the huge pyramidal crag is still hidden, and the image in the water still brighter.

But the Lyulph's Tower gleams like a ghost, dim and shadowy. The bright shadow thereof, how beautiful it is, cut across by that tongue of breezy water. Now the shadow is suddenly gone and the Tower itself rises emerging out of the mist, two-thirds wholly hidden, the turrets quite clear. In a moment all is snatched away – Realities and Shadows.

18 November

Monday morning – sitting on a tree stump at the brink of the lake by Mr Clarkson's,* perfect serenity. That round fat backside of a hill with its image in the water made together one absolutely indistinguishable form – a kite or a paddle or keel turned to you. The road appeared a sort of suture, in many places exactly as the weiblich tetragrammaton† is painted in anatomical books! I never saw so sweet an image!

November

Partridges towering [flying near vertically upwards] after being shot is a certain proof that they are mortally wounded.

In the North every brook, every crag, almost every field has a name – a proof of greater independence and a society more approaching in their laws and habits to nature.

All about Sockburn and indeed generally in Yorkshire, North Riding, and in Durham, asses are counted so lucky that they are almost universally found among cows in dairy farms. And if a man should happen to have a horse of great value, he immediately purchases an ass, for luck! The ass runs both with the horse and with the cows, especially with the cows, as in calving they are more subject to accidents.

27 November

A most interesting morning. Awoke from one of my painful coach sleeps, in the coach to London. It was a rich orange sky like that of a winter evening save that the fleecy dark blue clouds that rippled above it shewed it to be morning. These soon became of a glowing brass colour, brassy fleeces, woolpacks in shape, rising high up into the sky. The sun at length rose upon the flat plain, like a hill of fire in the distance, rose wholly, and in the water

*An anti-slavery enthusiast who lived at Eusemere, at the northern end of Ullswater.
†A female four-letter word.

that flooded part of the flat, a deep column of light. But as the coach went on, a hill rose and intercepted the sun, and the sun in a few minutes rose over it, a compleat second rising through other clouds and with a different glory. Soon after this I saw starlings in vast flights, borne along like smoke, mist, like a body unendued with voluntary power. Now it shaped itself into a circular area, inclined; now it formed a square, now a globe, now from a complete orb into an ellipse; then oblongated into a balloon with the car suspended, now a concave semicircle; still expanding, or contracting, thinning or condensing, now glimmering and shivering, now thickening, deepening, blackening!

When on his way to London in January 1804 for the last time before sailing for Malta, Coleridge made a similar observation of birds' flight at his friend Dr Crompton's house near Liverpool.

Friday Evening, Jan. 20, 1804. Observed in the garden of Eaton House the flight of the brown linnets, a large flock of whom I had repeatedly disturbed by my foot-fall as I walked by the thicket: 1. Twinkling of wings. 2. Heavy and swanlike rise and fall, yet so that while one was rising, another was falling. 3. Their sweet straight onward motion – they swam on, not with *speed* or haste, much less *hurry*, but with easy natural swiftness – and their graceful wheel round one half of a circle or more, and then cut straight the diameter of it. 4. Their change of position amongst themselves: right to left, hindward to the front, vanguard to the rear. These four motions all at once in one beautiful whole, like a machine.

29 November
Arrived in London 27 November. The immoveableness of all things through which so many men were moving – a harsh contrast compared with the universal motion, the harmonious system of motions, in the country and everywhere in nature. In this dim light London appeared to me as a huge place of sepulchres through which hosts of spirits were gliding.

ONCE BACK IN LONDON, COLERIDGE TOOK LODGINGS NEAR THE *Strand and began on a hectic round of journalism and dining out – with Charles Lamb, William Godwin, Humphry Davy and many others. He wrote seventy-six articles for the* Morning Post, *to whose editor, Daniel Stuart, he had been introduced by the Wedgwoods. He had overdrawn on their pension and needed to earn some money. Sara and Hartley joined him until March 1800, when he went to lodge with Lamb. In April he returned to the Lake Country for a month, staying at the Wordsworths' new home, Dove Cottage at Grasmere, while he looked round for a house for himself and his family. At the beginning of June he was back at Grasmere with Sara and Hartley. They finally moved into Greta Hall at Keswick on 24 July, where their son Derwent was born on 14 September.*

Wordsworth and Coleridge were planning a second edition of the Lyrical Ballads, *which was to contain* Christabel. *Coleridge seems to have finished the second part of this in September. In October Wordsworth suddenly decided that he no longer wanted it to be included. Coleridge appeared to accept this volte-face, but it had a profound affect on his behaviour and health. He started taking opium regularly and to suffer from nightmares and boils. Previously he had only taken it intermittently, and normally as a medicine to alleviate some other bodily illness or complaint. By January 1801 his health had broken down, though he continued reading deeply in metaphysics, particularly the work of Kant, whilst still drugging himself. In April he was able to say, 'With the fine weather I revive, like a parlour fly.'*

To William Godwin*   *Nether Stowey, 21 May 1800*

If I cannot procure a suitable house at Stowey I return to Cumberland and settle at Keswick, in a house of such a prospect, that if according to you and Hume, impressions and ideas *constitute* our being, I shall have a tendency to become a god, so sublime and beautiful will be the series of my visual existence.

*Political theorist and novelist. Husband of Mary Wollstonecraft, the pioneer feminist. Their daughter Mary married Shelley and was the author of *Frankenstein*.

Greta Hall, Keswick: 'a tenement in the possession of S.T. Coleridge, Esq.,
Gentleman-Poet and Philosopher in a mist' (p.81)

To Humphry Davy   *Dove Cottage, Grasmere, 15 July 1800*

We remove to our own house in Keswick on Tuesday week – my address is,
Mr Coleridge, Greta Hall, Keswick, Cumberland. My dear fellow, I would
that I could wrap up the view from my house in a pill of opium, and send it
to you! I should then be sure of seeing you in the fall of the year. But you
will come.

As soon as I have disembrangled my affairs by a couple of months'
industry, I shall attack chemistry, like a shark. In the meantime do not
forget to fulfil your promise of sending me a synopsis of your metaphysical

opinions. I am even *anxious* about this. I see your researches on the nitrous oxide [laughing gas] regularly advertised. Be so kind as to order one to be left for me at Longman's,* that it may be sent with my box. The difficulty of procuring books is the greatest disadvantage, under which I shall labor. The carriage from London by the waggon is cross-roadish, and insecure; that by the mail attacks the purse with seven hydra mouths all open.

Mid-July

Dungeon Gill Force. Stand to the right hand, close by the bellying rock, so as to see the top of the waterfall only by the daylight on the wet rock. The arch right above, the little imitation of the great waterfall (connections in nature). Between the arch and the great waterfall, an arch of trees: hollies, ash, and one birch. The stream widens from a foot to a yard and a half. As it widens, varying from a vivid white to a blue through all the intermediate shades. The second [pool?] divided from the first by a huge boulder contiguated to the two sides by rocks small and pendulous. Plumy ferns on the side and, over the second pool, the light umbrella of a young ash.

Going up to the Force, notice the sheepfold, the higher wall of whose parallelogram is faced with fern, one a plume, the rest bunches of parsley fern. The fold encloses a curve of the path of a mountain beck, as may be seen by the elegantly winding stream of pebbles close by the right-hand wall.

Ladies reading Gilpin's† etc. while passing by the very places instead of looking at the places.

23 July

About a quarter of a mile from Jakesson's enquired of an old woman the way to Watendlatter [Watendlath]. She was carrying hay into a barn with vigor. Four grandchildren sitting on the hay, lazily helping her. 'Which way to W?' 'Up the gap, a gay canny road.' 'How far?' 'Two miles and more.' 'Is there much to climb beyond the highest point we see?' 'As much again before you get level. 'Tis a gay canny climb. You may get there in an hour. I'self could ga there in an hour who's eighty and over.'

She was eighty-three. Her son had nine children and those we saw were the four youngest. Mr Jakesson's house blue slated – the corners, the woodwork of the windows, and the two chimneys painted gore-colour.

---

*The publisher with whom Coleridge had contracted to translate Schiller's play *Wallenstein* from the German.
†The fashionable guidebook to the Lakes.

To Humphry Davy   *Greta Hall, Keswick, 25 July 1800*

Work hard, and if success do not dance up like the bubbles in the salt (with the spirit lamp under it) may the Devil and his Dame take success! 'S death my dear fellow! from the window before me there is a great *camp* of mountains – Giants seem to have pitched their tents there. Each mountain is a Giant's tent – and how the light streams from them, and the shadows that travel upon them! Davy! I *ake* for you to be with us . . .

We drank tea the night before I left Grasmere, on the island in that lovely lake; our kettle swung over the fire hanging from the branch of a fir-tree, and I lay and saw the woods, and mountains, and lake all trembling, and as it were *idealized* through the subtle smoke which rose up from the clear red embers of the fir-apples, which we had collected; afterwards, we made a glorious bonfire on the margin, by some elder bushes, whose twigs heaved and sobbed in the uprushing column of smoke – and the image of the bonfire, and of us that danced round it – ruddy laughing faces in the twilight – the image of this in a lake smooth as that sea, to whose waves the Son of God had said, *Peace*! May God and all his Sons, love you as I do.

Sara desires her kind remembrances – Hartley is a spirit that dances on an aspen leaf – the air that yonder sallow-faced and yawning tourist is breathing, is to my babe a perpetual nitrous oxide. Never was more joyous creature born. Pain with him is so wholly trans-substantiated by the joys that had rolled on before, and rushed in after, that often-times five minutes after his mother had whipt him, he had gone up and asked her to whip again.

*To Samuel Purkis**   *Greta Hall, Keswick, 29 July 1800*

I write to you from the *leads* of Greta Hall, a tenement in the possession of S. T. Coleridge, Esq., Gentleman-Poet and Philosopher in a mist. This Greta Hall is a house on a small eminence, a furlong from Keswick in the county of Cumberland. Yes – my dear Sir! here I am – with Skiddaw at my back – on my right hand the Bassenthwaite Water with its majestic *case* of mountains, all of simplest outline – looking slant, direct over the feather of this infamous pen, I see the sun setting – my God! what a scene! Right before me is a great *camp* of single mountains – each in shape resembles a Giant's Tent; and to the left, but closer to it far than the Bassenthwaite Water to my right, is the lake of Keswick [Derwentwater], with its islands

*A tanner and man of letters like Thomas Poole, through whom Coleridge met him.

'Keswick Lake (Derwentwater) . . . *crowned* with green meadows' (p.84)

Sir Humphry Davy

and white sails, and glossy lights of evening – *crowned* with green meadows. But the three remaining sides are encircled by the most fantastic mountains, that ever earthquakes made in sport; as fantastic, as if Nature had *laughed* herself into the convulsion, in which they were made. Close behind me at the foot of Skiddaw flows the Greta, I hear its murmuring distinctly – then it curves round almost in a semicircle, and is now catching the purple lights of the scattered clouds above it directly before me. . . Till now I have been grievously indisposed – now I am enjoying the Godlikeness of the place, in which I am settled, with the voluptuous and joy-trembling nerves of convalescence. We arrived here last week – I was confined a fortnight at Grasmere. . .

Sara Coleridge is well – she expects to be confined in the first weeks of September. Hartley is all health and ecstasy.

To Thomas Poole   *Greta Hall, Keswick, 14 August 1800*

Your two letters I received exactly four days ago – some days they must have been lying at Ambleside before they were sent to Grasmere, and some days at Grasmere before they moved to Keswick. . . It grieved me that you had felt so much from my silence. Believe me, I have been harassed with business, and shall remain so for the remainder of this year. Our house is a delightful residence, something less than half a mile from the lake of Keswick and something more than a furlong from the town. It commands both that lake and the lake of Bassenthwaite. Skiddaw is behind us; to the left, the right, and in front mountains of all shapes and sizes. The waterfall of Lodore is distinctly visible. In garden, etc., we are uncommonly well off, and our landlord, who resides next door in this twofold house, is already much attached to us.* He is a quiet, sensible man, with as large a library as yours – and perhaps rather larger – well stored with encyclopædias, dictionaries, and histories, etc., all modern. The gentry of the country, titled and untitled, have all called or are about to call on me, and I shall have free access to the magnificent library of Sir Gilfrid Lawson. I wish you could come here in October after your harvesting, and stand godfather at the christening of my child. In October the country is in all its blaze of beauty.

. . . I was standing at the very top of Skiddaw, by a little shed of slate stones on which I had scribbled with a bit of slate my name among the other names. A lean-expression-faced man came up the hill, stood beside

*For more about William Jackson, owner of Greta Hall, see p. 108.

me a little while, then, on running over the names, exclaimed, 'Coleridge! I lay my life that is the *poet Coleridge!*'

God bless you, and for God's sake never doubt that I am attached to you beyond all other men.

July, August

The Rydal Lake glittering and rippled all over. Only, on the Rydal side of the oval island of trees that lies athwart the Lake, a long round-pointed wedge of black glossy calm. Rocky island across the narrow, like the fragment of some huge bridge, now overgrown with moss and trees. Silver How casts its black shadow in two lakes – Rydal and Grasmere.

The Druids and Hebrews, in piling stones *in honorem genii loci* [to honour the genius of the place], suffered them not to be defiled by a tool.

In the parish of Bewcastle, schoolmaster hired for £10 a year, and goes about with the scholars begging for victuals by rotation. The custom is called 'Whittlegate'.

24 August

Walked to Latrigg with Sara and Hartley. The sun set with columns of misty light slanted from him, the light a bright buff. Walla Crag purple red, the lake a deep dingy purple blue, that Torrent Crag opposite Elder Seat a maroon. But the clouds – that great egg, almost one twentieth of the whole Heaven in appearance, a fine smoke-flame. Beyond, a huge flight of steps to a temple. The helm on Skiddaw – in that huge semicircular hollow, a bridge of clouds over the bend of the circle, and the blue sky seen under it. The helm itself, a well defined ridge of lead-coloured clouds. As we turn round on our return, we see a moving pillar of clouds, flame and smoke, rising, bending, arching, and in swift motion. From what God's chimney does it issue? I scarcely ever saw in the sky such variety of shapes and colours, and colours floating over colours. Solemnly now lie the black masses on the blue firmament of – not quite night – for still at the foot of Bassenthwaite there is a smoky russet light. 'Tis nine o'clock.

25 August

Tour up Saddleback. Passing Windy Brow and Wood, came to a stream which runs between Latrigg and Skiddaw. Mounted above High Row. The Derwent Water and the Greta meandering, its right bank being Latrigg, hollow and woody. Two vales on my left. Mount and mount and mount, the vale now fronting me as I stand. Lay down: beautiful effect of the Vale

Rydal Lake

Derwentwater with Skiddaw in the centre distance

of St John's with Withburne Water [Thirlmere] on the right in the distance. Endless squares of land, whose multiplicity, by multitude, acquires unity.

Now at length come to Saddleback properly so called, and see beneath me those precipices and ridges which from the vale of St John's appear tents. The stones burnt evidently. Ascend again and again. Leave the precipices and tents behind me. Descend northward, and ascend, and thence see the Tarn [Scales Tarn]: a round basin of vast depth, the west arc an almost perpendicular precipice of naked shelving crags (each crag a precipice with a small shelf). To the east the outlet. Northwest between a narrow chasm a little sike [rivulet] wound down over very green moss. At every fall the water fell off in little liquid icicles from the points of moss jelly

bags. In one place a semi-round stone with sixteen of these. The northern wall of the basin green with huge scars of bare blue stone dust, and whiter stones. On the green slips within the scars, sheep. No noise but that of loose stones rolling away from the feet of the sheep, that move slowly along these perilous ledges.

An eminently beautiful object is fern, on a hillside, scattered thick but growing single – and all shaking themselves in the wind.

A child scolding a flower in the words in which he had himself been scolded and whipt, is *poetry*: past passion with pleasure.

'A Thought suggested by a View of Saddleback in Cumberland'

On stern Blencartha's* perilous height
 The winds are tyrannous and strong;
And flashing forth unsteady light
From stern Blencartha's skiey height,
 As loud the torrents throng!
Beneath the moon, in gentle weather,
They bind the earth and sky together.
But oh! the sky and all its forms, how quiet!
The things that seek the earth, how full of noise and riot!

26 August
A day of clouds and threatening showrlets. The helm on Skiddaw resolved itself into a cloud connected with the great burthens of the sky. Visit – Applethwaite – a divine village!

27 August
Morning, six o'clock. Clouds in motion half down Skiddaw, capping and veiling Wanthwaite. No sun, no absolute gleam, but the mountains in and beyond Borrowdale were bright and washed, and the vale of Newlands silent and bright. All the crags that enbason the Derwentwater very dark, especially Walla Crag; the Crag such a very gloomy purple, its treeage such a very black green. Shortly after the Castle Crag and Grange became illuminated, but all soon darkened, a mere gloom of cloudiness.

 N.B. What is it that makes the silent bright of the morning vale so different from that other silence and bright gleams of late evening? Is it in

*Blencartha, or more properly Blencathra, is another name for Saddleback.

A morning scene in Borrowdale

the mind or is there any physical cause? Our house, in all else a true temple of Nature, is unfortunately placed for the water lights, Derwentwater being to the S and Bassenthwaite to the N, and the latter likewise too distant . . .

Half-past eight. In this whole basin, from the mountains of Borrowdale to the hill behind Ouse bridge, but one field is sunny – that with a white cottage. The grass yellow green, so bright. The white cottage sparkles like a diamond in the surrounding gloom.

Borrowdale: 'what a view of mountains' (p.94)

The first half of 'A Stranger Minstrel' follows, which Coleridge wrote to Mrs Perdita Robinson 'a few weeks before her death' in December 1800. Sometime mistress of the Prince of Wales and then of Charles James Fox, actress, poet and gothick novelist, she was greatly admired by Coleridge, who had met her the previous winter in London.

As late on Skiddaw's mount I lay supine,
Midway th' ascent, in that repose divine
When the soul centred in the heart's recess
Hath quaff'd its fill of Nature's loveliness,
Yet still beside the fountain's marge will stay
   And fain would thirst again, again to quaff;
Then when the tear, slow travelling on its way,
   Fills up the wrinkles of a silent laugh –
In that sweet mood of sad and humorous thought
A form within me rose, within me wrought
With such strong magic, that I cried aloud,
'Thou ancient Skiddaw by thy helm of cloud,
And by thy many-colour'd chasms deep,
And by their shadows that for ever sleep,
By yon small flaky mists that love to creep
Along the edges of those spots of light,
Those sunny islands on thy smooth green height,
   And by yon shepherds with their sheep,
   And dogs and boys, a gladsome crowd,
   That rush e'en now with clamour loud
   Sudden from forth thy topmost cloud,
   And by this laugh, and by this tear,
   I would, old Skiddaw, she were here!
   A lady of sweet song is she,
   Her soft blue eye was made for thee!
   O ancient Skiddaw, by this tear,
   I would, I would that she were here!'

Then ancient Skiddaw, stern and proud,
   In sullen majesty replying,
Thus spake from out his helm of cloud
   (His voice was like an echo dying!) –
'She dwells belike in scenes more fair,
And scorns a mount so bleak and bare.'

28 August

A morning of masses of clouds rolling in sunshine; the Grange well lighted up. It rained a trifle.

Sunset lights slanted Newlands Hollows. Smoke flame over Wanthwaite and under that mass, a *wedge* of light on the cliff. But soon the whole of Wanthwaite drunk with a black-hued *scarlet*. The distances of Borrowdale duskily coloured long after the set. The end of the lake was crimsoned during the sunset.

As I sate on the side of Skiddaw at one o'clock in the noon of this day, saw the shore of the lake and those of its island hemmed with silver in the misty, cloudy, rain-spattered lake.

Eleven o'clock at night. That conical volcano of coal, half an inch high, ejaculating its inverted cone of smoke. The smoke in what a furious wind, this way and that way – and what a noise!

> The poet's eye in his tipsy hour
> Hath a magnifying power
> Or rather his soul emancipates his eyes
> Of the accidents of size.
> In unctuous cones of kindling coal
> Or smoke from his pipe's bowl
> His eye can see
> Phantoms of sublimity.

Twelve o'clock at night. No moon. Heard a nick! nick! at the window panes. Went with the candle. Saw at both windows an amazing quantity of flies or small gnats and a spider whose web was on the outside, as busy as a successful poacher.

29 August

Friday evening saw the force of Saddleback Tarn beck about forty feet high. For the first eight or nine feet it falls perpendicular, water-colour, then meets a rock and rushes down in a steep slope, all foam, till the last two feet when the rock ceases but the water preserves the same colour and inclination as if it were there. The pool into which it falls is almost a circle, ten yards in diameter with blue slates at the bottom. A young mountain ash with one unripe and never to be ripe cluster is growing athwart it. The fall, when perpendicular, is about a good yard across; when it runs slope, no more than a foot and a half. But in winter and after rain no doubt it fills the whole capacity of its scoop, and will then be a yard and a half in breadth.

Something more than a furlong from the force, not ten yards from the beck, on the hill eight heaps of moss . . . each an exact grave, each in the descent somewhat longer than the one higher up, the first four feet in length, the lowest eight and a half feet. You have then an august view of Cove Crag (a sloping edge) with a tree on it. A few yards further a small force with a fine mountain ash over it, and a beautifully long smooth bathing pool at its foot, six or seven yards long. A little further down, a third force, uninteresting, but then what a view of that half-moon crag before me, and the inverted crescent on its right hand. Ran along and in a half-furlong another beck joined my fellow traveller. I looked up it into a magnificent embracement of cliff, an embracement two-thirds of an oval. 'Another tarn! Another tarn!' I cried. I ran and ran. As I approached, 'Psha!' said I. 'Where are my wits? 'Tis the same as I before visited and I have been blundering.' Every moment this conviction increased and now I saw every minute object of my old friend. But, behold! When I came up there was no tarn awhile. It might be made a noble tarn by a couple of stout men in a day's time. . . What a noise of kites! How the sheep stand, each on the green ledge-top of its black violet naked clifflet.

31 August
Left my house, crossed the Greta, past Window [Windy, Whinny] Brow, went on through the wood by Westcote and kept the road till it joins the great turnpike a little above Threlkeld. Crossed the Glenderatara then, scaling stone fences, wound up along the stony knot at the foot of the green fells under the Whitepike. A hot cloudy day. Ascended straight up for at least an hour and O! how glad was I at last to see the blue sky on the other side. Walked by a more leisurely ascent to the very summit of Whitepike. . .

Trudge on over a heathy, boggy ground, over the rotten wet scarlet and yellow moss, over ground which, in wet time would, I suppose, be unsafe. With a little descent and a little ascent come to a blunt cone-hill white with stones, a sheepfold at the bottom of it. Surely this must be Whitepike! and then what is the name of that high round hill which I have left?. . . To my left two or three green mountains and Helvellyn. Its deep torrent-chasmy crags bound the view, so high, so perpendicularly steep. . . In front, a most delicious view. What a universal convention of mountains ending in that vale which goes from Thirlmere to Keswick . . . the ridge that runs up between the vales into Threlkeld, how fine, with torrent-worn raspberry and milk-coloured crags. . .

From this point I hear swelling and sinking a murmur – is it of water? Or is it of falling screes? Fine columns of misty sunshine sailing slowly over the

A different view of Derwentwater with 'ancient' Skiddaw in the distance

crags. I make for the water; it runs down that green mountain which is so directly behind that which I first ascended, and somewhat higher than it. I drank and was refreshed. Ascend this green mountain. That opposite which immediately fronts Saddleback and seems to say, 'I am as high as thou', is surely not Whitepike. I think I see Whitepike, peeping up on its slope like a wart between me and Souterfell – and what is the name of that with the sheepfold?

How populous is this landscape. Between the mountains and the clouds, and slanting adown the clouds, and adown the mountains, are columns or arches of misty light! From the utmost points of Great Gable to the head of Derwentwater they extend – I count twenty-five of them. What a view of mountains. Looking over into the Buttermere country I count seven great

mountains, one behind another, and I can look in no direction from Lang-dale to Whinlatter but there are four distances. In one direction I count nine, yea ten. I left the mountain beck behind me and went towards St John's Vale. Then, wending up the mountain, had St John's at my back as I climb, till I reach the summit. . . Beheld (O joy for me!) Patterdale and Ullswater. . . down to Mr Clarkson's. I think I see his house, but I am sure I see that round *backside* hill that the Wordsworths and I laughed at there*. . . Derwentwater (the higher third of it) a dusky yellow richness, indented and tongued, and with a rim of *brightness*. . . My next object, that sugarloaf on the mountain that looks down on Wythburn. . .

*See entry for 18 November 1799.

I reached the sugarloaf, an uncommonly well built cone of stones. . . The sugarloaf point is rather a high shoulder, and that green to which I am bending a monstrous high one. I reach it . . . descend, soon to ascend. What a scene of horrible desolateness the ascent is, so scarified with peat holes, on its left running down with white cliffs – Whiteside I suppose – and its top so rugged with white cliffs. This place is evidently Styx Top [Sticks Pass between St John's Vale and Patterdale]. . . Passed by the ragged stones on top, scor[ace]ious as the dross of a smelting house. The evening now lating, I had resolved to pass by it; but Nature twitched me at my heart strings. I ascended it, thanks to her! Thanks to her, what a scene! Nothing behind me, as if it would be an affront to that which fronts me! Two complete reaches of Ullswater, then a noble tongue of a hill (Glenruddin Screes, where the King of Patterdale* keeps his goats). . . Away up in the mountains on the right two tarns and close on my right those precipices stained with green amid their nakedness, and ridges, tents, embracing semicircles. I front to them – there are two and a narrow ridge between them. I will go up it. Descended. As I bounded down, noticed the moving stones under the soft moss, hurting my feet.

Ascended that steep and narrow ridge. On my right that precipice and the morass at its feet. On my left the two tarns and another precipice twice as lofty as the other, but its white stones more coated and lined with moss. Am now at the top of Helvellyn. . . Travelling along the ridge I came to the other side of those precipices and down below me on the left – no – no! No words can convey any idea of this prodigious wildness. That precipice fine on this side was but its ridge, sharp as a jagged knife, level so long, and then ascending so boldly. What a frightful bulgy precipice I stand on and to my right how the crag which corresponds to the other, how it plunges down like a waterfall, reaches a level steepness, and again plunges!

The moon is above Fairfield almost at the full. Now descended over a perilous peat-moss then down a hill of stones all dark, and darkling. I climbed stone after stone down a half-dry torrent and came out at the Raise Gap. And O! my God! how did that opposite precipice look in the moonshine – its name Stile Crags.†

*The owners of the Mounsey estate there who had never paid rents or done homage to the king or to anyone else.
†'At eleven o'clock Coleridge came, when I was walking in the still, clear moonshine in the garden. . . We sate and chatted till half-past three, W. in his dressing-gown. Coleridge read us a part of *Christabel*.'

Dorothy Wordsworth's *Grasmere Journal, 31 August 1800*

1 September
The beards of thistle and dandelions flying above the lonely mountains like life, and I saw them through the trees skimming the lake like swallows.

2 September
Passed the lake [Grasmere], crossed over Hammerscar and the slate quarries, Warthwaite Chapel stile, Harry Place, Raw Head; bower or rather arch. . . all flower-gem'd with honeysuckles in the garden of the cottage. Climbed up by the Knots to the [Stickle] Tarn, Langdale Pike at the side nearest the vale. Fronting me a stupendous perpendicular crag [Harrison Stickle]. Ascend that; meet rocks overgrown as with limpets, exact pyramids.

To William Godwin   *Greta Hall, Keswick, 8 September 1800*

Of North Wales my recollections are faint, and as to Wicklow I only know from the newspapers that it is a mountainous country.* As far as my memory will permit me to decide on the grander parts of Carnarvonshire, I may say that the single objects are superior to any which I have seen elsewhere, but there is a deficiency in combination. I know of no mountain in the North equal to Snowdon, but then we have an encampment of huge mountains, in no harmony perhaps to the eye of the mere painter, but always interesting, various and, as it were nutritive. Height is assuredly an advantage, as it connects the earth with the sky, by the clouds that are ever skimming the summits or climbing up, or creeping down the sides, or rising from the chasm, like smoke from a cauldron, or veiling or bridging the higher parts or lower parts of waterfalls. That you were less impressed by North Wales I can easily believe; it is possible that the scenes of Wicklow may be superior, but it is certain that you were in a finer irritability of spirit to enjoy them. The first pause and silence after a return from a very interesting visit is somewhat connected with langour in all of us. Besides, as you have observed, mountains and mountainous scenery taken collectively and cursorily, must depend for their charms on their novelty. They put on their immortal interest then first, when we have resided among them, and learnt to understand their language, their written character and intelligible sounds, and all their eloquence, so various, so unwearied.

*Godwin went to Dublin in the summer of 1800 to stay with John Philpot Curran, the lawyer who had defended the leaders of the United Irishmen when they were tried in 1798.

Helvellyn: 'this prodigious
wildness' (p.96)

9 September
Crossed the meadows to the Lake [Derwentwater], a heavenly walk this.
Noticed the houses with the woods at their back, in the best style of the
picturesque. A little way down the river a boat-house of bushes, high as a
large cottage, with two fine ashes growing high above it . . . a perfect model
of a boat-house, with gable ends a perfect triangle, the base a loft for dry
wood, etc. . . Came to a peat-ground full of Dutch myrtle and so to Swinside . . . The colour of this hill is owing to the red, yellow, and rusty green
mingled everywhere with the grass, as the colour of the Barrow is owing to
the black ling and green fern. From the point of Swinside the Vale of
Newlands . . . is so arborous as to look almost like a Somersetshire vale; the
winding river with its arched bridges, hid chiefly where houses by its side
have more and higher trees, lovely . . .

Went down the lane, crossed the bridge, O lovely bridge . . . came to Barrow Gill, it runs through a bed of rock. Almost at the foot of Rolling End a well-ivied bridge. Beautiful pools and waterslides in this gill and an eminently beautiful spout and pool under the bridge. The walls of the bridge reach only to my ankle, but the stonework above the arch is at least two yards. Followed this gill, winding along with Causey Pike on my left . . . Spotty Skiddaw with his chasms and ribs in sunshine looked in on me, and Latrigg so so soft a pea green, its soft knobbly gable end yellow . . .

I now came to a level, passed a moss peat, and beheld a narrow bottom. On the other side a hill, how high I cannot see for the cloud; grass and ling most magnificently *streamed* with purple and scarlet screes. Made up to some shepherds by a sheepfold, whom I had seen running down the hill through the mist . . . That so streamed is called Long Ridge . . . then Force Crag . . . the narrow bottom is called Cowdale [Coledale] . . . On the left of Cowdale runs Grisdale Pike.

10 September

On Saturday morning, a spectacle etc., the body of an infant etc. From the length of time the body had remained in the water the legs had assumed a greenish hue, *probably from the weeds*, and the flesh was more yielding to the touch than is either necessary or agreeable to describe.

Catch hold of the bough as you climb, not to sustain, but balance. – *Moral use.*

19 September

A beautiful rainbow on Skiddaw, the foot of the arch in the third field under Ormathwaite, the other foot just under the nearest part of Skiddaw Dodd. The height of the arch just in the half-way height of Skiddaw Tent. It faded away into a green reflection, preserving its figure, yet so that if I had not seen it before, I should not have thought it a rainbow.

22 September

After the so unusual continuance of fine weather, the rain seems to have come at last. Lodore and the fall in Borrowdale whiten conspicuously. Yet ever and anon the sun is on the hills and mounts, the universal mist not *dissipated* but *attenuated*. Sometimes the mist will dissolve wholly from some field or eminence, that stands out from the rest of the landscape bright and newbathed. One column of watery sunshine falls upon the Grange. To the inverted arch in Newlands clear; at the arch a wall of impenetrable darkness. A pelting shower, then clear and a road of silver brightness from the woods far over the lake to the other side of the island. Vanishes. Beautiful appearance of moving mist over Newlands, in long dividuous flakes, the interspaces filled up by a thinner mist – all in sunlight.

29 September

After a most tremendous storm of hail, the lower half of the lake was bright silver. Over it and intercepting Borrowdale, a *thick palpable blue* up to the moon, save that at the very top of the blue the clouds rolled lead-coloured. Small detachments of these clouds running in thick flakes near the moon and drinking its light in amber and white. The moon in a clear azure sky – the mountains seen indeed, and only seen – I never saw aught so sublime!

10 October

White Water Dash, at the top of a horse shoe valley. The Dash a precipice of white rock and purple screes almost perpendicular. It laves its feet. A semicircular basin of craggy rocks, not very high, variegated with screes, heath, and moss – this is the upper part of the valley. It is by no means equal to the Churnmilk at Easedale, or the Wythburn Fall.

This I wrote seeing the whole Dash, but when I descended to the bottom, there I only saw the real *Fall* and the curve of the steep slope, and retracted. It is indeed, so seen, a fine thing. It falls parallel with a fine black rock for thirty feet and is more shattered, more completely atomized and white than any I have ever seen. The pool likewise is formed by a few high large stones and not a yard in breadth, [so] of course as white as the fall itself . . . The fall of the Dash is in a horse shoe basin of its own, wildly peopled with small ashes standing out of the rocks.

Crossed the stream by the white pool, and stood on the other side in a complete spray-rain. Here it assumes, I think, a still finer appearance. You see the vast ruggedness and angular points and upright cones of the black rock. The fall assumes a variety and complexity, parts rushing in wheels, other parts perpendicular, some in white horse-tails. While towards the right edge of the black, two or three leisurely fillets have escaped out of the turmoil.

11 October

Caldbeck town embosomed in low woody hills, a woody scattered village of Micklebeck, near the Howk. On the bank of the beck prodigious quantities of that huge-leafed plant (Burdock). Before you, stand fairies' parlours and fine cathedral seats overhung by the rock . . . Go again into the cavern and see another chamber, crawl into it. At the end one round hole through which I glimpse another waterfall. Shut my eyes: the noise of water like that when you are in a mill, a room off the great wheel. Climb out through the window hole . . . Rocks overhanging from a big square pillar three yards at least. Great swinging pendula of ivy almost down to the water. The inclined rocks make a natural bridge over the beck.

Climbed Carrock. Descended just over the last house in Swinside and almost broke my neck. Above Swinside, just at the bottom of that first winding of the valley (Swinside is at the head of the second winding) a very fine slope of water in the Caldew. A very large rock forms the whole channel and is about as much raised as a man lying and raising himself on his elbow, the water in the pool at the bottom for ever fighting up against the fierce descending army of foam . . . A lively image of a battle.

Burdock: 'that huge-leafed plant'
(p.101)

Coleridge became an aficionado of waterfalls
in the Lakes, noting the effects of changing
light and weather on them

As I passed under Caldbeck fells, with the Bowscale fells on my left, found on my plashy mossy path immense quantities of the Tremella.* In one either a mouse's or a mole's leg, with a bit of the skin of the thigh. On October 10th, the first snow fell on Skiddaw.

October

The Sopha of Sods – whole life – sliding down Latrigg – snow tree – planting and sowing – poem hid in a tin box – stooping from sublime thoughts to reckon how many lines the poem would make.†

To Humphry Davy   *Greta Hall, Keswick, 18 October 1800*

Our mountains northward end in the mountain Carrock – one huge, steep, enormous bulk of stones, desolately variegated with the heath plant; at its foot runs the river Calder, and a narrow vale between it and the mountain Bowscale, so narrow, that in its greatest width it is not more than a furlong. But that narrow vale is *so* green, *so* beautiful, there are moods in which a man might weep to look at it. On this mountain Carrock, at the summit of which are the remains of a vast Druid circle of stones, I was wandering, when a thick cloud came on, and wrapped me in such darkness that I could not see ten yards before me, and with the cloud a storm of wind and hail, the like of which I had never before seen and felt. At the very summit is a cone of stones, built by the shepherds, and called the Carrock Man. Such cones are on the tops of almost all our mountains, and they are all called *men*. At the bottom of the Carrock Man I seated myself for shelter, but the wind became so fearful and tyrannous, that I was apprehensive some of the stones might topple down upon me, so I groped my way farther down and came to three rocks . . . each one supported by the other like a child's house of cards, and in the hollow and screen which they made I sate for a long while sheltered, as if I had been in my own study in which I am now writing: there I sate with a total feeling worshipping the power and 'eternal link' of energy. The darkness vanished as by enchantment; far off, far, far off to the south, the mountains of Glaramara and Great Gable and their family appeared distinct, in deepest, sablest *blue*. I rose, and behind me was a rainbow bright as the brightest.

*A wobbly, jelly-like fungus.
†This seems to be the outline for a poem about a seat of sods which Coleridge, William and Dorothy Wordsworth had built at Windy Brow on the lower slopes of Latrigg on 13 August 1800. The poem never got written. That entitled 'Inscription for a Seat . . .' in Coleridge's *Complete Poetical Works* is a revision by him of one written by Wordsworth on the same subject. See also p.229.

I descended by the side of a torrent, and passed, or rather crawled (for I was forced to descend on all fours), by many a naked waterfall, till, fatigued and hungry (and with a finger almost broken, and which remains swelled to the size of two fingers), I reached the narrow vale, and the single house nestled in ash and sycamores. I entered to claim the universal hospitality of this country; but instead of the life and comfort usual in these lonely houses, I saw dirt and every appearance of misery – a pale woman sitting by a peat fire. I asked her for bread and milk, and she sent a small child to fetch it, but did not rise herself. I eat very heartily of the black, sour bread, and drank a bowl of milk, and asked her to permit me to pay her. 'Nay,' says she, 'we are not so scant as that – you are right welcome; but do you know any help for the rheumatics, for I have been so long ailing that I am almost fain to die?' So I advised her to eat a great deal of mustard, having seen in an advertisement something about essence of mustard curing the most obstinate cases of rheumatism. But do write me, and tell me some cure for the rheumatism; it is in her shoulders, and the small of her back chiefly. I wish much to go off with some bottles of stuff to the poor creature. I should walk the ten miles as ten yards.

21 October
Morning, two o'clock. Wind amid its [?brausen] makes every now and then such a deep moan of pain, that I think it my wife asleep in pain. A trembling Oo! Oo! like a wounded man on a field of battle whose wounds smarted with the cold.

October
Derwent laughed at six weeks old – the first thing he appeared to take notice of was the trees bending, etc., in the strong wind – this too at six weeks.

To Josiah Wedgwood   *Greta Hall, Keswick, 1 November 1800*

But immediately on my arrival in this country I undertook to finish a poem which I had begun, entitled Christabel, for a second volume of the Lyrical Ballads. I tried to perform my promise; but the deep unutterable disgust, which I had suffered in the translation of that accursed Wallenstein, seemed to have stricken me with barrenness – for I tried and tried, and nothing would come of it. I desisted with a deeper dejection than I am willing to remember. The wind from the Skiddaw and Borrowdale was often as loud as wind need be – and many a walk in the clouds on the mountains did I

The druidical circle near Keswick

Josiah Wedgwood II

take; but all would not do – till one day I dined out at the house of a neighbouring clergyman, and somehow or other drank so much wine, that I found some effort and dexterity requisite to balance myself on the hither edge of sobriety. The next day, my verse making faculties returned to me, and I proceeded successfully – till my poem grew so long and in Wordsworth's opinion so impressive, that he rejected it from his volume as disproportionate both in size and merit, and as discordant in its character. In the meantime, I had gotten myself entangled in the old Sorites of the old Sophist, Procrastination. I had suffered my necessary business to accumulate so terribly, that I neglected to write to any one – till the pain I suffered from not writing, made me waste as many hours in dreaming about it, as would have sufficed for the letter-writing of half a life. . .

The room in which I write commands six distinct landscapes – the two lakes, the vale, the river, and mountains and mists, and clouds, and sunshine make endless combinations, as if heaven and earth were for ever talking to each other. Often when in a deep study I have walked to the window and remained there *looking without seeing*; all at once the lake of Keswick and the fantastic mountains of Borrowdale at the head of it, have entered into my mind with a suddenness, as if I had been snatched out of Cheapside and placed for the first time, on the spot where I stood – and that is a delightful feeling – these fits and trances of *novelty* received from a long known object. The river of Greta flows behind our house, roaring like an untamed son of the hills, then winds round, and *glides* away in the front – so that we live in a peninsula. But besides this etherial eye-feeding, we have very substantial conveniences. We are close to the town, where we have respectable and neighbourly acquaintance, and a most sensible and truly excellent medical man. Our garden is part of a large nursery garden, which is the same to us and as private as if the whole had been our own, and thus too we have delightful walks without passing our garden gates.

My Landlord, who lives in the sister house (for the two houses are built so as to look like one great one), is a modest and kind man, of a singular character. By the severest economy he raised himself from a carrier into the possession of a comfortable independence. He was always very fond of reading, and has collected nearly 500 volumes of our most esteemed modern writers, such as Gibbon, Hume, Johnson, etc., etc. His habits of economy and simplicity remain with him – and yet so very disinterested a man I scarcely ever knew. Lately when I wished to settle with him about the rent of our house, he appeared much affected, told me that my living near him and the having so much of Hartley's company were great comforts to him and his housekeeper – that he had no children to provide for, and did not mean to marry – and in short, that he did not want any rent at all from me. This, of course, I laughed him out of; but he absolutely refused to receive any rent for the first half year, under the pretext, that the house was not completely finished. Hartley quite *lives* at the house – and it is as you may suppose no small joy to my wife to have a good affectionate motherly woman divided from her only by a wall.

Eighteen miles from our house lives Sir Gilfrid Lawson, who has a princely library, chiefly of natural history – a kind, and generous, but weak and ostentatious sort of man, who has been abundantly civil to me. Among other raree shews he keeps a wild beast or two, with some eagles, etc. The Master of the Beasts at Exeter change, sent him down a large bear – with it a long letter of directions concerning the food etc. of the animal, and many solicitations respecting other agreeable quadrupeds, which he was *desirous* to send to the Baronet, at a moderate price, concluding in this manner – 'and remain your Honor's most devoted humble servant, J. P. P s *Permit* me, Sir Gilfrid, to send you a Buffalo and a Rhinoceros.' As neat a postscript as I ever heard! – the tradesmanlike coolness with which these pretty little animals occurred to him just at the finishing of his letter!!

2 November
Night, eight o'clock. One of the sublimest scenes. It was moonlight but the mist was so thick on the Lake and between me and the mountains, that of the whole vast landscape I could see only Peach's house, the whole of Swineside and Pocklington's house [Barrow House]. One advantage of white houses – they shine in the moon.

6 November
Morning. Behind the Grange and the mountain above the Grange, a thick blanket of white woolly cloud which, thinning here and there, shewed bits and edges of the mountains behind in the most sublime style.

24 November
To butcher: 'Chickens – will you kill them?'
   'Neay, I don't much like it. I had far fainer kill an ox.'
   Rabbits hung out to air.

27 November
Hartley taken ill, white as a sheet. The snow-mountains almost covered with a fog, yet here and there and everywhere clear spots of bright yellow sunshine.

The lake of
Keswick with the
'fantastic
mountains of
Borrowdale at the
head of it' (p.108)

Barrow House on Pocklington's Island, Keswick Lake

29 November
Rydal looked more lovely than Grasmere, its fantastic variety being counter-acted and counterpoised by the uniformity of the snow everywhere. The sameness of Grasmere sombrous.

30 November
Cottage, garden high up the hill: favourite stocks etc., with three sticks roofed with slate, and stone to keep the slate down. Three recesses in the wall, each closed with a shutter. In one bees and a mouse trap; in another a

lover's chain in a broken white pint pot in a broken brown glazed pipkin – in the same recess a Sunday's cap hung to dry.

In the lawn by the wilderness of rocks, an oak bush with oblong carrotty leaves. Heard as I came near it, a noise like a spinning wheel or grasshopper. Observed one leaf in brisk motion, from whence this noise proceeded – only one of all the bush. Thought it must be some bird, woodpecker pecking, but no! This one leaf was by the bending in of its sides a complete scollop shell, and so placed as to catch the wind – hence the upheaval.

A stanza from the first part of Christabel, *completed early in 1798.*

> The night is chill; the forest bare;
> Is it the wind that moaneth bleak?
> There is not wind enough in the air
> To move away the ringlet curl
> From the lovely lady's cheek –
> There is not wind enough to twirl
> The one red leaf, the last of its clan,
> That dances as often as dance it can,
> Hanging so light, and hanging so high,
> On the topmost twig that looks up at the sky.

To Humphry Davy   *Greta Hall, Keswick, 2 December 1800*

There is a deep blue cloud over the heavens; the lake, and the vale, and the mountains are all in darkness; only the *summits* of all the mountains in long ridges, covered with snow, are bright to a dazzling excess. A glorious scene! Hartley was in my arms the other evening, looking at the sky; he saw the moon glide into a large cloud. Shortly after, at another part of the cloud, several stars sailed in. Says he, 'Pretty creatures! they are going in to see after their mother moon.'

*To Francis Wrangham**   *Greta Hall, Keswick, 19 December 1800*

In truth, my glass being opposite the window, I seldom shave without cutting myself. Some mountain or peak is rising out of the mist, or some slanting column of misty sunlight is sailing cross me, so that I offer up soap and blood daily, as an eye-servant of the Goddess Nature.

*An old university friend.

To Humphry Davy   *Greta Hall, Keswick, 11 January 1801*

Somewhat more than three weeks ago I walked to Grasmere, and was wet through. I changed immediately, but still the next day I was taken ill, and by the lettre de cachet of a rheumatic fever sentenced to the Bed-bastille. The fever left me, and on Friday before last I was well enough to be conveyed home in a chaise, but immediately took to my bed again, a most excruciating pain on the least motion, but not without motion, playing Robespierre and Marat in my left hip and the small of my back. Yet still my animal spirits bear me up, though I am so weak, that even from sitting up to write this note to you, I seem to sink in upon myself in a ruin, like a column of sand, informed and animated only by a whirl-blast of the desart. . .

You say Wordsworth's 'last poem is full of just pictures of what human life ought to be'. Believe me, that such scenes and such characters really exist in this country – the superiority of the small Estates-men, such as W. paints in old Michael, is a God compared to our peasants and small farmers in the South: and furnishes important documents of the kindly ministrations of local attachment and hereditary descent. Success, my dear Davy! to Galvanism and every other ism and schism that you are about.

Coleridge had more to say on this topic in the Biographia Literaria:

The thoughts, feelings, language, and manners of the shepherd-farmers in the vales of Cumberland and Westmoreland . . . may be accounted for from causes, which will and do produce the same results in every state of life, whether in town or country. As the two principal I rank that independence, which raises a man above servitude, or daily toil for the profit of others, yet not above the necessity of industry and a frugal simplicity of domestic life; and the accompanying unambitious, but solid and religious, education, which has rendered few books familiar, but the Bible, and the Liturgy or Hymn book. . .

I am convinced, that for the human soul to prosper in rustic life a certain vantage-ground is prerequisite. It is not every man that is likely to be improved by a country life or by country labours. Education, or original sensibility, or both, must pre-exist, if the changes, forms, and incidents of nature are to prove a sufficient stimulant. And where these are not sufficient, the mind contracts and hardens by want of stimulants: and the man becomes selfish, sensual, gross, and hard-hearted. Let the management of the Poor Laws in Liverpool, Manchester, or Bristol be compared with the ordinary dispensation of the poor rates in agricultural villages, where the farmers are the overseers and guardians of the poor. If my own experience have not been particularly unfortunate, as well as that of the many respectable country clergymen with whom I have conversed on the subject, the result would engender more than scepticism concerning the desirable influences of low and rustic life in and for itself. Whatever may be concluded on the other side, from the stronger local attachments and enterprising spirit of the Swiss, and other mountaineers, applies to a particular mode of pastoral life, under forms of property that permit and beget manners truly republican, not to rustic life in general, or to the absence of artificial cultivation. On the contrary the mountaineers, whose manners have been so often eulogized, are in general better educated and greater readers than men of equal rank elsewhere. But where this is not the case, as among the peasantry of North Wales, the ancient mountains, with all their terrors and all their glories, are pictures to the blind, and music to the deaf.

Early 1801
Old Willy Bank has a passion for old antique cupboards and drawers and, at different sales of the old farmers of the country, he has bought nineteen. Now how to reconcile this with his avarice? Why, he lets them out to poor people at a shilling a year each and they are to keep them in repair. He gets from fifteen to twenty per cent for his money as few have cost him more than three or four shillings.

17 March
Hartley, looking out of my study window, fixed his eyes steadily and for some time on the opposite prospect, and then said, 'Will yon mountains *always* be?' I shewed him the whole magnificent prospect in a looking glass and held it up, so that the whole was like a canopy or ceiling over his head. He struggled to express himself concerning the difference between the Thing and the Image almost with convulsive effort. I never before saw such an Abstract of *Thinking* as distinguished from *Thoughts*.

To Thomas Poole   *Greta Hall, Keswick, 24 March 1801*

Some time ago I mentioned to you a thought which had suggested itself to me, of making acorns more serviceable. I am convinced that this is practicable simply by malting them. There was a total failure of acorns in this country last year, or I would have tried it. But last week as I was turning up some ground in my garden, I found a few acorns just beginning to sprout –

and I ate them. They were, as I had anticipated, perfectly *sweet* and fine-flavored, and wholly and absolutely without any of that particular and offensive taste which acorns, when crude, leave upon the palate, and throat. I have no doubt that they would make both bread and beer, of an excellent taste and nutritious quality. It may be objected – suppose this – what gain? They fatten pigs at present. This is however inaccurately stated. Where there are large woods of oak, a few pigs may be fattened, but acorns are so uncertain a crop, that except in large woods pigs can never be kept on that speculation, and in truth, of the acorns dropped every year nine-tenths are wasted. Secondly, pigs fed with only acorns have a bad flavor. Thirdly, *pigs* are likewise and more regularly fatted with potatoes and barley-meal – and if the objection, which I have stated, held good against the *humanization* of acorns it would have held good against the introduction of potatoes and barley, as human food – nay, it actually has been made in Germany and France against potatoes. What gain, said they? – they are already useful – we fatten our pigs with them.

In this country oaks thrive uncommonly well, and in very bleak and rocky places – and I have little doubt, that by extending and properly managing the plantation of oaks, there might be twenty families maintained where now there is one. For corn in this country is a most uncertain crop; but it so happens, that those very seasons which utterly destroy corn produce an overflow of acorns, and those seasons, which are particularly favorable to corn, prevent the harvest of acorns. Thus, the summer before last all the corn was spoilt, but there was a prodigious crop of acorns. Last summer there was a fine crop of excellent corn in these counties (which never want as much moisture as corn needs) but no acorns. If my hopes should be realized by my experiments, it would add another to the innumerable instances of the Almighty's wisdom and love – making the valleys and the mountains supply, each the failure of the other. When the mountains are struck with drouth, the valleys give corn – when the valleys are rotted with rain, the mountains yield acorns. The great objection at present to the planting of oaks is their slow growth (the young wood which is weeded out not paying sufficient for the *board and lodging* of the wood destined for timber), but very young trees bear a certain proportion of acorns. Oaks, I apprehend, draw, even more than other trees, their nourishment from the moisture et cetera of the air, for they thrive in dry soils alone; yet are most fruitful in wet seasons. It is worth trying whether the oak would be injured if the leaves were taken off after the acorns have fallen. They make a food for horses, cows, and sheep. Should it be true, that the oak is fructified by superficial irrigation, what a delightful thing it would be if in every plot adjacent to mountain cottages stood half a dozen noble oaks, and the little red-apple-cheeked children in drouthy seasons were turning [the jet from] a small fire engine into the air so as to fall on them! Merciful God! what a contrast to the employment of these dear beings by a wheel or a machine in a hellish cotton factory! – 'See! see! what a pretty rainbow *I* have made!' – etc. etc. *Write to me* – I cannot express to you what a consolation, I receive from your letters! S. T. C.

My Wife has a violent cold – Derwent is quite well – and Hartley has the worms. Do not forget to ask Chester for Greenough's address. Love to your dear Mother.

The farmers in these northern counties are getting rich. Their crops last year were excellent; but the county itself is starving. If it were found, that potatoes would bear carriage as well as grain, there would be no food left in the county. It would all go to Liverpool and Manchester, etc.

To William Godwin   *Greta Hall, Keswick, 25 March 1801*

I fear, your Tragedy* will find me in a very unfit state of mind to sit in judgement on it. I have been, during the last three months, undergoing a process of intellectual *exsiccation*. In my long illness I had compelled into hours of delight many a sleepless, painful hour of darkness by chasing down metaphysical game – and since then I have continued the hunt, till I found myself unaware at the root of pure mathematics – and up that tall smooth tree, whose few poor branches are all at its very summit, am I climbing by pure adhesive strength of arms and thighs, still slipping down, still renewing my ascent. You would not know me! All sounds of similitude keep at such a distance from each other in my mind, that I have *forgotten* how to make a rhyme – I look at the mountains (that visible God Almighty that looks in at all my windows) I look at the mountains only for the curves of their outlines; the stars, as I behold them, form themselves into triangles – and my hands are scarred with scratches from a cat, whose back I was rubbing in the dark in order to see whether the sparks from it were refrangible by a prism. The Poet is dead in me – my imagination (or rather the somewhat that had been imaginative) lies, like a cold snuff on the circular rim of a brass candle-stick, without even a stink of tallow to remind you that it was once cloathed and mitred with flame. That is past by! I was once a volume of gold leaf, rising and riding on every breath of fancy – but I have beaten myself back into weight and density, and now I sink in quicksilver, yea,

*This was *Abbas, King of Persia*, which was not performed.

remain squat and square on the earth amid the hurricane, that makes oaks and straws join in one dance, fifty yards high in the element.

However, I will do what I can – taste and feeling have I none, but what I have, give I unto thee. But I repeat, that I am unfit to decide on any but works of severe logic. . .

God bless you
& S. T. Coleridge

I have inoculated my youngest child, Derwent, with the cowpox – he passed through it without any sickness. I myself am the Slave of Rheumatism – indeed, though in a certain sense I *am recovered* from my sickness, yet I have by no means *recovered* it. I congratulate you on the settlement of Davy in London. I hope that his enchanting manners will not draw too many idlers round him, to harrass and vex his mornings.

25 March
Afternoon. Abed, nervous, had noticed prismatic colours transmitted from the tumbler. Wordsworth came; I talked with him; he left me alone. I shut my eyes: beauteous spectra of two colours, orange and violet, then of green which immediately changed to peagreen, and then actually *grew* to my eye into a beautiful moss, the same as is on the mantle-piece at Grasmere. Abstract ideas – and unconscious links!

William Godwin

V ❧ June 1801 – December 1802

IN JUNE 1801 COLERIDGE SUFFERED A RELAPSE AND HIS OPIUM *dosing continued. In July he went to see the Hutchinsons, using the excuse that he wanted to consult the cathedral library at Durham. He began his return journey on 9 August. In November he went to London and was not back in Keswick until mid-March 1802. He was escaping from his increasingly unhappy marriage and earning much-needed money from journalism for the* Morning Post. *Dorothy Wordsworth wrote to Mary Hutchinson on 29 April 1801, 'Mrs Coleridge is much, very much, to be pitied, for when one party is ill matched the other must necessarily be so too. She would have made a very good wife to many another man, but for Coleridge!! Her radical fault is want of sensibility, and what can such a woman be to Coleridge?' He saw Sara (Asra) Hutchinson in early March 1802 before going on to Keswick and must then have agreed with her what Richard Holmes in his recent biography calls 'a form of renunciation'. They could go on seeing each other, for instance when she came to stay with the Wordsworths, but what at that stage seemed the likely transition from a highly charged platonic relationship to their becoming lovers was not to be.*

At the end of March 1802 Wordsworth came over to Keswick, bringing with him the first four stanzas of his ode on 'Intimations of Immortality'. This prompted Coleridge to start his own great poem, 'Dejection'. Dorothy and William Wordsworth left Grasmere in July for a visit to William's former love, Annette Vallon, in France: this was made possible by the short-lived Peace of Amiens. In August Coleridge went on his famous Scafell walking tour. In September Charles Lamb and his sister Mary came to stay. They found Coleridge 'quite enveloped on all sides by a net of mountains: great floundering bears and monsters they seemed, all couchant and asleep . . . We have clambered up to the top of Skiddaw, and I have waded up the bed of Lodore. In fine, I have satisfied myself that there is such a thing as that which tourists call romantic, *which I very much suspected before . . .' (Lamb to Thomas Manning, 24/9/1802).*

In November Coleridge set off for a trip to South Wales with the increasingly ill and erratic Tom Wedgwood. He then delayed in London, writing more journalism, so was not back in Keswick until Christmas Eve, just too late for the premature birth of his daughter Sara.

18 June

A hollow place in the rock like a coffin, a sycamore bush at the head, enough to give a shadow for my face, and just at the foot one tall foxglove. Exactly my own length. There I lay and slept; it was quite soft.

To Thomas Poole   *Greta Hall, Keswick, 7 July 1801*

That beastly Bishop,* that blustering fool, Watson, a native of this vicinity, a pretty constant resident here, and who has for many years kept a rain-gage, considers it as a vulgar error that the climate of this County is particularly wet. He says, the opinion originates in this – that the rain here falls more certainly in certain months, and these happen to be the months, in which the tourists visit us. William Coates said to me at Bristol – 'Keswick, Sir! is said to be the rainiest place in the Kingdom – it always rains there, Sir! I was there myself three days, and it rained the whole of the time.' Men's memories are not much to be relied on in cases of weather; but judging from what I remember of Stowey and Devon, Keswick has not been, since I have been here, wetter than the former, and not so wet as Devonshire.

Coleridge's 'Ode to the Rain', published in 1802, rather contradicts his defence of Lakeland weather. Here is the second verse of this lighthearted poem.

> O Rain! with your dull two-fold sound,
> The clash hard by, and the murmur all round!
> You know, if you know aught, that we,
> Both night and day, but ill agree:
> For days and months, and almost years,
> Have limped on through this vale of tears,
> Since body of mine, and rainy weather,
> Have lived on easy terms together.
> Yet if, as soon as it is light,
> O Rain! you will but take your flight,
> Though you should come again tomorrow,
> And bring with you both pain and sorrow;
> Though stomach should sicken and knees should swell –
> I'll nothing speak of you but well.
> But only now for this one day,
> Do go, dear Rain! do go away!

Summer 1801
The half-knit stocking in the kitchen-table drawer.

Ants having dim notions of the architecture of the whole system of the world, and imitating it according to their notion in their ant-heaps – and even these little ant-heaps no uncomely parts of that great architecture.

*Of Llandaff. See footnote on p.64.

Hartley's intense wish to have ant-heaps near our house, his *Brahman* love and awe of life. N.B. to commence his education with natural history.

On 12 December 1804, when he was in Malta, Coleridge took himself to task for anthropomorphizing.

I addressed a butterfly on a pea-blossom thus, 'Beautiful Psyche, soul of a blossom, that art visiting and hovering over thy former friends whom thou hast left!' Had I forgot the caterpillar? Or did I dream like a mad metaphysician that the caterpillar's hunger for plants was self-love, recollection, and a lust that in its next state, refined itself into love?

Many years later, on 2 May 1830 as recorded in Table Talk, *Coleridge returned to the subject of insects.*

Plants exist *in* themselves, insects *by*, or by means of, themselves. Men, *for* themselves. The perfection of irrational animals is that which is best for *them*; the perfection of man is that which is absolutely best. There is growth only in plants; but there is irritability, or, a better word, instinctivity, in insects.

There is also a vignette of Coleridge the entomologist in Wordsworth's 'Stanzas in Thomson's Castle of Indolence' written in May 1802:

> Long blades of grass, plucked round him as he lay,
> Made, to his ear attentively applied,
> A pipe on which the wind would deftly play;
> Glasses he had, that little things display,
> The beetle panoplied in gems and gold . . .

10 August
At Ingleby: peacock's feather round the bright pewter, and fox's tail in the plates, in the lath-and-thatched-ceiling parlour. A new map of the Promised Land, half map, half pictures. On the chimney piece two glasses and a sailor in plaister, and King George in basso relievo. A manuscript prodigious adorned and framed in black. The Landlord's caution to his customers: Wit and Folly in a maze – and a true lover knot. The latter two very puzzling indeed, but with no space of green, red, and gamboge. From the thatch hangs a large buttock of hung beef and a bell close beside it fastened in the thatch. The string is gone in. Three little pictures such as are sold by the Italians, probably bought at the same time with Ben the Sailor, or cap crimper.

23 August
Bowes, church clock striking eleven – this quiet village. Looking up at the moon in the pane of a window I see its shadow dance on the top of it, like a figure 8, the upper part dim and dancing.

A thousand clouds in the sky, and not one which the moon did not bless in its fringes. I could have with ease counted all the stars, had not mine eye been too lazy to roll round the heaven, and my mood too placid.

September
The spring with the little tiny cone of loose sand ever rising and sinking at the bottom, but its surface without a wrinkle. – W. W., M. H., D. W., S. H. [William Wordsworth, Mary Hutchinson, Dorothy Wordsworth, Sara Hutchinson]

The poem 'Inscription for a Fountain on a Heath', published in 1802, takes its origin from this entry.

> This Sycamore, oft musical with bees, –
> Such tents the Patriarchs loved! O long unharmed
> May all its agéd boughs o'er-canopy
> The small round basin, which this jutting stone
> Keeps pure from falling leaves! Long may the Spring,
> Quietly as a sleeping infant's breath,
> Send up cold waters to the traveller
> With soft and even pulse! Nor ever cease
> Yon tiny cone of sand its soundless dance,
> Which at the bottom, like a Fairy's Page,
> As merry and no taller, dances still,
> Nor wrinkles the smooth surface of the Fount.
> Here Twilight is and Coolness: here is moss,
> A soft seat, and a deep and ample shade.
> Thou may'st toil far and find no second tree.
> Drink, Pilgrim, here; Here rest! and if thy heart
> Be innocent, here too shalt thou refresh
> Thy spirit, listening to some gentle sound,
> Or passing gale or hum of murmuring bees!

14 September
Northern lights remarkably fine, chiefly a purple blue in shooting pyramids. Moved from over Bassenthwaite behind Skiddaw. Derwent's birthday, one year old.

15 September

Observed the great half moon setting behind the mountain ridge and watched the shapes its various segments presented as it slowly sunk. First, the foot of a boot, all but the heel; then, a little pyramid; then a star of the first magnitude. Indeed it was not distinguishable from the Evening Star at the largest. Then rapidly a smaller, a small, a very small star – and as it diminished in size, so it grew paler in tint. And now where is it? Unseen; but a little fleecy cloud hangs above the mountain ridge and is rich, with an amber light.

19 October

On the Greta over the bridge by Mr Edmondson's Father-in-law, the ashes, their leaves of that light yellow which Autumn gives them, cast a reflection on the river like a painter's sun shine.

22 October

All the mountains black and tremendously obscure, except Swinside. . . At this time, I saw one after the other, nearly in the same place, two perfect moon rainbows – the one foot in the field below my garden, the other in the field nearest but two to the church. It was grey-moonlight-mist-colour.

1 November

Hartley breeched. Dancing to the jingle of the money, but eager and solemn joy, not his usual whirl-about gladness – but solemn to and fro eager looks, as befitted the importance of the aera.

13 November

Left Eusemere half past six, Penrith at nine. In the heavy coach. A new horse put in, which fell in at Emont Bridge, taken out, the coach drawn by the three over the Bridge and the new horse put in as a leader. Plunged, etc., etc., and tore all the harness, and another horse sent for.

A certain quantity of water in which lime has been dissolved and whitened by the fine particles of that substance, be mixed with ley of ashes or with soapy water that has been even used for washing, it will destroy the offensive smell. Thus a tub with five or six pounds of quick lime, a small quantity of ashes, and two buckets of water, with a seat, makes an admirable and healthy close stool.

Winter 1801
When in the strong and regular wind the snow keeps weaving its strong warp – and darting its white threads down its inclined plane.

Spring 1802
The larches in spring push out their separate bundles of leaves first into green brushes or pencils, which soon then are only small tassels.

Quiet stream, with all its eddies and the moonlight playing on them, quiet as if they were Ideas in the divine mind anterior to the Creation.

Waterfall – tiny – and leaf: still attracted, still repelled.

16 April
From the summit above Walla Crag, Skiddaw and Saddleback form one beautiful ellipse. The vales of Threlkeld and Hutton become one with Keswick, the islands in the lake more dishy than ever, the mountains from Borrowdale inclusive to Grisdale Pike more than anywhere a rude jumble. After I had written this I descended from the Man of Stones and came unawares on Walla Crag – tremendous indeed. There is nothing on Helvellyn so terrible. It is absolutely and strictly perpendicular on all sides and in its outline forms an awful forehead and aquiline nose – on the saddle of the nose a tree and a bunch of juniper, I believe.

Came in a few yards to a noble ravine, one side rough and treeless rock, the other mossy and shrubby green. In a hundred yards more, to a grand slope and one *leaning tower*, on its top a green shorn *poll* or crown of head, railed off with wooden rails. Above the ravine another small precipice and here too is one of the noblest ravines ever seen: rock on both sides, grey with white lichens.

The long bracken, unreapt, wet and rotting, lying, strait dangling, from the mossy stone-hillocks like unkempt red brown hair. Good Friday.

20 April
Tuesday evening, half after seven. Cut out my name and Dorothy's over the S. H. at Sara's Rock.*

*The Rock of Names near Wythburn on the east side of Thirlmere. It was moved to higher ground when the water level was raised.

23 April
Discovered the *Double-bower* among Rydal Rocks – ivy, oak, hawthorn, mountain ash, common ash, holly, yews, fern and wild sage, juniper, etc. Carpet of moss – and rocks.*

April – May
To believe that trees were made by a great maggot worm of the same kind with that which eats out the rude shapes of trees in the wood of old gates, etc.

From the Cedar of Lebanon to the mould of a Cheshire Cheese.

The yellow hammer sings like one working on steel, or the file in a brazier's shop.

The thrush, gurgling, quavering, shooting forth long notes. Then with short emissions as of pushing up against a stream.

The old woman on an hot evening gone out to walk, but could not get warmth in her, so came in and spread her poor arms out to the sticks flaming under the teakettles in the inn kitchen.

Sea celandine (Chelidonium Glaucium) [Yellow Horned Poppy]: the highest winds do not affect its petals, and yet it is difficult to pluck the flowers without some of them falling off. Nature and Man!

*Dorothy Wordsworth describes this in her Journal entry for the same day.

Saddleback, 'stern Blencartha', and part of Skiddaw

The rocks and stones put on a vital semblance; and Life itself thereby seemed to forego its restlessness, to anticipate in its own nature an infinite repose, and to become, as it were, compatible with immoveability. Kirk-stone.

Moon, owl a ventriloquist. What should we think? That the man in the moon had a toothache?

The proportion of cow calfs to bull calfs, very extraordinary in different years: almost all bull calfs this year. Never any fell ewes (or *very* seldom) yean two lambs; in Norfolk seldom.

A light breeze upon the *smooth* of the river and the shadows of the tree turn into two-edged cherub's swords.

The trout leaping in the sunshine spreads on the bottom of the river concentric circles of light.

8 June
Grisdale Tarn, rolling towards its outlet like a sea. The gust on the broad beck snatching up water made the smooth and level water as full of small breakers and white waves as the rough and steep part. The spray fell upon me, *lownded* [sheltered] in the rock, like rain. The Sun setting behind the hill behind me made a rainbow in the spray across the beck (twenty yards from the Tarn) every time the gust came.

To William Sotheby*   *Greta Hall, Keswick, 13 July 1802*

We have had little else but rain and squally weather since you left us till within the last three days. But showery weather is no evil to us; and even that most oppressive of all weathers, hot, small *drizzle*, exhibits the mountains the best of any. It produced such new combinations of ridges in the Lodore and Borrowdale mountains on Saturday morning that I declare, had I been blindfolded and so brought to the prospect, I should scarcely have known them again. It was a dream such as lovers have – a wild and transfiguring, yet enchantingly lovely dream, of an object lying by the side of the sleeper. Wordsworth, who has walked through Switzerland, declared that he never saw anything superior, perhaps nothing equal, in the Alps.

To William Sotheby   *Greta Hall, Keswick, 19 July 1802*

I wished to force myself out of metaphysical trains of thought, which, when I wished to write a poem, beat up game of far other kind. Instead of a covey of poetic partridges with whirring wings of music, or wild ducks *shaping* their rapid flight in forms always regular (a still better image of verse), up came a metaphysical bustard, urging its slow, heavy, laborious, earth-skimming flight over dreary and level wastes. To have done with poetical prose (which is a very vile Olio), sickness and some other and worse afflictions first forced me into downright metaphysics. For I believe that by nature I have more of the poet in me. In a poem written during that dejection, to Wordsworth, and the greater part of a private nature, I thus expressed the thought in language more forcible than harmonious:

[*Verses I, II, III and part of verse VII from 'Dejection: an ode', written on 4 April 1802, not to Wordsworth, but to Sara Hutchinson.*]

> Late, late yestreen I saw the new Moon,
> With the old Moon in her arms;
> And I fear, I fear, my Master dear!
> We shall have a deadly storm.
> *Ballad of Sir Patrick Spence*

I

Well! If the Bard was weather-wise, who made
The grand old ballad of Sir Patrick Spence,

*Poet and dramatist who had just visited Greta Hall. He and Coleridge entered into a literary correspondence.

This night, so tranquil now, will not go hence
Unroused by winds, that ply a busier trade
Than those which mould yon cloud in lazy flakes,
Or the dull sobbing draft, that moans and rakes
Upon the strings of this Aeolian lute,
    Which better far were mute.
  For lo! the New-moon winter-bright!
  And overspread with phantom light,
  (With swimming phantom light o'erspread
  But rimmed and circled by a silver thread)
I see the old Moon in her lap, foretelling
  The coming-on of rain and squally blast.
And oh! that even now the gust were swelling,
  And the slant night-shower driving loud and fast!
Those sounds which oft have raised me, whilst they awed,
    And sent my soul abroad,
Might now perhaps their wonted impulse give,
Might startle this dull pain, and make it move and live!

II
A grief without a pang, void, dark, and drear,
  A stifled, drowsy, unimpassioned grief,
  Which finds no natural outlet, no relief,
    In word, or sigh, or tear –
O Lady! in this wan and heartless mood,
To other thoughts by yonder throstle woo'd,
  All this long eve, so balmy and serene,
Have I been gazing on the western sky,
  And its peculiar tint of yellow green:
And still I gaze – and with how blank an eye!
And those thin clouds above, in flakes and bars,
That give away their motion to the stars;
Those stars, that glide behind them or between,
Now sparkling, now bedimmed, but always seen:
Yon crescent Moon, as fixed as if it grew
In its own cloudless, starless lake of blue;
I see them all so excellently fair,
I see, not feel, how beautiful they are!

Mountains in Borrowdale. This scene looks towards Gate Crag, with Castle Crag to the left. The old Keswick road can just be seen on the shoulder of the hill on the right

III

My genial spirits fail;
And what can these avail
To lift the smothering weight from off my breast?
It were a vain endeavour,
Though I should gaze for ever
On that green light that lingers in the west:
I may not hope from outward forms to win
The passion and the life, whose fountains are within.

VII

Hence, viper thoughts, that coil around my mind,
  Reality's dark dream!
I turn from you, and listen to the wind,
  Which long has raved unnoticed. What a scream
Of agony by torture lengthened out
That lute sent forth! Thou Wind, that rav'st without,
  Bare crag, or mountain-tairn, or blasted tree,
Or pine-grove whither woodman never clomb,
Or lonely house, long held the witches' home,
  Methinks were fitter instruments for thee,
Mad Lutanist! who in this month of showers,
Of dark-brown gardens, and of peeping flowers,
Mak'st Devils' yule, with worse than wintry song,
The blossoms, buds, and timorous leaves among.

My dear sir! ought I to make an apology for troubling you with such a long, verse-cramm'd letter? Oh, that instead of it, I could but send to you the image now before my eyes, over Bassenthwaite. The sun is setting in a glorious, rich, brassy light, on the top of Skiddaw, and one third adown it is a huge, enormous mountain of cloud, with the outlines of a mountain. This is of a starchy grey, but floating past along it, and upon it, are various patches of sack-like clouds, bags and woolsacks, of a shade lighter than the brassy light. Of the clouds that hide the setting sun – a fine yellow-red, somewhat more than sandy light, and these, the farthest from the sun, are suffused with the darkness of a stormy colour. Marvellous creatures! how they pass along!

To Sara Hutchinson   *Greta Hall, Keswick, 27 July 1802*

If the weather with you be what it is here, our dear Friends* must have had a miserable day yesterday. It rained almost incessantly at Keswick; till the late evening, when it fell a deep calm, and even the leaves, the very topmost leaves, of the poplars and aspens had holiday, and like an overworked boy, consumed it in sound sleep. The whole vale presented a curious spectacle: the clouds were scattered by the wind and rain in all shapes and heights, above the mountains, on their sides, and low down to their bases – some masses in the middle of the valley, when the wind and rain dropt down, and died. And for two hours all the clouds, white and fleecy all of them, remained without motion, forming an appearance not very unlike the Moon as seen through a telescope. On the mountains directly opposite to our house (in Stoddart's tobacco-juice picture) the clouds lay in two ridges with a broad, strait *road* between them, they being the *walls* of the road. Blessings on the mountains! to the eye and ear they are always faithful. I have often thought of writing a set of *play-bills* for the vale of Keswick – for every day in the year – announcing each day the performances, by his Supreme Majesty's Servants, Clouds, Waters, Sun, Moon, Stars, et cetera. Today the weather is mild – though (as Mrs Bancroft informed my wife in a note last week) '*the humid Aspect of the general Atmosphere is eminently hostile to my fondly-cherished Hopes.*' For I wait only for a truly fine day to walk off to St Bees. Best compliments to the River Bee, and if he have any commands to the Saint, his relation, I shall be happy to communicate the same.

*William and Dorothy Wordsworth had been staying at Gallow Hill near Malton in Yorkshire with Sara Hutchinson on their way to London, and France.

A storm on Keswick Lake

Buttermere with part of Crummock Water beyond

Newlands Vale

Sara Hutchinson, Coleridge's Asra

To Sara Hutchinson   *The top of Scafell, 5 August 1802*

On Sunday August 1st – half after twelve – I had a shirt, cravat, two pair of stockings, a little paper and half a dozen pens, a German book (Voss's Poems) and a little tea and sugar, with my night cap, packed up in my natty green oil-skin, neatly squared, and put into my *net* knapsack. The knapsack on my back and the besom stick in my hand, which for want of a better, and in spite of Mrs C. and Mary, who both raised their voices against it, especially as I left the besom scattered on the kitchen floor, off I sallied over the bridge, through the hop-field, through the Prospect Bridge at Portinscale, so on by the tall birch that grows out of the centre of the huge oak, along into Newlands. Newlands is indeed a lovely place – the houses, each in its little shelter of ashes and sycamores, just under the road, so that in some places you might leap down on the roof, seemingly at least – the exceeding greenness and pastoral beauty of the Vale itself, with the savage wildness of the mountains, their coves, and long arm-shaped and elbow-shaped ridges – yet this wildness softened down into a congruity with the Vale by the semicircular lines of the crags, and of the bason-like concavities. The cataract between Newlands and Kescadale had but little water in it [so] of course, was of no particular interest.

I passed on through the green steep smooth bare Kescadale, a sort of unfurnished passage or antechamber between Newlands and Buttermere, came out on Buttermere and drank tea at the little inn, and read the greater part of the Revelations – the only part of the New Testament which the Scotch cobbler read – because why? *Because it was the only part that he understood.* O 'twas a wise cobler! Conceive an enormous round bason mountain-high of solid stone cracked in half and one half gone: exactly in the remaining half of this enormous bason, does Buttermere lie, in this beautiful and stern embracement of rock. I left it, passed by Scale Force, the white downfall of which glimmered through the trees, that hang before it like bushy hair over a madman's eyes, and climbed 'till I gained the first level. Here it was 'every man his own pathmaker,' and I went directly cross it upon soft mossy ground, with many a hop, skip, and jump, and many an occasion for observing the truth of the old saying: where rushes grow, a man may go. Red Pike, a dolphin-shaped peak of a deep red, looked in upon me from over the fell on my left; on my right I had, first Melbreak (the mountain on the right of Crummock, as you ascend the Lake) then a vale running down with a pretty stream in it, to Loweswater, then Heck [Hen] Coomb, a fell of the same height and running in the same direction with Melbreak, a vale on the other side too – and at the bottom of both these vales the Loweswater Fells running abreast. Again I reached an ascent, climbed up, and came to a ruined sheepfold – a wild green view all around me, bleating of sheep and noise of waters. I sate there near twenty minutes, the sun setting on the hill behind with a soft watery gleam; and in front of me the upper halves of huge deep-furrowed Grasmire [Grassmoor] (the mountain on the other side of Crummock) and the huge Newland and Buttermere Mountains, and peeping in from behind, the top of Saddleback. Two fields were visible, the highest cultivated ground on the Newland side of Buttermere, and the trees in those fields were the only trees visible in the whole prospect. I left the sheepfold with regret – for of all things a ruined sheepfold in a desolate place is the dearest to me, and fills me most with dreams and visions and tender thoughts of those I love best.

Well! I passed a bulging roundish-headed green hill to my left (and to the left of it was a frightful crag), with a very high round-head right before me; this latter is called Ennerdale-Dodd, and bisects the ridge between Ennerdale and Buttermere and Crummock. I took it on my right hand, and came to the top of the bulging green hill, on which I found a small tarn, called Flatern [Floutern] Tarn, about 100 yards in length, and not more than seven or eight in breadth, but O! what a grand precipice it lay at the foot of! The half of this precipice (called Herd house [Herdus]) nearest to Ennerdale was black, with green moss-cushions on the ledges; the half nearest to Buttermere a pale pink, and divided from the black part by a

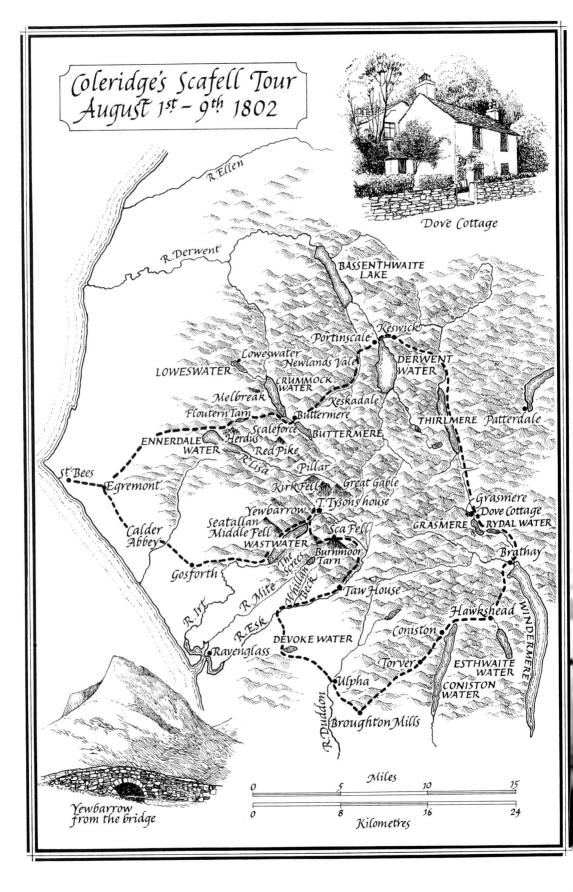

Coleridge's Scafell Tour
August 1st – 9th 1802

Dove Cottage

R. Ellen

R. Derwent

BASSENTHWAITE LAKE

Keswick

Portinscale

Loweswater

LOWESWATER

Newlands Vale

DERWENT WATER

CRUMMOCK WATER

Melbreak

Keskadale

Floutern Tarn

Buttermere

THIRLMERE

Patterdale

Scaleforce

BUTTERMERE

ENNERDALE WATER

Herdus

Red Pike

Scc Bees

R. Lisa

Pillar

Egremont

Kirk Fell

Great Gable

Grasmere

Dove Cottage

T. Tysons house

Yewbarrow

GRASMERE

RYDAL WATER

Calder Abbey

Seatallan Middle Fell

Sca Fell

WASTWATER

Brathay

The Screes

Burnmoor Tarn

Gosforth

R. Mite

Whillan Beck

R. Irt

R. Esk

Taw House

Hawkshead

WINDERMERE

Coniston

DEVOKE WATER

Ravenglass

Torver

ESTHWAITE WATER

Ulpha

CONISTON WATER

R. Duddon

Broughton Mills

Miles

| 0 | | 5 | | 10 | | 15 |

| 0 | | 8 | | 16 | | 24 |

Kilometres

Yewbarrow from the bridge

great streamy torrent of crimson shiver, and screes, or shilly (as they call it). I never saw a more heart-raising scene. I turned and looked on the scene which I had left behind, a marvellous group of mountains, wonderfully and admirably arranged – not a single minute object to interrupt the oneness of the view, excepting those two green fields in Buttermere – but before me the glorious Sea with the high coast and mountains of the Isle of Man, perfectly distinct – and three ships in view.

A little further on, the Lake of Ennerdale (the lower part of it) came in view, shaped like a clumsy battledore – but it is, in reality, exactly *fiddle-shaped*. The further bank and the higher part, steep, lofty, bare bulging crags; the nether bank green and pastoral, with houses in the shelter of their own dear trees. On the opposite shore in the middle and narrow part of the Lake there bulges out a huge crag, called Angling Stone – being a famous station for anglers – and the reflection of this crag in the water is admirable – pillars or rather it looks like the pipes of some enormous organ in a rich golden color. I travelled on to Long Moor, two miles below the foot of the Lake, and met a very hearty welcome from John Ponsonby, a Friend of Mr Jackson's. Here I stayed the night [1 August], and the greater part of Monday. The old man went to the head of the Lake with me. The mountains at the head of this Lake and Wastdale are the Monsters of the Country, bare bleak heads, evermore doing deeds of darkness, weather-plots, and storm-conspiracies in the clouds. Their names are Herd House, Bowness, Wha Head, Great Gavel, the Steeple, the Pillar, and Seat Allian [Seatallan].

I left Long Moor after tea, and proceeded to Egremont, five miles, through a very pleasant country, part of the way by the River Enna [Ehen], with well wooded banks, and nice green fields, and pretty houses with trees, and two huge sail-cloth manufactories. Went to Girtskill, a mercer, for whom I had a letter, but he was at Workington, so I walked on to St Bees, three miles from Egremont. When I came there could not get a bed – at last got an apology for one, at a miserable pot-house; slept [2 August] or rather dozed, in my clothes – breakfasted there – and went to the School and Church ruins. Had read in the history of Cumbd. that there was an 'excellent library presented to the School by Sr James Lowther,' which proved to be some thirty odd volumes of commentaries on the Scripture utterly worthless – and which with all my passion for ragged old folios I should certainly make serviceable for fire-lighting. Men who write Tours and County histories I have by woeful experience found out to be *damned liars*, harsh words, but true! It was a wet woeful oppressive morning – I was sore with my bad night – walked down to the beach, which is a very nice hard sand for more than a mile. But the St Bees Head which I had read much of as a noble cliff, might be made a song of on the flats of the Dutch Coast – but in England 'twill scarcely bear a looking-at.

Returned to Egremont [3 August], a miserable walk – dined there, visited the Castle, the views from which are uncommonly interesting. I looked through an old wild arch – slovenly black houses, and gardens, as wild as a dream, over the hills beyond them, which slip down in one place making a noticeable gap. Had a good bed, slept well – and left Egremont this morning [4 August] after breakfast. Had a pleasant walk to Calder Abbey – an elegant but not very interesting ruin, joining to a very handsome gentleman's house built of red freestone, which has the comfortable warm look of brick without its meanness and multitude of puny squares. This place lies just within the line of circumference of *a circle* of woody hills – the area, a pretty plain half a mile perhaps in diameter – and completely cloathed and hid with wood, except one red hollow in these low steep hills, and except behind the Abbey, where the hills are far higher, and consist of green fields almost (but not quite) to the top. Just opposite to Calder Abbey, and on the line of the circumference, rises Ponsonby Hill, the village of Calder Bridge, and its interesting mill, all in wood, some hidden, some roofs just on a line with the trees, some higher, but Ponsonby Hall far higher than the rest. I regained the road, and came to Bonewood, a single alehouse on the top of the hill above the village Gosforth – drank a pint of beer. (I forgot to tell you that the whole of my expences at St Bees, a glass of gin and water, my bed, and breakfast amounted to 11d.)

From this Bonewood is a noble view of the Isle of Man on the one side, and on the other side all the bold dread tops of the Ennerdale and Wastdale mountains. Indeed the whole way from Egremont I had beautiful sea views, the low hills to my right dipping down into inverted arches, or angles, and the sea, often with a ship seen through. While on my left the Steeple, and Scafell facing each other, far above the other fells, formed in their interspace a great gap in the Heaven. So I went on, turned eastward, up the Irt, the sea behind and Wastdale mountains before. And here I am – Wed. afternoon half past three, August 4th 1802 – [in] Wastdale, a mile and a half below the foot of the Lake, at an alehouse without a sign, twenty strides from the door, under the shade of a huge sycamore tree, without my coat – but that I will now put on, in prudence. Yes here I am, and have been for something more than an hour, and have enjoyed a good dish of tea (I carried my tea and sugar with me) under this delightful tree. In the house there are only an old feeble woman, and a '*Tallyeur*' lad upon the table – all the rest of the Wastdale World is a haymaking, rejoicing and thanking God for this first downright summer day that we have had since the beginning of May. And now I must go and see the Lake, for immediately at the foot of the Lake runs a low ridge so that you can see nothing of the water till you are at its very edge.

Between the Lake and the mountains on the left, a low ridge of hill runs parallel with the Lake, for more than half its length; and just at the foot of the Lake there is a bank even and smooth and low like a grassy bank in a gentleman's park. Along the hilly ridge I walked through a lane of green hazels, with hay-fields and haymakers on my right, beyond the River Irt, and on the other side of the River, Irton Fell with a deep perpendicular ravine, and a curious fretted pillar of clay crosier-shaped, standing up in it. Next to Irton Fells and in the same line are the Screes, and you can look at nothing but the Screes though there were twenty quaint pillars close by you. The Lake is wholly hidden 'till your very feet touch it, as one may say, and to a stranger the burst would be almost overwhelming. The Lake itself seen from its foot appears indeed of too regular shape; exactly like the sheet of paper on which I am writing, except it is still narrower in respect of its length. (In reality however the Lake widens as it ascends, and at the head is very considerably broader than at the foot.) But yet, in spite of this it is a marvellous sight: a sheet of water between three and four miles in length, the whole (or very nearly the whole) of its right bank formed by the Screes, or facing of bare rock of enormous height, two thirds of its height downwards absolutely perpendicular; and then slanting off in *screes*, or shiver, consisting of fine red streaks running in broad stripes through a stone colour – slanting off from the perpendicular, as steep as the meal newly ground from the miller's spout. So it is at the foot of the Lake; but higher up this streaky shiver occupies two thirds of the whole height, like a pointed decanter in shape, or an outspread fan, or a long-waisted old maid with a fine prim apron, or – no, other things that would only fill up the paper.

When I first came the Lake was a perfect mirror; and what must have been the glory of the reflections in it! This huge facing of rock *said* to be half a mile in perpendicular height, with deep ravines, the whole *winded* [wrinkled?] and torrent-worn, except where the pink-striped screes come in, as smooth as silk – all this reflected, turned into pillars, dells, and a whole new-world of images in the water! The head of the Lake is crowned by three huge pyramidal mountains, Yewbarrow, Scafell, and the great Gavel; Yewbarrow and Scafell nearly opposite to each other, yet so that the ness (or ridge-line, like the line of a fine nose) of Scafell runs in behind that of Yewbarrow, while the ness of great Gavel is still farther back, between the two others, and of course, instead of running athwart the Vale it directly faces you. The Lake and Vale run nearly from East to West. . .

The mountains of Upper Borrowdale with Great Gable in the distance

Melfell [Middle Fell] (lying north of the Lake) consists of great mountain steps decreasing in size as they approach the Lake.

My road led along under Melfell and by Yewbarrow – and now I came in sight of its other side called Keppel Crag and then a huge enormous bason-like cove called Green Crag [Red Pike?], as I suppose, from there being no single patch of green to be seen on any one of its perpendicular sides – so on to Kirk Fell, at the foot of which is Thomas Tyson's House where Wordsworth and I slept Novr. will be three years – and there I was welcomed kindly, had a good bed, and left it after breakfast.

Thursday Morning, Augt. 5th – went down the Vale almost to the water head, and ascended the low reach between Scafell and the Screes, and soon after I had gained its height came in sight of Burnmoor Water, a large tarn . . . [flounder-shaped] its tail towards Scafell, at its head a gap forming

an inverted arch with Black Coomb and a peep of the sea seen through it. It lies directly at the back of the Screes, and the stream that flows from it down through the gap, is called the Mite – and runs through a vale of its own called Miterdale, parallel with the lower part of Wastdale, and divided from it by the high ridge called Irton Fells. I ascended Scafell by the side of a torrent, and climbed and rested, rested and climbed, 'till I gained the very summit of Scafell – believed by the shepherds here to be higher than either Helvellyn or Skiddaw. Even to Black Coomb – before me all the mountains die away, running down westward to the sea, apparently in eleven ridges and three parallel vales with their three rivers, seen from their very sources to their falling into the sea, where they form (excepting their screw-like flexures) the *Trident* of the Irish Channel at Ravenglass. O my God! what enormous mountains these are close by me, and yet below the hill I stand on: Great Gavel, Kirk Fell, Green Crag, and behind the Pillar, then the Steeple, then the Hay Cock – on the other side and behind me, Great End, Esk Carse [Hause], Bow-fell and close to my back two huge pyramids, nearly as high as Scafell itself, and indeed parts and parts of Scafell known far and near by these names, the hither one of Broad Crag, and the next to it but divided from it by a low ridge Doe Crag,* which is indeed of itself a great mountain of stones from a pound to 20 ton weight embedded in wooly moss.

And here I am *lounded* – so fully lounded [sheltered] – that though the wind is strong, and the clouds are hast'ning hither from the sea – and the whole air seaward has a lurid look – and we shall certainly have thunder – yet here (but that I am hunger'd and provisionless) *here* I could lie warm, and wait methinks for tomorrow's Sun. And on a nice stone table am I now at this moment writing to you – between two and three o'clock as I guess – surely the first letter ever written from the top of Scafell! But O! what a look down just under my feet! The frightfullest cove that might ever be seen, huge perpendicular precipices, and one sheep upon its only ledge, that surely must be crag! Tyson told me of this place, and called it Hollow Stones. Just by it and joining together, rise two huge pillars of bare lead-coloured stone. I am no measurer, but their height and depth is terrible. I know how unfair it is to judge of these things by a comparison of past impressions with present – but I have no shadow of hesitation in saying that the coves and precipices of Helvellyn are nothing to these! But from this sweet lounding place I see directly through Borrowdale, the Castle Crag, the whole of Derwent Water, and but for the haziness of the air I could see my own house – I see clear enough where it stands.

Here I will fold up this letter – I have wafers in my inkhorn – and you shall call this letter when it passes before you the Scafell Letter. I must now drop down, how I may, into Eskdale – that lies under to my right – the upper part of it the wildest and savagest surely of all the vales that were ever seen from the top of an English mountain, and the lower part the loveliest.

To Sara Hutchinson   *At an Estate House called Toes [Taw House]*
in Eskdale, 6 August 1802

There is one sort of gambling, to which I am much addicted; and that not of the least criminal kind for a man who has children and a concern. It is this. When I find it convenient to descend from a mountain, I am too

*Doe Crag is Scafell Pike.

confident and too indolent to look round about and wind about 'till I find a track or other symptom of safety; but I wander on, and where it is first *possible* to descend, there I go – relying upon fortune for how far down this possibility will continue. So it was yesterday afternoon. I passed down from Broadcrag, skirted the Precipices, and found myself cut off from a most sublime crag-summit, that seemed to rival Scafell Man in height, and to outdo it in fierceness. A ridge of hill* lay low down, and divided this crag (called Doe-Crag) and Broad-Crag – even as the hyphen divides the words broad and crag. I determined to go thither; the first place I came to, that was not direct rock, I slipped down, and went on for a while with tolerable ease – but now I came (it was midway down) to a smooth perpendicular rock about seven feet high – this was nothing. I put my hands on the ledge, and dropped down. In a few yards came just such another; I *dropped* that too, and yet another, seemed not higher – I would not stand for a trifle, so I dropped that too. But the stretching of the muscles of my hands and arms, and the jolt of the fall on my feet, put my whole limbs in a *tremble*, and I paused, and looking down, saw that I had little else to encounter but a succession of these little precipices. It was in truth a path that in a very hard rain is, no doubt, the channel of a most splendid waterfall.

So I began to suspect that I ought not to go on, but then unfortunately, though I could with ease drop down a smooth rock seven feet high, I could not *climb* it, so go on I must – and on I went. The next three drops were not half a foot, at least not a foot more than my own height, but every drop increased the palsy of my limbs. I shook all over, Heaven knows without the least influence of fear. And now I had only two more to drop down – to return was impossible – but of these two the first was tremendous. It was twice my own height, and the ledge at the bottom was so exceedingly narrow, that if I dropt down upon it I must of necessity have fallen backwards and of course killed myself. My limbs were all in a tremble – I lay upon my back to rest myself, and was beginning according to my custom to laugh at myself for a madman, when the sight of the crags above me on each side, and the impetuous clouds just over them, posting so luridly and so rapidly northward, overawed me. I lay in a state of almost prophetic trance and delight, and blessed God aloud, for the powers of Reason and the Will, which remaining no danger can overpower us! O God, I exclaimed aloud – how calm, how blessed am I now. I know not how to proceed, how to return, but I am calm and fearless and confident. If this reality were a dream, if I were asleep, what agonies had I suffered! what screams! When

*Mickledore Ridge.

The Derwentwater amphitheatre looking from Skiddaw towards Scafell

the Reason and the Will are away, what remain to us but darkness and dimness and a bewildering shame, and pain that is utterly lord over us, or fantastic pleasure, that draws the soul along swimming through the air in many shapes, even as a flight of starlings in a wind.*

I arose, and looking down saw at the bottom a heap of stones – which had fallen abroad – and rendered the narrow ledge on which they had been piled, doubly dangerous. At the bottom of the third rock that I dropt from,

*See the Notebook entry for 27 November 1799 on p.77.

I met a dead sheep quite rotten. This heap of stones, I guessed, and have since found that I guessed aright, had been piled up by the shepherd to enable him to climb up and free the poor creature whom he had observed to be crag-fast – but seeing nothing but rock over rock, he had desisted and gone for help – and in the mean time the poor creature had fallen down and killed itself. As I was looking at these I glanced my eye to my left, and observed that the rock was rent from top to bottom. I measured the breadth of the rent, and found that there was no danger of my being *wedged* in, so I put my knap-sack round to my side and slipped down as between two walls, without any danger or difficulty. The next drop brought me down on the ridge called the How. I hunted out my besom stick, which I had flung before me when I first came to the rocks, and wisely gave over all thoughts of ascending Doe-Crag, for now the clouds were again coming in most tumultuously. So I began to descend, when I felt an odd sensation across my whole breast – not pain nor itching – and putting my hand on it I found it all bumpy, and on looking saw the whole of my breast from my neck to my navel, and exactly all that my kamell-hair breast-shield covers, filled with great red heat-bumps, so thick that no hair could lie between them. They still remain, but are evidently less, and I have no doubt will wholly disappear in a few days. It was however a startling proof to me of the violent exertions which I had made.

I descended this low hill which was all hollow beneath me and like the rough green quilt of a bed of waters. At length two streams burst out and took their way down, one on one side a high ground upon this ridge, the other on the other. I took that to my right (having on my left this high ground, and the other stream, and beyond that Doe-Crag, on the other side of which is Esk Halse, where the headspring of the Esk rises, and running down the hill and in upon the vale looks and actually deceived me, as a great turnpike road – in which, as in many other respects, the Head of Eskdale much resembles Langdale) and soon the channel sank all at once, at least 40 yards, and formed a magnificent waterfall – and close under this a succession of waterfalls seven in number [Cam Spouts], the third of which is nearly as high as the first. When I had almost reached the bottom of the hill, I stood so as to command the whole eight waterfalls, with the great triangle-crag looking in above them, and on the one side of them the enormous and more than perpendicular precipices and *bull's-brows*, of Scafell! And now the thunder-storm was coming on, again and again! Just at the bottom of the hill I saw on before me in the vale, lying just above the river on the side of a hill, one, two, three, four objects, I could not distinguish whether peat-hovels, or hovel-shaped stones. I thought in my mind, that three of them would turn out to be stone, but that the fourth was certainly a hovel. I went on toward them, crossing and recrossing the becks and the river, and found that they were all huge stones. The one nearest the beck, which I had determined to be really a hovel, retained its likeness when I was close beside. In size it is nearly equal to the famous Bowder Stone, but in every other respect greatly superior to it. It has a complete roof, and that perfectly *thatched* with weeds, and heath, and mountain-ash bushes.

I now was obliged to ascend again, as the river ran greatly to the left, and the vale was nothing more than the channel of the river, all the rest of the interspace between the mountains was a tossing up and down of hills of all sizes – and the place at which I am now writing is called – *Te-as*, and spelt, *Toes* – as the Toes of Scafell. It is not possible that any name can be more descriptive of the Head of Eskdale. I ascended close under Scafell, and came to a little village of sheep-folds; there were five together and the redding stuff, and the shears, and an old pot, was in the passage of the first of them. Here I found an imperfect shelter from a thunder-shower – accompanied with such echoes! O God! what thoughts were mine! O how I wished for health and strength that I might wander about for a month together, in the stormiest month of the year, among these places, so lonely and savage and full of sounds!

After the thunder-storm I shouted out all your names in the sheep-fold – when echo came upon echo – and then Hartley and Derwent, and then I laughed and shouted Joanna. It leaves all the echoes I ever heard far far behind, in number, distinctness and *humanness* of voice – and then not to forget an old friend I made them all say Dr Dodd* et cetera.

After the Storm I passed on and came to a great peat-road, that wound down a hill, called Maddock How, and now came out upon the first cultivated land which begins with a bridge that goes over a stream, a waterfall of considerable height and beautifully wooded above you, and a great water-slope under you. The gill down which it falls, is called Scale Gill – and the fall Scale Gill Force. (The word Scale and Scales is common in this Country – and is said to be derived from the Saxon Sceala; the wattling of sheep – but judging from the places themselves, *Scale Force* and this Scale Gill Force – I think it as probable that it is derived from Scalle – which signifies a deafening noise.) Well, I passed through some sweet pretty fields, and came to a large farm-house where I am now writing. The place is called Toes or *Te* as – the master's name John Vicars Towers – they received me hospitably. I drank tea here and they begged me to pass the

*Dr William Dodd, the forger.

night, which I did and supped of some excellent salmonlings, which Towers had brought from Ravenglass whither he had been, as holding under the Earl of Egremont, and obliged 'to ride the Fair' – a custom introduced during the times of insecurity and piratical incursion for the protection of Ravenglass Fair. They were a fine family – and a girl who did not look more than twelve years old, but was nearly fifteen, was very beautiful – with hair like vine-tendrils. She had been long ill and was a sickly child – 'Ah poor bairn! (said the Mother) worse luck for her, she looks like a quality bairn, as you may say.' This man's ancestors have been time out of mind in the vale and here I found that the common names, Towers and Tozers, are the same; *er* signifies 'upon' – as Mite-er-dale the Dale upon the River Mite, Donnerdale – a contraction of Duddon-er-dale, the Dale upon the River Duddon. So Towers, pronounced in the Vale *Te*-ars – and Tozers are those who live on *the toes* – i.e. upon the *knobby* feet of the Mountain. Mr *Te*ars has mended my pen.

This morning after breakfast I went out with him, and passed up the vale again due East, along a higher road, over a heathy upland, crossed the upper part of Scale Gill, came out upon Maddock How, and then ascending turned directly Northward, into the heart of the mountains; on my left the wild crags under which flows the Scale Gill Beck, the most remarkable of them called Cat Crag (a wild cat being killed there) and on my right hand six great crags, which appeared in the mist all in a file – and they were all, though of different sizes, yet the same shape all triangles. Other crags far above them, higher up the vale, appeared and disappeared as the mists passed and came: one with a waterfall, called Spout Crag – and another most tremendous one, called Earn [Heron] Crag. I passed on, a little way, till I came close under a huge crag, called Buck Crag – and immediately under this is Four-foot Stone – having on it the clear marks of four foot-steps. The Stone is in its whole breadth just 36 inches (I measured it exactly), but the part that contains the marks is raised above the other part, and is just $20\frac{1}{2}$ inches. The length of the Stone is $32\frac{1}{2}$ inches. The first foot-mark is an ox's foot – nothing can be conceived more exact – this is $5\frac{3}{4}$ inches wide. The second is a boy's shoe in the snow, $9\frac{1}{2}$ inches in length; this too is the very thing itself, the heel, the bend of the foot, et cetera. The third is the foot-step to the very life of a mastiff dog – and the fourth *is Derwent's very own first little shoe*, 4 inches in length and O! it is the sweetest baby shoe that ever was seen. The wie-foot in Borrowdale is contemptible; but this really does work upon my imagination very powerfully and I will try to construct a tale upon it. The place too is so very, very wild. I delighted the shepherd by my admiration. The Four-foot Stone is my own christening, and Towers

Hartley Coleridge

'The huge enormous
mountains in Wastdale'

undertakes it shall hereafter go by that name for hitherto it has been nameless.

And so I returned and have found a pedlar here of an interesting physiognomy – and here I must leave off – for dinner is ready.

Coleridge never completed his description of this walking tour for Sara Hutchinson, but we have his Notebook entries covering the rest of it. Before these, however, there are a few short passages from the pages of the Notebook covering the tour so far, which contain material not included in the Scafell Letter or its successor.

Under Barter Crag, the famous bield [shelter] of foxes, five cubs – eighty lambs, geese, hares, mice, moles, frogs, dogs – thirty-eight hours without food by the fox's bield, because the two foxes would have taken away their young. Tod, a Fox.

Iron Crag, back of this wild cat fell into the water, four hounds and a terrier with it. When they came up, they were all of a mat, each hold of the cat, the cat of all of them. Five minutes under the water.

Fox (last killed) just in Bowness – tumbled off the crag and broke his hind back. Old man, in the house, bedrid, heard the hounds, and got up and out. Fox trailing his back and fighting – old man got him before the hunters.

Sheep clinging like flies to a grass.

The huge enormous mountains of Wastdale all bare and iron-red – and on them *a forest* of cloud-shadows, all motionless.

Burnmoor Tarn – O for wealth to wood these tarns – weeping birches with mountain ash and laburnum, with hollies for underwood.

Dial plate flower and wild thyme roam up the fells, in company with them the fox's tail, fern, rushes, etc.

Wast-dale-Head, near Wast-Water, in Cumberland. – August 1781

6 August

Dined at Towers' – and quitted him at half past one. Eskdale, more descriptively Eskerdales, for it is a dale by the reluctant mercy of the mountains, and the hills, their children (some but babes, others striplings, who stand breast-high to their fathers); it is mainly however two dales, like Stanley's in St John's, only that the intervening ridge of hills is higher than those of Leathes' water and lower than the Naddle Fell. The Esk runs down the left hand of the ridge (as you go down). Both vales are in their course of very unequal breadths, often little more than the river channel in the one, and as much space as would serve for the bed of a good river in the other. Now [and] then the hill-ridge intermits and the vales become one. But never sure were lovelier human dwellings than these nested in trees at the foot of the fells, and in among the intervening hills. After you have left Scafell and his progeny behind you, the fells on each side are low, rough, and ragged with brushwood.

Inclosures made on the screes partly for saving the sheep from falling down, partly to reserve the grass for the *hogs* [year-old sheep].

After the junction and re-disjunction of the vales came to a beck, with a bridge which I crossed – a pretty beck with well wooded banks, chiefly oak, ash, alder, and birch, not without thorns, hazels, and hollies. Two or three houses very pleasantly situated on the Esk side of the Bridge, and on the other side a grand picture view of the ridge and top of Scafell seen through a [gap] with a road at the bottom. This beck slants from the bridge directly into the Esk, and in a few hundred yards after, the vale narrows, unites, and you walk by the side of the Esk, now as broad as the Greta; the front side of the last hill a pretty regular farmhouse with a noble *back* of wood, situated just as the House by the Brig at Great How, only the hill is not a quarter as high.

I walk however not a furlong, before the Esk slants away from me to the left again, but presents a beautiful reach . . . That beck which I crossed the bridge over, is Whillah Beck, comes from Burnmoor Tairn. On my right I have low fells, Eskdale Moors, exceedingly rocky and woody, huge perpend. smooth stones, now hidden, and encircled by young wood, now starting out. The *regular house* is a shooting seat of Mr Stanley's. I come again to a view of the river over some hayfields and an islet in the river, the opposite fells Birker Fells.

Come to the Public House, with a beautiful low hill of wood and rock close behind, cross the Esk Bridge, and pass at the end of Birker Moor, a piece of wooded rock – grander, exactly like the other side of Grasmere, opposite Tail End front-windows, except that it rises and falls in full large obtuse triangles, and not so much in small nipple-work. At the end of this Eskdale becomes a broad spacious vale, completely land-locked, though the fells at the end are low, indeed only green cultivated hills. The vale now seems to consist of very large fields, with corn and potatoes and grass land growing, all in one field, in broad stripes. To the right hand Muncaster Fell, to the left Easterfield Common, over which I ascended by a peat road. It seems I have gone two miles round about and ought to have crossed over at Dalegarth Hall (from Stanley's shooting box). Sate and wrote this near the top of Easterfield Common (fern, heath, and moss) – a pretty view of the sea through a sink in Muncaster, a small dip in the shape of an inverted triangle – the sea, and a triangle of green coast.

Descended on the other side of Easterfield Common, crossed a moss, and ascended another and came out upon Devock, a good large tarn with naked banks, and a tiny island covered with sea fowl, two of which and afterwards four, flew round about above me, wailing and [?barking/baiting], then dipped down low, and made a dead *dart* along over my head, so that I could hear the clang of the wings, and altering its note to a noise of anger and menace. I stand in the ruins of the city of Barnscar . . . but nevertheless I found nothing, after most patient search, that I could distinguish from any part of the fell.* Two heaps of stones, on each of which some boys had built up a shelter in the shape of a large chimney, wanting the one side fronting the Lake. It is a flat-round hill . . . However the view is very fine – sauce better than the fish. Behind to my left a noble sea-view, to my right a break in the fells, and a bold view of the huge mountains at the head of Wastdale directly across the Lake and in front of me. Corney Fell, Stones' Head Fell, Black Coomb, of a very wild, various, and angular outline, running in ridges, rising in triangles, sinking in inverting arches, or darting down in nesses – mountain seen behind mountain, either the backward overtopping the hitherward, or the nearer mountain dipping down in an inverted arch or triangle. At the bottom of Devock, i.e. between the mountain view and the water, and forming its immediate [companion] is a small hill with a curious round large stoney head. I shall ascend to my right, gain a still more extensive view of the sea, and go round to it.

The angry clapper of the bird's bill, as it passed over my head.

I was not in the City of Barnscar, it is half a mile from the foot of the lake, toward Muncaster . . . Devock Lake is prettily shaped, and runs from South to North. At the bottom, just under *Wadness How*, or *Seat How* by the boat-house, standing, the bank to my left is strait, [and] . . . is pretty in bays, and

*Bronze-Age urns have been found at this site.

Coniston: 'the head of the lake is an admirable junction of awful and of pleasing simplicity' (p.158)

the island close on its left bank is pretty with some trees and bushes on it. If the whole of its right bank, which is an ascent of 120 yards perhaps, were compleatly cloathed with wood, and the other banks judiciously planted, it would cap 'em [all] – sea views and fell views! . . .

Passed over a common, wild, and dreary, and descending a hill came down upon Ulpha Kirk, with a sweet view up the river, with a large mirror over a rapid. Ulpha Kirk is a most romantic vale, the mountains that embosom it, low and of a remarkably wild outline, and higher mountains looking in from behind. The view from the bridge, consisting of a reach of the river, the road and the kirk to the left at the end of the reach. The kirk standing on the low rough hill up which the road climbs, the fields level and high, beyond that; and then the different flights of mountains in the background, with wild ridges from the right and the left, running like arms and confining the middle view to these level fields on high ground is eminently picturesque. A little step (50 or 60 yards) beyond the bridge, you gain a compleatly different picture – the houses and the kirk forming more important parts, and the view bounded at once by a high wooded rock, shaped as an obtuse-triangle, or segments of a circle forming an angle at their point of junction, now compleat in a mirror and equally delightful as a view.

7 August

I pass along for a furlong or so upon the road, the river winding through the narrow vale, and then turn off to my left athwart a cove on Donnerdale Fell – a very rocky fell, yew-trees on the rocks (each crag a lownding-place for sheep). The outer line running in the segment of a circle so as to form the cove athwart which I went – this outline most wildly saw-toothed and sheep-tracks every where – O lovely lovely Vale!

Here it was seated on this mount, on Saturday, August 7, that I resolved to write under the name of The Soother of Absence, the topographical poem which I had long mummel'd about in my mind, and the day before thought of under the name of the Bards of Helvellyn or the Stone Hovels. The public house at Ulpha a very nice one and the landlord, a very intelligent man [?Danny/Dumny] Bloomfield.* I climb over the fell, taking to my left a little, wind around under and between low crags, and come to two dubs in the shape of an 8, the hither one with thirty or forty little islets, each of a yard or so of breadth. Now suddenly burst upon me a blunt-angled triangle hill, a peak of great height and singularity, rocky, and heathery, with patches of yellow green pasture intermixed. Behind me, right over the Dubbs, a fine water view, of rivers and flat land, and the Sea. It must have been here that I lost my way, for I now went on till I found myself coming down upon Ulpha again, about a mile above the house and kirk which I had just quitted. However I was not sorry, to have another view of that lovely place, and it brought me full in sight of a fine water fall on the opposite hill on the other side of the Duddon, seemingly a short mile above the kirk. I saw houses to my right, and an old man with his daughter, a sweet girl, burning bracken – went up to him and talked with him and the

*Coleridge spent the night of 6 August at Ulpha.

lovely girl in the midst of the huge volumes of smoke, and found I had gone two miles wrong – which yet I could scarcely believe. However he sent me to the road, which ran hard by, and winded down through Donnerdale Halse, a sloping vale between the Donnerdale Common and Donnerdale Fell, a most lovely narrow vale with several houses. After I had passed the first house, on my right the sound of a beck, deep hidden and with a woody bank between me and it, and its other bank a hill with a ravin bisecting it, but all covered with fine wood, and completely hidden, ravin and all. And now, being a short mile from Broughton Mills, this wood-covered hill and sounding beck to my right, there burst on me a lovely prospect – about a quarter of a mile on before me the woody hill ran down with a very gentle descent in a long ness, and the hilly ridge, directly in front of me, cultivated and inclosed to the top, ran down in a ness far on behind the ness of the woody hill, and so as to form an inverted obtuse-angled triangle with the upper half of the woody nose, and through this the sea, and an island in the distance. Two or three houses immediately upon the sea-ness and, just where the wood-ness reached the ground, a beautiful road came in sight leading up the cultivated hill, with houses and trees and hedges directly on to the little village upon the ness. As I proceed a few yards, the view is completely altered, and a round smooth [hill] rises up beyond the sea-ness, and bisects the distance, and on the other side of the round hill is the high land on the coast.

Now I descend, and cross the wood-beck, which preserves its character to the last, running all under alders, into a beck of a similar character from the woods on Donnerdale Fell – and now come into a lovely vale, and a bridge covered with ivy, its wall twenty yards in length. The vale is completely land-locked by segments of circles folding in behind each other. Before me a strait ridge slants across, the hill on my right folds in in a long *ellipse* behind, while the hill on my left in more of a segment of a circle folds in before it: so is it, with my back to the sea, and my face looking up the stream that runs between alders and birch elms. The name of the beck Little Beck, that springs out of Coe Moss. Turning round and looking sea-ward the hill that is now to my left and makes an elliptical line to my back, curves in a circle-segment, while the hill to my right folds round about it. The place Broughton Mills, Corn Hills; the hill that I came upon when I lost my way, Stickle Knot.

Dined on oatcake and cheese, with a pint of ale, and two glasses of rum and water sweetened with preserved gooseberries at the ale house – Cassons'. The son, William Casson, got a pleurisy and abscess in his side by over-heating himself and then starving himself in breaking up the ice for the Mill – but being a scholar, he gets his cloathes and a little money besides by teaching a 'lile lock of bairns'. His Father and Mother that keep the Public House, give him his meat. The road to Torvill or Torva [Torver] turns off at the Inn, the views on your left hand exceedingly interesting. A few hundred yards from the inn [is] one eminently picturesque – a cottage among the hills with nine main features of sight having their point of unity in it. But all the way for a mile by our left is a great bulging rocky hill covered with wood, with two or three deep wooded ravines in it, and the unseen ever-heard brook winding at its feet – between the road and the brook inclosed fields, of steep descent, and near to the head of the woody hill-bank a house and outhouses with 10 tall firs at its back. The roads upon and between the hills from here a very interesting part of the picture and views to the right were of open fields, steep ascending. Beyond the house with the firs . . . the brook becomes visible sloping down a descent. I still ascend, ferny common to my right, to my left woods with fields and in-closures intermixed, and above the woods. Now nearly in the bottom you see a house with two outhouses, the house itself ivied all over its sea-ward gavel, and from this house the line of the beck runs almost straight up to its fountain head. A beautiful road serpentizes over the hill just above its head, and for a small space down along its hither bank. It rises or seems to rise between two round stony hills, each of which the mountain-ridges now rise over, now sink under, in a jagged saw-toothed outline. I am sitting in the road, with the ivied house beneath me, and right opposite to me, through an inverted arch in the fells, a very singular pike looks in. . .

   At this ivied house another beck comes from the fells, close by my road, and joins the former. Now a ridge rises gradually like a fish, increasing all the way from the tail up to the head, between my road and the source of the former beck. About a furlong higher up, a bridge crosses the latter beck and the road which I before observed serpentizing at the head of the main beck runs down in a sweet curve upon the bridge; and goes by the beck side down to the ivied house in a strait line. All before me, as far as I can see, which indeed is not more than $\frac{1}{4}$ mile, a gentle ascent, ferny common steep on my right, the wider view on my left a descending fell with green stony bulging hills on either side, which unite at its head in a shelving ridge, over behind which a higher ridge shelves in the same direction. I now pass on, beyond the source of the hither beck, to the top of the hill along which and up which my road had been ever winding, and see behind me to my right a grand seaview and the flat lands upon the sea, with three hills, the largest of which looks like a Paradise in the wild, the fields so sweetly shaped and so green; the smaller is not unlike it, the hither one is bleak. I go on, descend a little and to my right a low cultivated dell, with stony fells above it; to my

Hawkshead and Esthwaite

left a bleak common, and stony fells over which the clouds are sweeping, and on my right far onward long ridges of fells, all running abreast with long arms sea-ward, and seen either by the dips and gaps in the hithermost ridges, or by the superior height of the furthermost – but all alike – grey and stoney. It is a day of sun and clouds, with a thousand shadows on the hills.

8 August

Coniston is doubtless a worthy compeer of the stateliest, an equal coheir of nature with Keswick, Wyndermere, and Ullswater. Its distinguishing character I think is its perfect and easy comprehensibility. At its foot the hills are low, but of a various outline. From the foot to within a mile of the head, the hills on either side are of no great permanent interest, though susceptible no doubt of a very high one from the accidents of nature, that must be so frequent here, of broken sunlights, clouds, and storm. The head of the lake is an admirable junction of awful and of pleasing simplicity. It is beyond all the other lakes perfectly intelligible. Conceive a crescent of hills, or rather a crescent hill, enfolding the first mile of water, this hill of various height and various outline, but nowhere high. Above this hill at the head of the Lake, but somewhat to the left of it (as you ascend the Lake) high mountains of a remarkable sternness and simplicity, one-colored, as seen at a distance, and dark-colored. Its boldest parts are first, the Bell and the Scrow, two black peaks, perfectly breast-shaped and lying abreast of each other, the whole Bosom of a Brobdignag Negress, and on one side of them the Lever's water-fall. Second, the very bold ness called Yewdale Crag [Long Crag?], its ridge line rounded; and about 150 yards from Gateskarth's, the house close upon the Lake, at its very head, the simple, most unfantastic Yewdale Crag seen through a dip in the woody pastoral crescent below, this dip a very gentle curve, the under half of an ellipse. The houses, gardens, fields, and woodland upon this crescent hill are all in admirable *keeping*, various as heart can wish, yet all sweet brothers and sisters – so various that when together you see small likeness, so like that when separate, you might mistake one for the other. I pass by Gateskarth, and go for Skelleth. Add Coniston Hall as the first bold feature, with its four round chimneys, two cloathed so warmly cap à pie with ivy and down on the wall far below.

Observe from Torva through Coniston the force of imitation in the gardens and sweet porches, and every where clipped yews, in obelisks, and fine arches. About two miles from Coniston (just where [the road joins from] Hawkshead and Esthwaite with Priest-Pot,* its floating isle with trees, then at the farther end, nearest Esthwaite, fifteen yards long) there is on your left [a house], belonging to one John Swainson, with a compleate colonnade of clipped yews. An old man with his wife – had small else to do – was a tanner, but long given over – has children, they are grown up and married off. Some time before this I came upon the view of Wyndermere.

To Sara Hutchinson   *Greta Hall, Keswick, 10 August 1802*

More rain coming! I broke off writing to look at the sky. It was exactly thirty-five minutes after seven, which was four minutes after the real sunset, and long long after the apparent sun-set behind our vales – and I saw such a sight as I never before saw. Beyond Bassenthwaite at the end of the view was a sky of bright yellow-green; but over that and extending all over Bassenthwaite, and almost up to Keswick church a cloud-sky of the deepest most fiery orange – Bassenthwaite Lake look'd like a lake of 'blood-red wine' – and the River Greta, in all its winding, before our house, and the upper part of the Keswick Lake, were fiery red – even as I once saw the Thames when the huge Albion Mills were burning, amid the shouts of an exulting mob – but with one foot upon Walla Crag, and the other foot exactly upon Calvert's House at Windy Brow was one great rainbow, *red* and *all* red, entirely formed by the clouds. I have now seen all the rainbows,

*A floating islet in Esthwaite

that, I suppose, are possible – the Solar rainbow, with its many colors, the grey lunar rainbow, and a fiery red rainbow, wholly from the clouds after sunset! . . .

I slept at Bratha on Sunday night and did not go on to Grasmere, though I had time enough, and was not over-fatigued; but though I have no objection to sleep in a lonely house, I did not like to sleep in *their* lonely house.* I called the next day – went into the garden – pulled some peas, and shelled and drest them and eat them for my dinner with one rasher of bacon boiled – but I did not go up stairs, nor indeed any where but the kitchen. Partly I was very wet and my boots very dirty – and Molly had set the pride of her heart upon its niceness – and still more – I had small desire to go up! . . .

In the course of my tour (and I was absent nine days) I gave away to bairns, and foot-sore wayfarers four shillings, and some odd pence; and I *spent* nine shillings – sum total, £0 13s 0d – but to this must be added the wear and tear of my boots, which are gone to be mended; and sixpence for a great knee-patch for my pantaloons, which will not however be worn an hour the shorter time for the said large knee-patch. I have now *no clothes but what are patched at the elbows, and knees, and in the seat* – and I am determined to wear them *out and out*, and to have none till after Christmas.

Hartley is in good spirits; but he does not look well. Derwent too looks less rosy than usual for we cannot keep him from the gooseberries. Hartley says, 'He is far over wicked; but it's all owing to Adam, who did the same thing in Paradise.' Derwent can *repeat* all the letters; and can point out six or seven. O! that you could see his darling mouth, when he shouts out Q. But notwithstanding his *erudition*, he is very backward in his tongue. Lloyd's children are nice fair babies; but there is nothing *lovely* in their countenances or manners. I have seldom seen children, I was so little inclined to caress, fair and clean, as they were. O how many a cottage bairn have I kissed or long'd to kiss, whose cheeks I could scarce see for the healthy dirt – but these I had no wish to kiss! There is a something in children that makes Love flow out upon them, distinct from beauty, and still more distinct from good-behaviour. I cannot say, God knows! that our children are even decently well-behaved – and Hartley is no beauty – and yet it has been the lot of the two children to be beloved. They are the general darlings of the whole town: and wherever they go, love is their natural heritage.

*Coleridge stayed with Charles Lloyd at Bratha (Brathay), rather than at Dove Cottage in Grasmere, since William and Dorothy Wordsworth were in France. Molly was their servant.

Mrs Coleridge is now pretty well.

God bless my darling Sara! and thee, dear Mary! I will finish my long Letter, as soon as possible.

To Sara Hutchinson　　　　　　　　　　　*Greta Hall, Keswick, 25 August 1802*

. . . All night it rained incessantly – and in a hard storm of rain this morning at half past ten, I set off and drove away toward Newlands. There is a waterfall [Moss Force], that divides Great Robinson from Buttermere Halse Fell, which when Mary and Tom [Hutchinson], and I passed, we stopped and said – what a wonderful creature it would be in a hard rain. Dear Mary was especially struck with its latent greatness – and since that time I have never passed it without a haunting wish to see it in its fury – it is just eight miles from Keswick. I had a glorious walk – the rain sailing along those black crags and green steeps, white as the wooly down on the under side of a willow leaf, and soft as floss silk. Silver fillets of water down every mountain from top to bottom that were as fine as bridegrooms. I soon arrived at the Halse and climbed up by the waterfall as near as I could, to the very top of the Fell. But it was so craggy – the crags covered with spongy soaky moss, and when bare so jagged as to wound one's hands fearfully – and the gusts came so very sudden and strong, that the going up was slow, and difficult and earnest – and the coming down, not only all that, but likewise extremely dangerous. However, I have always found this *stretched and anxious* state of mind favorable to depth of pleasurable impression, in the resting places and *lownding* coves. The thing repaid me amply: it is a great torrent from the top of the mountain to the bottom. The lower part of it is not the least interesting, where it is beginning to slope to a level – the mad water rushes through its *sinuous* bed, or rather prison of rock, with such rapid curves, as if it turned the corners not from the mechanic force, but with foreknowledge, like a fierce and skilful driver. Great masses of water, one after the other, that in twilight one might have feelingly compared them to a vast crowd of huge white bears, rushing, one over the other, against the wind – their long white hair shattering abroad in the wind.

The remainder of the torrent is marked out by three great waterfalls – the lowermost apron-shaped, and though the rock down which it rushes is an inclined plane, it shoots off in such an independence of the rock as shews that its direction was given it by the force of the water from above. The middle, which in peaceable times would be two tinkling falls, formed in this furious rain one great *water-wheel* endlessly revolving and double the size and height of the lowest. The third and highest is a mighty one indeed; it is

Dove Cottage: 'I did not like to sleep in *their* lonely house' (p.160)

twice the height of both the others added together, nearly as high as Scale Force, but it rushes down an inclined plane – and does not *fall*, like Scale Force. However, if the plane had been smooth, it is so near a perpendicular that it would have *appeared* to fall – but it is indeed so fearfully savage, and black, and jagged, that it tears the flood to pieces – and one great black outjutment divides the water, and overbrows and keeps uncovered a long slip of jagged black rock beneath, which gives a marked *character* to the whole force. What a sight it is to look down on such a cataract! – the wheels, that circumvolve in it – the leaping up and plunging forward of that infinity of pearls and glass bulbs – the continual *change* of the *Matter*, the perpetual *sameness* of the *Form* – it is an awful Image and Shadow of God and the World. When I reached the very top, where the stream flows level, there were feeding three darling sheep, with their red ochre letters on their sides, as quiet as if they were by a rill in a flat meadow, flowing clear over smooth tressy water-weeds, and through by long grass – Bless their dear hearts what darlings mountain sheep are! A little above the summit of the waterfall I had a very striking view – the Lake and part of Keswick in a remarkably interesting point of view seen at the end of the vista formed by the Vale of Newlands – this was on my right – and as I turned to my left, the Sun burst out – and I saw close by me part of the Lake of Buttermere, but not an inch of any one of its shores or of the Vale – but over away beside Crummock a white shining dazzling view of the Vale of Lorton and the sea beyond it.

I went to Lodore on Sunday [29 August] – it was finer than I had ever seen it before. Never were there three waterfalls so different from each other, as Lodore, Buttermere Halse Fall, and Scale Force. Scale Force is a proper fall between two very high and narrow walls of rock, well tree'd – yet so that the trees rather add to, than lessen the precipice walls. Buttermere Halse Fall is a narrow, open, naked torrent with three great water-slopes individualized in it one above another, large, larger, largest. Lodore has its walls, but they are scarcely walls, they are wide apart, and not upright, and their beauty and exceeding majesty take away the terror – and the torrent is broad and wide, and from top to bottom it is small waterfalls, abreast, and abreast. Buttermere Halse Fall is the War-song of a Scandinavian Bard. Lodore is the Precipitation of the fallen Angels from Heaven, Flight and Confusion, and Distraction, but all harmonized into one majestic Thing by the genius of Milton, who describes it. Lodore is beyond all rivalry the first and best thing of the whole Lake Country. Indeed (but we cannot judge at all from prints) I have seen nothing equal to it in the prints and sketches of the Scotch and Swiss Cataracts.

To William Sotheby   *Greta Hall, Keswick, 27 September 1802*

The river is full, and Lodore is full, and silver-fillets come out of clouds and glitter in every ravine of all the mountains; and the hail lies like snow, upon their tops, and the impetuous gusts from Borrowdale snatch the water up high, and continually. At the bottom of the lake it is not distinguishable from snow slanting before the wind – and under this seeming snowdrift the sunshine *gleams*, and over all the nether half of the lake it is *bright* and *dazzles*, a cauldron of melted silver boiling! It is in very truth a sunny, misty, cloudy, dazzling, howling, omniform day, and I have been looking at as pretty a sight as a father's eyes could well see – Hartley and little Derwent running in the green where the gusts blow most madly, both with their hair floating and tossing, a miniature of the agitated trees, below which they were playing, inebriate both with the pleasure – Hartley whirling round for joy, Derwent eddying, half-willingly, half by the force of the gust – driven backward, struggling forward, and shouting his little hymn of joy.

September
The old stump of the tree, with briar roses and bramble leaves, wreathed round and round: a bramble arch, a foxglove in the centre.

October
The stedfast rainbow in the fast-moving, hurrying, hail-mist! What a congregation of images and feelings, of fantastic permanence amidst the rapid change of tempest – quietness the daughter of storm.

19 October
Midnight, sitting up in my bed, which I had drawn alongside the fire, with my head to the great window and the foot to the bookcase, my candle on the green table close by me – as I was reading – a flash of lightning came so vivid as for the moment to extinguish in appearance both the candle and the bright fire. It was followed by a clap of thunder that made the window belly in as in a violent gust of wind, the window that looks out on Newlands, through which the lightning came.

20 October
My 30th birthday. A windy, showery day with great columns of misty sunshine travelling along the lake toward Borrowdale, the heavens a confusion of white clouds in masses, and bright blue sky. Sunshine on the Bassenthwaite window while rain and hail was scourging the Newlands window. The whole vale shadow and sunshine, in broad masses. No clouds on the tops of the mountains. . .

Half past one. The whole of Newlands full of a shower mist drunk and dazzling with sunshine in one part transparent, and Great Robinson and the Green Ridge and hollow below or seen through it. It passed off and floated across the Lake toward Lodore in flossy silk. The birches, auburn and gold, shew themselves among the oak grove. The white flossy sun-mist floats along and now Borrowdale looks through it. The upper segment of the arch of the sky is all blue, bright blue, and the descent on all sides white massy clouds, thrusting their heads into the blue, in mountain shapes.

28 October
The sun set directly opposite, in a straight line to our door, behind the edgy ridge between Sale and Causey Pike. Of course, after its departure Newlands is in a blaze of light. A great beam runs athwart Borrowdale, above and behind the Castle [Castle Crag], and behind Grange Fells – a *sandy*-pink, a pillar lying lengthways, just below the mountain tops and parallel with the gaps. Fine lights on Skiddaw after the sunset.

4 November
Left Keswick, went to Penrith, could not get a place in the Mail. Passed the day with Sara at Miss Monkhouses. A large round of beef, sirloin of beef, a ham, 4 geese, 4 fowls, a hare, 2 giblet pies, 1 veal pie, 12 puddings, vegetables of all sorts: 1s and 6d a head, at the annual hunt-feast at Culthwaite, seven miles from Penrith on the Thursday before Martinmas, twenty-eight persons present – ale included.

To Sara Coleridge   *St Clear, Caermarthen, 16 November 1802*

I write to you from the New Passage. Saturday morning, November 13, we had a favourable passage,* dined on the other side, and proceeded in a post-chaise to Usk, and from thence to Abergavenny, where we supped and slept and breakfasted – a vile supper, vile beds, and vile breakfast. From Abergavenny to Brecon, through the vale of Usk, I believe, nineteen miles of most delightful country. It is not indeed comparable with the meanest part of our Lake Country, but hills, vale, and river, cottages and woods are nobly blended, and, thank Heaven, I seldom permit my past greater pleasures to lessen my enjoyment of present charms. Of the things which this nineteen miles has in common with our whole vale of Keswick (which is about nineteen miles long), I may say that the two vales and the two rivers are equal to each other, that the Keswick vale beats the Welsh one all hollow in cottages, but is as much surpassed by it in woods and timber trees. I am persuaded that every tree in the south of England has three times the number of *leaves* that a tree of the same sort and size has in Cumberland or Westmoreland, and there is an incomparably larger number of very large trees. Even the Scotch firs luxuriate into beauty and pluminess, and the larches are magnificent creatures indeed, in S. Wales. I must not deceive you, however, with all the advantages. S. Wales, if you came into it with the very pictures of Keswick, Ullswater, Grasmere, etc.,

*Across the Severn Estuary.

Lodore Falls: 'beyond all rivalry the first and best thing in the whole Lake country'

in your fancy, and were determined to hold them together, S. Wales, with all its richer fields, woods, and ancient trees, would needs appear flat and tame as ditchwater. I have no firmer persuasion than this, that there is no place in our island (and, saving Switzerland, none in Europe perhaps), which really equals the vale of Keswick, including Borrowdale, Newlands, and Bassenthwaite. O Heaven! that it had but a more genial climate! It is now going on for the eighteenth week since they have had any rain here, more than a few casual refreshing showers, and we have monopolized the rain of the whole kingdom.

From Brecon to Trecastle – a churchyard, two or three miles from Brecon, is belted by a circle of the largest and noblest yews I ever saw – in a belt, to wit; they are not so large as the yew in Borrowdale or that in Lorton, but so many, so large and noble, I never saw before – and quite *glowing* with those heavenly-coloured, silky-pink-scarlet berries. From Trecastle to Llandovery, where we found a nice inn, an excellent supper, and good beds. From Llandovery to Llandilo – from Llandilo to Caermarthen, a large town all whitewashed – the roofs of the houses all whitewashed! a great town in a confectioner's shop, on Twelfth-cake-Day, or a huge snowpiece at a distance. It is nobly situated along a hill among hills, at the head of a very extensive vale. From Caermarthen after dinner to St Clear, a little hamlet nine miles from Caermarthen, three miles from the sea (the nearest seaport being Llangan, pronounced *Larne* [Laugharne], on Caermarthen Bay – look in the map), and not quite a hundred miles from Bristol. The country immediately round is exceedingly bleak and dreary – just the sort of country that there is around Shurton, etc. But the inn, the *Blue Boar*, is the most comfortable little public house I was ever in.

17 November
Arrived at St Clear, November 15th. Fire in the kitchen [of the Blue Boar] never out for nine years: twenty-four miles from coals – balls, or rather great wasp-maggots, or large kidney potatoes, or penny rolls, six inches from head to tail, of clay and coal.

Walked from St Clear to Larn (or Laugern) the vale on each side of me deep, the hills high, not unwooded or uncottaged, yet on the whole little impressive. The first view of Larn with its fine richly ivied castle close upon the sea and its *white and all white* houses, interesting. Unfortunately at low tide, or I should have seen the Castle washed by the sea. The Bay is a great river of greenish water taking one bend among fieldy hills. The outline sufficiently various and the whole breastwork of the hills sinking and swelling very playfully being low tide. Many tongues and many islands of mud-sand, with its little brooks from the salt-water marshes showing stately lines. Four, five or six promontories, like boars' heads, some of them with pretty cottages on the slope.

Take castles in Wales not as curiosities but as the *stans quantitas* [fixtures], the lay brother of the Church, and you will find them very interesting.

Sand brooks etc., opposite the promontory, then flat saltmarshes at the back of the hill on which I stand. Long jagged line of low clay cliffs fenced off from the main sea. High land to my right, seemingly three hands. Mallows, furze, lichens. Cottage with its dunghill of cockle shells, and sea-worn wood pushing up among it. The murmur of the main sea and the barking, yelping, whining, wailing of the various sea fowls. One third of the furze bushes in plentiful blossom. Daisies and tansy with the white petals fallen off and only lingering a few on the yellow head; periwinkle by the cockleshell dunghill.

The recesses and little gills of the promontories. . .

The ivy on the Castle I observed to be a beautiful yellow green when it faced the sea, but a deep dark green on the sheltered sides, and even in the sheltered recesses of the seaward side.

A number of handsome *glassy* houses in Larn, never saw such a profusion of tall broad windows, except in Hamburg. Before one of the doors two large cages with two fine parrots screaming away. A hen and two or three large chicks perching upon one cage, but unscared, and a handsome cock on the other with its bold brave old England face. I waited for him to crow, but he did not.

Cottages favourable only to vegetable life – hot bed of wild weeds on their roofs and ivy on their walls – but the shrivelled shrimps of cold and hunger, their swarthied tenants.

White church with grey steeple a furlong or so from the Town near the bottom of a hillside. [Various epitaphs copied down by STC follow.] When I took the copy, the groundsel showered its white beard on me: groundsel and fern on the grave, and the thorns growing that had been bound over it. On a square tomb as high as half up my thigh . . . the tom tits with their black velvet caps showered down the lovely yew-berries on me.

24 November

November 21st at Crescelly. Returned to St Clear's on Monday. Left it on Tuesday for Narberth. Mem. the various noises of the house and mem! the great sheep dog that burst crashing the pane of the window, the upper

Tom Wedgwood

pane, while I was writing to Luff for T. Wedgwood. *Felix sit!** *Crash* and down fell the dog into the room, just on my back. The bottom of this large sash window level with a back street and the window splashed with mud like a London cellar window.

Men and women, servants, drivers, waiters, master and mistress – all talking at once, very loud, and one or two laughs always, when it was not scolding. Women scolding the children; children trampling, laughing, screaming in play, yowling in earnest (boys etc., on the street, level with the last pane of the window); bells ringing; dogs barking.

The above sounds imitated in its own scream by a parrot and someone talking to the parrot in a low voice. Finis: window crash and mad dog fall. All duly performed at the White Hart [Narberth] without interspace the whole evening of Tuesday November 23rd and morning of Wednesday 24th.

30 November

Visited St Gowen's Rocks and dined at Pembroke. The half moon, the cavern a thoroughfare of the high tide, and the gull heaving on the waves.

December

All animals have a sense of *joke* – calfs with their horns, dogs biting, women abusing their infants.

Gavel end of house covered with fern, all waving in the wind beautifully.

Gay Xmas look of the hawthorn bush with a background of ivy – the berries wet and the sun shining on them.

19 December

Every season Nature converts me from some unloving heresy and will make a *Catholic* of me at last – the pear trees in the lovely vale of Teme.

20 December

Two laughing chimney sweeps on a white horse – spur, rod, sneezing fine brown soot.

23 December

Between Garstang and Lancaster. Himself [Tom Wedgwood] and his idea of himself forms a compleat circle, like a one-arched bridge over a smooth clear stream.

*'May it bring a happy outcome.' Captain Luff was a Lake District friend of the Wordsworths and the hope was that T. Wedgwood could stay with him.

AT THE END OF JANUARY 1803 COLERIDGE SET OFF AGAIN, THIS time for the West Country, with Tom Wedgwood. In February the two of them experimented with the drug 'bang' or Indian hemp, obtained from Sir Joseph Banks, the President of the Royal Society. Coleridge returned to Keswick in April, after a stay in London when he insured his life. Undoubtedly his opium habit continued. In July William Hazlitt, now twenty-five, came to the Lakes. Coleridge, in a letter to Tom Wedgwood, called him 'a thinking, observant, original man . . . His manners are ninety-nine in a hundred singularly repulsive: brow hanging, shoe contemplative, strange. . . He is, I verily believe, kindly natured. . . He is strangely confused and dark in his conversation and delivers himself of almost all his conceptions with a forceps, yet he says more than any man I ever knew. . .'

In mid-August Coleridge set out on a Scottish tour with Dorothy and William Wordsworth. William was by now married to Mary Hutchinson, but she stayed behind to look after their new-born child. The tour was seen as a way of weaning Coleridge from his addiction. It is interesting to compare Dorothy Wordsworth's parallel account, until the Wordsworths separated from Coleridge at Loch Lomond, in her Recollections of a Tour made in Scotland 1803. *Dorothy wrote her account from memory once she had got back to Grasmere from Scotland and it is therefore a much more self-consciously literary and contrived essay than Coleridge's Notebook entries. Here is a passage describing some scenes shortly after they had left the top of Nithsdale:*

Just as we had begun to climb the hill we saw three boys who came down the cleft of a brow on our left; one carried a fishing rod, and the hats of all were braided with honeysuckles; they ran after one another as wanton as the wind. I cannot express what a character of *beauty* those few honeysuckles in the hats of the three boys gave the place: what bower could they have come from? We walked up the hill, met two well-dressed travellers, the woman barefoot. Our little lads before they had gone far were joined by some half-dozen of their companions, all without shoes or stockings. They told us they lived in Wanlockhead, the village above, pointing to the top of the hill; they went to school and learned Latin (Vergil), and some of them Greek (Homer), but when Coleridge began to inquire further, off they ran, poor things! I suppose afraid of being examined.

We saw . . . a tall upright building of grey stone, with several men standing on the roof, as if they were looking out over battlements. It stood beyond the village [Wanlockhead], upon higher ground, as if presiding over it – a kind of enchanter's castle, which it might have been, a place which Don Quixote would have gloried in. When we drew nearer we saw, coming out of the side of the building, a large machine or lever, in appearance like a great forge-hammer, as we supposed for raising water out of the [lead] mines. It heaved upwards once in half a minute with a slow motion, and seemed to rest to take breath at the bottom, its motion being accompanied with a sound between a groan and *jike* [creaking noise]. There would have been something in this object very striking in any place, as it was impossible not to invest the machine with some faculty of intellect; it seemed to have made the first step from brute matter to life and purpose, showing its progress by great power. William made a remark to this effect, and Coleridge observed it was like a giant with one idea.

Southey and his wife, Edith, were now installed at Greta Hall with her sister, Sara Coleridge – the first part of a plan of which the second was that Coleridge should take himself abroad with his life heavily insured. In December Derwent and he went to stay with the Wordsworths at Grasmere. On 14 January he walked over the hills to Kendal on his way to London and then Malta, Sicily and Italy.

To Robert Southey   *Greta Hall, Keswick, 8 January 1803*

On the 30th of December I accompanied Wedgwood to Patterdale, at the head of Ullswater, to Mr Luff's – whom he has some thoughts, I believe, of getting as a companion. On New Year's Day I walked over Kirkstone, an awful road over a sublime mountain by tairn and waterfall, to Ambleside and Grasmere. The next day, I walked more than halfway to Keswick to meet Miss Wordsworth, and back again, but unfortunately got wet in my feet. On the day after, Monday, January 3 in the evening I had an attack of dysentery, in kind the same, and in degree nearly equal, to that which I had at Keswick when Stoddart and Edith were there. Dear Edith will remember it well. The same deadly sweats, the same frightful profluvium of burning dregs, like melted lead, with quantities of bloody mucus from the coats of the intestines. I was better after and had a good night, and was so well the next day, that I determined to perform the promise I had made and accordingly walked back again to Mr Luff's over Kirkstone, just fifteen miles from Grasmere. I stayed Wednesday at Luff's – and on Thursday Wedgwood seemed to have made up his plans, and I found I could go to my home, for a week or so – but having something of importance to talk to Wordsworth about concerning Luff I was forced to go by Grasmere. But took a little pony and a woman to bring it back again, to take me to the top of the mountain; but before I got half way up, the storm was so horrid and pitiless that the woman seemed frightened – and I thought it unmanly to let her go on. So I dismounted, and sent her home with the storm to her back. I am no novice in storms; but such as this I never before witnessed, combining the violence of the wind and rain with the intensity of the cold. My hands were shrivelled like a washer-woman's: and the rain was pelted, or rather *slung*, by the wind against my face, like splinters of flint; and seemed to *cut* my flesh. A violent pain attacked my right eye which, I own, greatly alarmed me. On turning the mountain, at the first step of descent, all was calm, breathless. It seemed as if there was a great fountain of wind and tempest at the summit that rolled down a Niagara of air towards Patterdale. I arrived at Grasmere soaked through – and the next day walked to Keswick – but in consequence of all this, I have had another attack of dysentery.

To Thomas Wedgwood   *Greta Hall, Keswick, 14 January 1803*

You ask, in God's name, why I did not return when I saw the state of the weather? The true reason is simple, though it may be somewhat strange – the thought never once entered my head. The *cause* of this I suppose to be, that (I do not remember it at least) I never once in my whole life turned back in fear of the weather. Prudence is a plant, of which I, no doubt, possess some valuable specimens – but they are always in my hot-house, never out of the glasses – and least of all things would endure the climate of the mountains. In simple earnest, I never find myself alone within the embracement of rocks and hills, a traveller up an alpine road, but my spirit courses, drives, and eddies, like a leaf in Autumn: a wild activity, of thoughts, imaginations, feelings, and impulses of motion, rises up from within me – a sort of *bottom-wind*, that blows to no point of the compass, and comes from I know not whence, but agitates the whole of me; my whole Being is filled with waves, as it were, that roll and stumble, one this way, and one that way, like things that have no common master. I think that my soul must have pre-existed in the body of a chamois-chaser; the simple image of the old object has been obliterated – but the feelings, and impulsive habits, and incipient actions, are in me, and the old scenery awakens them. The farther I ascend from animated Nature, from men, and cattle, and the common birds of the woods, and fields, the greater becomes in me the intensity of the feeling of Life; Life seems to me then a universal spirit, that neither has, nor can have, an opposite. God is every where, I have exclaimed, and works

Ambleside

every where; and where is there *room* for Death? In these moments it has
been my creed, that Death exists only because Ideas exist; that Life is
limitless Sensation; that Death is a child of the organic senses, chiefly of the
Sight; that Feelings die by flowing into the mould of the Intellect, and
becoming Ideas; and that Ideas passing forth into action re-instate themselves again in the world of Life. And I do believe, that Truth lies inveloped
in these loose generalizations.

I do not think it possible, that any bodily pains could eat out the love and
joy, that is so substantially part of me, towards hills, and rocks, and steep
waters! And I have had some trial. On Monday Night I had an attack in
my stomach, and right side, which in pain and the length of its continuance

appeared to me by the far the severest, I ever had. I was under the necessity of having a person sit up with me till three in the morning, though about one o'clock the pain passed out of my stomach, like lightning from a cloud, into the extremities of my right foot – my toe swelled and throbbed – and I was in a state of delicious ease, which the pain in my toe did not seem at all to interfere with. On Tuesday I was uncommonly well all the morning, and ate an excellent dinner; but playing too long and too rompingly with Hartley and Derwent I was very unwell that evening. On Wednesday I was well, and after dinner wrapt myself up warm, and walked with Sara Hutchinson to Lodore. I never beheld any thing more impressive than the wild outline of the *black* masses of mountain, over Lodore and so on to the

Gorge of Borrowdale seen through the bare twigs of a grove of birch trees, through which the road passes – and on emerging from the Grove, a red planet (so very red that I never saw a star so red, being clear and bright at the same time), stood. . . It seemed to have sky behind it – it *started*, as it were, from the Heaven, like an eye-ball of fire. I wished aloud for you to have been with me at that moment.

6 July
Derwent to whom I was explaining what his senses were for: he had never once thought of connecting sight with his eyes, etc. I asked him what his tongue was for, and I told him. To convince [him] I held his tongue. He was not at all affected having been used to having his voluntary power controlled by others. Sometime after I asked him again; he had forgotten. I bade him hold his tongue and try to say, 'Papa'. He did, and finding that he could not speak, he turned pale as death and in the reaction from fear flushed red, and gave me a blow in the face. Two years and eight months old, within eight days.

10 July
Derwent fever-hot. The day before he ran round and round in the kitchen so long that for the first time in his consciousness he became giddy. He turned pale with fright and repeatedly cried 'the kissen is walking away from Derwent', pawing out his hands as if stopping it.

July
A row of crisp curly oaks reflected in Grasmere Lake with the field at the end of which they stood, looked lank and smooth, like seaweed tresses from a green sea rock.

Butterfly let loose, how very high, how madly, how purposeless it pushes the air under it and runs up the stairs of the air. Butterflies, an image of the restless fondness of two young lovers. Goose, would be a noble bird if it did not remind us of the swan, = Wyndham:Burke.*

Pretty incident of an old man resting in the shade in a hot noon. I accost him, sit beside him, talk to him and he to me. Become interested, we leave our resting place and he walks 100 yards or more, and then discovers that he has left his staff at the resting place.

*William Windham was the friend and ally of Edmund Burke in the House of Commons.

19 July
Intensely hot day. Left off a waistcoat and for yarn wore silk stockings.
About 9 o'clock had unpleasant chillinesses; heard a noise which I thought
Derwent's in sleep. Listened anxiously; found it was a calf bellowing. Instantly came on my mind that night I slept out at Ottery [aged seven] and
the calf in the field across the river whose lowing had so deeply impressed
me: chill + child + calf-lowing, probably the rivers Greta and Otter.

15 August
Monday morning, twenty minutes after eleven, August 15, 1803, W. and D.
Wordsworth, and S. T. Coleridge left Keswick, in the jaunting car, for
Scotland. . .
   Seat of limestone, in the limestone bank of the Dell Brook [at Caldbeck],
coming out from the rock, like a thick slate, or London flag stone – above it
some four or five feet, a low ruined garden wall, overgrown with gooseberry
trees, which formed a thick bushy *shed* over the seat, and above these a
double-blossomed cherry tree in its barren pomp, stretching out beyond the
shed, and dropping its glinting blossoms into the river.
   At Hesket we stayed at Younghusband's, The Sign of the Queen's Head
where I was before – a striking and noble-looking girl, with a flat face, but
yet with large features and large eyes, a noble one. Out of the little parlour
window looking across the market place and over the market house, a
group of ashes, of which the hithermost hath its topmost twig exactly like a
rook or magpie perching. N.B. The manifest magnitude which this twig
attained by its assimilation to a familiar form, the size of which had been
exempted by its old acquaintance, Queen Imagination, from all changes of
perspective.
   The sanded stone floor with the spitting pot full of sand dust, two pictures
of young Master and Miss with their round birds' eyes and parlour dress, he
with a paroquet on his hand, horizontal, the other hand pushed forward
just below it – she with a rose in her uplifted perpend. hand, the other hand
grasping it to support it in that posture. The whole Room struck me as
cleanliness quarreling with tobacco ghosts.

16 August
Tuesday Morning, left Hesket at 9 o'clock, our whole expences £0 18s 10d.
A fine view behind us from the first hill, and a pleasant country of hills and
woods and dells and valleys – in the manner of the Yorkshire Dales . . .
   We come to the bridge over the Caldew by Rose Castle, look S.W. up the
bed of the river, glittering down a gentle slope about 400 yards, thinly

'It seemed as if there was a great fountain of wind and tempest . . . that rolled down a Niagara of air towards Patterdale' (p.173)

wooded with low woods, single trees, on its banks. Then a large bank of wood, and Carrock over beyond it, but 30 yards from the bridge to my left hand as I look up the river, the most glorious tree, a beech elm, I believe, that I have seen this many a year. It is on a green platform, a small nook formed by the river, the high woody bank, and the bridge, all which are a harmony of shade and coolness.

We are delighted with Rose Castle, the thickset green fence to the garden, the two walls, the lower making a terrace, the house, the orchard crowding round it, the chestnuts, the masses of ivy over the gateway, from one great root. This stands on the other side of the wall to my left as I face the gateway. Go in, the ivy over the coach house belonging to the same mass – the horns of the dark old mulberry tree among it – the swallows and their shadows on the castle-house walls, the green shaven bank, like the roof of a house, between the main building and the castle, properly so called, the great nets on this castle, to cover the fruit trees – all, all perfect – Cottage Comfort and Ancestral Dignity!

Come to Hawksdale Bridge. All above the bridge very pretty, but all below it a plain of ugliest desolation, flooded with stones and sand by the winter torrents. In the bed of the river, great hogsheads of stones, for what purpose I did not learn. On the other side of the river a Sodom and Gomorrah cotton manufactory. So on to Dalston. Nothing very impressive in the first view of Carlisle.

17 August
At Carlisle, dined. At half past eight in the evening arrived at Longtown, Graham Arms – left it, Wednesday 9 o'clock. At Carlisle I alarmed the whole Court, judges, counsellors, tipstaves, jurymen, witnesses, and spectators by hallooing to Wordsworth, who was in a window on the other side of the hall – *Dinner!* Walked on the wall – the divine pearly whiteness of those rich fleecy clouds, so deliciously shaded toward the top of their component fleecy parts. Think of this often.

Then visited Hatfield, impelled by Miss Wordsworth – *vain*, a hypocrite. It is not by mere thought, I can understand this man.*

Enter Scotland, on foot over a bridge of the scanty River Sark, that winds like the convex edge of a crescent of sand then rolls dark over its red brown stones, a peat-moss river with a 1000 leisurely circles and ellipses of foam . . .

Come to the village of Springfield, 12 years old. Then there was but one clay house. Sir William Maxwell, of Spring . . . ground, a penny a foot to build on, as a grouped row and to every house four acres, some at 20 s., some 30 s. the acre, most of them weavers. O what dreary melancholy things are villages built by great men, cast-iron hovels. How ill does the dirt and misery combine with the formal regular shapes. Are they cells of

*Hatfield was a confidence-trickster who, claiming to be an MP, had seduced the Beauty of Buttermere, a Lakeland innkeeper's daughter. Coleridge had written a series of sensational articles about the affair for the *Morning Post* the previous year. Such an impersonation was a capital offence and Hatfield was hanged a few days later.

Carlisle

prisons? It is the feeling of a jail. Here at the public house the marriage ceremony is performed – Gretna Green – about half a mile a handsome nice-looking 'New Inn' on your right hand down a treeey lane where the new married elopers consummate. The chapel and burial ground crowded with flat grave stones, as high as from one's knee to one's hip, commands a view of Solway Firth, and the flat land between and the mountains beyond.

On the road from Gretna Green, immediately, and close in and about the village, a good number of trees – but yet all so dreary. A public house with a

gaudy daub of *Hope*. 'To crown returning Hope' – no beer! – What then?
Whisky, gin, and rum – cries a pale squalid girl at the door, a true offspring
of whiskey-gin-and-rum-drinking parents. At Springfield I was led into
reflections on the contrast between the Providence of God and the *Providence*
of man. The latter, while it gives, is sure to *prevent;* man's providence
provides *moulds*, hard iron moulds; but God's gives the growing principle.
We arrived at Dumfries, in the evening, having previously baited the horse,
and dined, at Annan.

18 August
Thursday Morning, half past eleven we left Dumfries, W. and Dorothy
Wordsworth having spent the morning in visiting Burns's house and grave,
and W. having called *to* and *on* [Samuel] Rogers.* A hot ride up the
pleasant Valley of Nith, which strongly reminded me of Gallow Hill, every
feature greatly magnified – to a single public house, called Brown Hill, at
which our dinner and apartments gave me the first specimen of the difference
between English and Scotch inns. We have had a great difficulty started
about beds, and I cut the knot, by offering, if anybody came, to sleep on the
chairs in the parlour. We must expect many of these inconveniences during
the tour, we wanting three beds for three persons.

The groundsel everywhere in the hedges, instead of the fox glove, lychnis
[ragged robin], and fifty other *Englishmen*. Say what you will, 'the naked
feet' is disgusting more so in Scotland than in Germany, from the *tawdry* or
squalid appearance of the bare-footed. In Germany there is a uniform dress
in the class that go bare-footed and they always have their shoes in their
hands or on their heads. In Scotland cabin gowns, white petticoat, all
tawdry fine, and naked legs, and naked splaid-feet, and gouty ancles.

19 August
Friday, left Brownhill and along by the Nith. This an interesting valley, the
Nith a rough rocky stream, the rocks like those on a low but savage sea
coast. The hills now thickly, now thinly wooded, now with single trees, and
now bare; here and there a cottage on them, but all single storied. We come
to Drumlanrigg, through a village, long, and all of thickset short single
storied cottages, to contrast with the huge monster crowned with pepper
castors, straight before us. Here I entered into a long reflection on the Duke
of Queensburie's Character ['Old Q' – a notorious rake].

*A mediocre poet famous for his breakfasts in London where he entertained society
and the literary world.

20 August

Left Leadhill, Saturday, through a like country, now not differing from the inside of moorish mountains in general, where the hills [angle in steeply] and the bottom is now just large enough for the road and the stream, running side by side, now admitting a little green boggy valley for the stream. Now the road climbs on the side of the hill a 100 yards leaving the stream on one's right beneath it in its green ellipse of grassiness. A cottage at the end of this, a gavel end wall upstanding, in ruin, the other part inhabited, seven trees, three of them blighted and one thin thing among potatoes – green turf fence.*

21 August

Sunday morning [Lanark – the Falls of Clyde]. Huge cotton mills, with rocky river, the hills that form its banks, finely wooded, deeply and variously ravined and gullied, perpendicular, transverse, horizontal. No inclosures consequently no styles – the men and women in their Sunday finery straggle like cattle, each in his own path.† Thus as you move on you behold the grand red precipices glooming through the trees. A clump of trees at the end of a wood on my left had a fine effect. This precipice is part of that round theatrical wall of rock which embraces the pool at the foot of the Cora Lynn on the left. The general colour of this wall a dim white with patches of green, and patches and streaks of red and yellow. The half farthest from the falls pushes out young elms from its clefts, and a little coppice of young elms grow at its feet.

The pool, ample and almost round, harmonizes very well with the broad *flight-of-stairs* fall. The water runs in a slant direction, and the *screen* of rock close beside it on the right is beautifully fringed with trees, which shade and

*From Dorothy Wordsworth's *Recollections*: 'We discovered a woman sitting right in the middle of the field, alone, wrapped up in a grey cloak or plaid. She sat motionless all the time we looked at her, which might be nearly half an hour. We could not conceive why she sat there, for there were neither sheep nor cattle in the field; her appearance was very melancholy. . . There was so much obscurity and uncertainty about her, and her figure agreed so well with the desolation of the place, that we were indebted to the chance of her being there for some of the most interesting feelings that we had ever had from natural objects connected with man in dreary solitariness.'

†From Dorothy Wordsworth's *Recollections*: 'It was delightful to see the lasses in gay dresses running like cattle among the broom, making their way straight forward towards the river, here and there, as it might chance.' These were probably workers from Robert Owen's mills at New Lanark which he ran on enlightened model lines from 1801. He was a pioneer of the Co-operative movement.

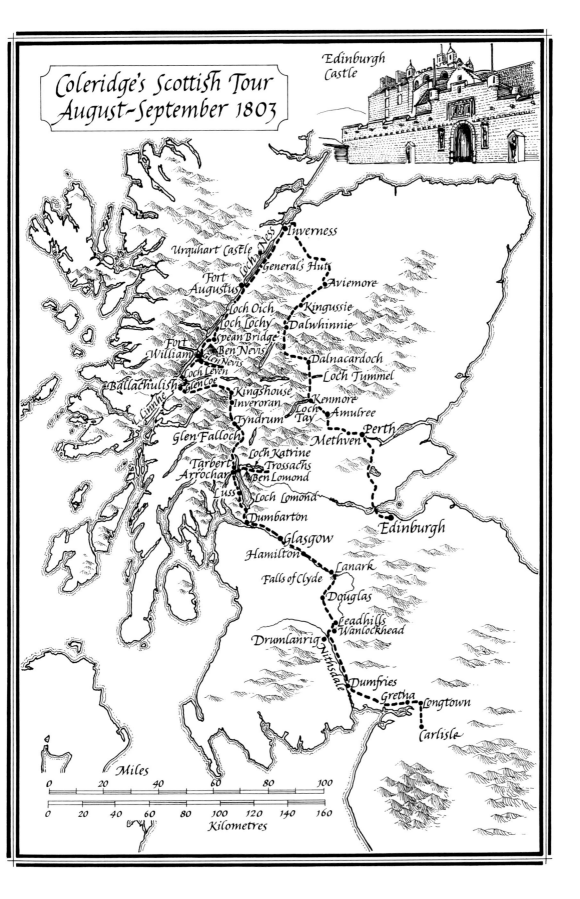

Coleridge's Scottish Tour
August–September 1803

Edinburgh Castle

Inverness

Urquhart Castle
Loch Ness
General's Hut
Aviemore
Fort Augustus
Loch Oich
Kingussie
Loch Lochy
Dalwhinnie
Spean Bridge
Fort William
Ben Nevis
Glen Nevis
Loch Leven
Dalnacardoch
Ballachulish
Glen Coe
Loch Tummel
Linnhe
Kingshouse
Inveroran
Kenmore
Tyndrum
Loch Tay
Amulree
Glen Falloch
Perth
Methven
Loch Katrine
Trossachs
Tarbert
Ben Lomond
Arrochar
Luss
Loch Lomond
Dumbarton
Edinburgh
Glasgow
Hamilton
Lanark
Falls of Clyde
Douglas
Leadhills
Wanlockhead
Drumlanrig
Nithsdale
Dumfries
Gretha
Longtown
Carlisle

Miles
0   20   40   60   80   100

0   20   40   60   80   100   120   140   160
Kilometres

lattice the third part of the lower fall, and half of the higher. Between the lower and higher fall (the higher *seeming* here about one-third as large as the lower) is a smooth slope of rock thirty yards in length perhaps, over which the water spreads itself thin and black, rocks just white enough from some unevennesses on this slope to be a bond of connection between the two masses of white above it and below it. On the left of the fall, right above this slope, is a red path, which has a good effect, and about a 100 yards from this path, the whole interspace filled with trees, overhanging the wall-rock are three firs which had a very fine effect. First they made a new feature, and a striking one; secondly their straightness and tallness gave perhaps some dim association of the human form (at least, they did certainly impress on my mind a distinct breezelet of fear); and lastly, the trees with which this whole semicircle of wall-rock is crowned, are so various, that this variety acted upon you without acting so obtrusively as to offend. O that I had seen this in the evening a thumbsbreadth from sunset; the solemn motions of the trees is, on such nights, harmonious with the dimmer shape and deeper colour.

As I write this, I turn my head, and close by me I see a birch, so placed as among a number of trees it alone is in full sunshine, and the shadows of its leaves playing on its silver bark, an image that delighted my boyhood, when I had no waterfalls to see. Moving higher and winding till we climb up directly over the place where I first sate, we see the whole fall, the higher, the lower and the interslope, with only a fragment of the wall-rock and the pool – the whole at once, with the white conical rock, with a cloak of mosses, and bushes and fir trees growing out of them, and the old round tower on the top of all. The little girl sent to *dog* and guide us, yawning with stretching limbs, a droll dissonance with Dorothy's raptures.

So we go to the top of all, and look down on both, a noble precipitation. . . The lower fall has two wheels, the first grey-green, the lower and larger, white and loose with the delicate shade as of diluted black, among it and upon it. The path of the river above the fall, still through the unroofed antechamber or passage of rock, sometimes naked and sometimes bushy. So we come to the moss house exactly like a hay-stack scooped out: lath and the moss apparently beaten into it, for it is smooth bruised not cut smooth. A curious table of moss, like an axis on a tripod, or rather stem with three branches, grows out of the ground. Then the round bason, a little hole at the bottom where it rises, and a little hole on the marge where it escapes. Close half a mile from Cora Lynn is another fall, the course of the river between the two through a passage of rocks, with occasional bays and coves – till we reach and overhang the Fall . . . it is awful indeed. O for evening

Dorothy Wordsworth

and solitude: such cathedral steeples, broken arches; so overboughed; such sounds, such shapes, such motions above the fall. The banks of the river fall at once into mild and cultivated green hills and fields.

See the shapes below me, in three yards of water: smooth water in a vault, smooth water close to the smooth rock, a hollow unquiet and changeful between the waters, water with glassy wrinkles, water with a thousand wrinkles all lengthways, water all puckered and all over dimples, over smooth rock rough with tiny roughnesses, the boiling foam below this fall.

Carland Crags – [O Asra] wherever I am, and am impressed, my heart akes for you, and I know a deal of the heart of man, that I otherwise should not know.

Reaches, short and quite land-locked, the rocks of each from 460 to 500 feet high, as high as any possible effect could require: now one green drapery of flowing woods from the summit to the very water; now blank, naked, and staring; now half clad, now in patches. The rocks now retiring in bays and now bulging out in buttresses; now in giant stairs, now in needle points, now in huge towers with chimneys on the top. The single trees on the very edge of the top, birch and ash, O how lovely! Pity there is any water or that it is not clear. Now the lower half wood and the higher bare;

Luss Glen near Loch Lomond

now the higher wooded and the lower bare. Sometimes one great huge spreading tree, all branches, and no trunk, starts out of a starting rock, and over-canopies half the stream. Sometimes top and bottom thick wooded and the middle bare; sometimes the nakedness running transverse or curvingly a whole reach together. Once a huge bulging ragged 1000-angled crag on whose endless surface one might read hieroglyphics, whole naked but greeted at the edge of its summit by branching trees: ashes and birches and hazels and one great oak in a center, all shooting out their branches far far over the bulge of the crag; but the oak seeming to canopy the stream in the bottom. At the foot of this great semicircular convexity of naked rock, one tall slender ash tree with no branches save only at its very top.

Larches and firs a repetition of units in time rather than an assemblage in space; units without union consequently without greatness, no character of relationship . . . tamed down by exceeding number and the exclusion of all things to be compared with.

The country by the Clyde tossing, playful, surface patchy with an odd mixture of fertility and barrenness, the hills often delved with gullies. But the last hour of the ride to Hamilton changed into large square corn fields upon hills of more ordinary outline.

22 August

Arrived at Hamilton, Sunday night, 9 o'clock. Walked next morning to Barrancluch, a wild terrace garden over the Avon, terrace above terrace, five terraces. The opposite bank of the river clothed richly with trees. Observed here the dragon scales of the bark of old sycamores. Yew trees cut out into all shapes contrasted with the wild beauty of the opposite bank.

N.B. The mirror of steel placed at the top of the room opposite the window that looks out on that vast waterfall with all its rocks and trees.

Monday Noon, August 22, left Hamilton for Glasgow, where we arrived at 4 o'clock, having seen Douglas Castle on the way. The Castle of massive red freestone, surrounded with rose beds, shrubs and climbers indigenous and planted. Over the Clyde the more perfectly impressive Abbey of Ballantyre [Blantyre Priory].

At Glasgow, the hurry and crowd of people and of carts, marking a populous trading city, but no coaches or carriages! Here I stood beside an asthmatic town-cryer, a ludicrous combination. A woman-shaver, and a man with his lathered chin most amorously ogling her as she had him by the nose. I was most pleased by the two great washinghouses and drying grounds, four square cloysters, with an open square, and the cauldron in the middle. Each woman pays a $\frac{1}{2}$d for her tub and $\frac{1}{2}$d, sometimes in scarce times 1d, for a tub of hot water, a penny to the watcher. So that the poorest person who can get cloathes to wash may earn their living, whereas in other cities those only can do it who can pay for lodgings with fire and washing utensils etc. I suppose there might be 120 women in each house.

24 August
Shadows over corn and woods like the motion of the air in sails. First view in a field of Loch Lomond, most like the view from Mr Clarkson's, but inferior. But about a short mile onward you see it as you mount a little ascent of the road under the boughs of trees that stretch all across the road, as under the arch of a bridge; the water, the island as a low ridge of mountain, and then Lomond towering behind that! Most lovely and most simple.

The lake ceased to interest me till within two miles of Luss a wooded cliff all green rises up, and bare Ben Lomond in a like ridge rises up behind it. Here too I saw for the first time a larch wound round with ivy, from the top of the stem to the bottom. Another curious larch by the side of a farm house bending like an arbor across the whole road. Yet another right opposite to the first inn at Luss, close by a shed, and having for its neighbour a gigantic sycamore. This larch is spread into an arbor perfectly round, like the expansion of an oak, with its limbs twisted in among this round spread of boughs in the wildest shapes, knees, and elbows, and crosses, and loops, and figures of eight.

25 August
Thursday Morning, side of the Loch Lomond. Observed the fern-roofed cottages, the fern stalks, of glossy polish ending in half an inch of black, lie like tiles on the bedde form[?] beneath. The round chimneys, or *stool*-shaped of four sticks: on them a slate and on the slate a stone. Ben Lomond from the lake rises up, and goes *bounding* down, its outline divided into six great segments, scolloped like many leaves, with five or six small scollops in each great segment, of the same shape.

Mount Inchdevannoch, by a path most judiciously winding up this mountain-isle and everywhere shewing to our right the delicious islands. One close by us in contrasted and perfect flatness, another *so* close to us, a hilly isle, that the water in two points disappears and the intermediate water forms a compleat little lake. The endless variety of shapes, of bays, of tongues, the varying lights on the various shores, some sandy, some rocky, some green with grass, some dark-green with forest trees. The most striking, and frequent form of bay, is the hook. Look at that black-green isle, in shape like the sword-fish, inclosed within a circular island of melted-silver-white sunshine. The broad low hills at the bottom of the lake are in fine keeping with the island character, and where they sink in a long gentle under curve of an ellipse you see the two points of Dumbarton Rocks . . .

What? though the World praise me, I have no dear heart that loves my verses. I never hear them in snatches from a beloved voice, fitted to some sweet occasion, of natural prospect, in winds at night.

Landed on the island, where the bark hut is. Went into the hut where the woodmen sleep. Straw beds inclosed by thick sticks, one raised off the ground like a bed-stock, and in the middle the fire place (stone) with the crooked stick to hang the pot on – the smutty wooden crock. The woodman's roof-shaped hut, with two straight gavel ends, and slanting door; clay, sods, and brush wood, one gavel end supported by two silver birches – the wooden hammer for ripping on the ground by the straw beds. Note the bark rick, the deep orange with the tarnished silver, with masses of sunshine and shade on it.

As we ascend, the lake becomes very like Ullswater, with a character of Crommock. Ben Lomond is indeed a thing betwixt Melbreak, and Place Fell. Higher still the lake gains a character of its own, nesses running down into the lake on each side, at certain distance appearing to run in behind each other, at other distances to meet and close up the lake. Now they seem opposite, and the lake runs up endlessly between them, the road and the mountains close by my left hand – wild, and steep, but not particularly interesting and everywhere we miss the 'Statesmen's Houses', and sweet spots of Cumberland cultivation. Every where there is a distressing sense of local unrememberableness. On the descent of the hill close upon Tarbet, we had to our left a view of the wild broken cliff, called the Cobbler, looking in over a smooth ridge. I knew it instantly, from recollection of Mr Wilkinson's Drawing.

Two children, in the rain, under one cloak, their arms round each other, their two faces, a pair! – the drapery, etc., very picturesque. A fisherman's hut: the oar, the one end on the ground, leaning on the cottage, the broad end rising a few inches above the little chimney – an image for a poet. The view from the parlor window at E. Tarbet – and all the walk for more than two miles above so deludingly like Ullswater by Patterdale and Glenridden. (Alas! too few houses, too little motion.) The most striking feature an ascending terrace of cultivated fields with frequent interruption of wooded bushy rocks, a steep mountain above, a perpendicular precipice below it. both the mountain and precipice bushy.

Loch Lomond

In a nook formed by the turn of a brook, a stone's throw from a cottage, a whole forest of raspberries – only old people in the cottage.

26 August
Friday. Took a couple of fowls from our inn, our hospitable inn, at E. Tarbet, went with the Jacobin traitor of a boatman to Rob Roy's Cave. Such caves are always and of necessity where huge masses of stone in great numbers have fallen down on one another; but the masses, the bushes and trees, and the half-wooded precipice above, all most impressive. We returned half a mile to the ferry, a cottage with a few fields among trees by a wild waterfall. So we ascended into moorland, with strong views behind us of the three pyramidal mountains of the opposite coast of Ben Lomond. These,

when all becomes moorland desolation, combine awfully with two lofty houses, each with a smaller one attached to it. We wondered how they came there, but afterwards, found they were a garrison. We move on about three miles to a little lake [Loch Arklet], like Burnmoor Tarn, and in about two miles to a sheepfold at the edge of Loch Ketterin [Katrine], a fine body of water in an elbow bend, but the mountains were all too dreary and not very impressive in their forms or combinations. There was wood on them, but a total want of cultivated land and happy cottages. We wound along over a hill into a very interesting moorland till we came in sight of what I may call the haft or handle of the lake, with two farm houses – here called gentlemen's houses. This first reach of the lake, two miles perhaps in length, has four islands, sweet bays, and island-like promontories, one shaped like a dolphin, another like a sea-lion. Still as we moved along, there formed new pictures, sometimes shutting out, sometimes admitting a peep, sometimes pouring in a full view of the large mass of water. But our road, our wild moorland path [was] through the most luxuriant heaths, the purple, the white, the pale purple, the deep crimson, or rose-color purple; through a mountain pass, like a giant gate-way – while on each side the mountain sides were cloathed wildly with willow trees, in ravines or around bulging rocks, and the edges of the mountains wildly broken.

The rocks, by which we passed, under the brow of one of which I sate, beside an old blasted tree, seemed the very link by which Nature connected wood and stone. The rock substance was not distinguishable in grain, cracks, and colors from old scathed trees, age- or lightning-burnt. Right opposite to me [were] the willowy mountains with the broken wild craggy summits, and half way up one very large blasted tree, white and leafless. Here too I heard with a deep feeling the swelling unequal noise of mountain water from the streams in the ravines. We now found that our expedition to the Trossachs was rashly undertaken. We were at least nine miles from the Trossachs, no public house there or here. It was almost too late to return, and if we did, the Loch Lomond ferry boat uncertain. We proceeded to the first house in the first reach, and threw ourselves upon the hospitality of the gentleman, who after some demur with Wordsworth did offer us a bed, and his wife, a sweet and matronly woman, made tea for us most hospitably. Best possible butter, white cheese, tea, and barley bannocks.

27, 28, 29 August
Saturday morning, left the house. A little before we reached the second white house, a perfect *picture* from the two hooks, one of a promontory, and another of an island seeming a *promontory*, within another larger hook, and

in the foreground a fisherman's hut with the oars. So we went on, the white house, 'green to the very door'. Here Rob Roy died; we passed by his burial ground (each house has a square inclosure for burying).*

The path now led up, then along, the breast of the mountain. Hazels, ashes, birches, above us to the height, with starting cliffs, of the *wood-fibre* stone. Below the eye made its way through tangles and little openings, down a steep of hazels and wood, down upon the summit of a flat wood, in upon the ever-sounding lake. The mountain from many distances looking in upon my right hand [was] Ben Lomond, and behind those three pyrami-dal mountains in mist, opposite the ferry on Loch Lomond.

We came to the ferry house [on Loch Katrine] where W. and D. took boat – I declined it – lost my road, clambered among woods almost to the top of the fells, but regained it in about a mile. The road a most delightful one, all along by the side of the lake, now open, now inclosed, now a broad road, now a brown pathway through a green lane. About two miles from the ferry, the views of the foot of the loch begin to be highly interesting and the lake itself always highly so from the multitude and fine shape of its bays. But here as I leaned against an ash tree, I saw such a visionary scene! One promontory from the right ran down into the lake like a stretched out arm bent downwards, with a *bend* as if to support something, then a long island midway the Lake, then from the left another promontory much resembling the former, but varying in the steepness of its segments. Again from the right a high headland falling down steep and high as far as the tower and in the far distance and exact center of the view a small sugar loaf hill – all these in exquisite harmony, every ridge branch out [?], every intervening distance softened by the rainy air.

Still as I went on, the view varied and improved in distinctness – promon-tories that could not be distinguished from islands, island mistaken for promontory – till I arrived at the foot, in the heart of the Trossachs. I exclaimed Galilæe vicisti ['You, of Galilee, have conquered.' It was as] if the Lake of Keswick were to push up a mile into Borrowdale, and interweave itself among the mountains, and if those mountains were built up still more detachedly in a universal harmonious *dislocation* of all its component cliffs – those cliffs all wooded, variously wooded, young wood chiefly from *stumps* of huge trees, weeping birches surmounting steep precipices, as large as the largest weeping willows. But I must see it again!

I returned to the ferryman's house, and soon after my friends and an artist [?Wilson], of Edinburgh. We had a merry meal in the hovel, black

*This is incorrect. Rob Roy's grave is in Balquhidder, fifteen or twenty miles away.

The Trossachs

and varnished and glistering with peat smoak, the fowls roosting in the chimney amid the cloud of Smoke. We slept in the barn upon the hay. My friend and the artist had a sort of hay bed with blankets spread on the ground, but I preferred the hay rick, and was right. The brook ran as if running under my hay pillow! Next morning [Sunday 28 August] we went in the boat to the end of the lake, and so on by the old path by the garrison to the ferry house by Loch Lomond, where now the fall was in all its fury, and formed with the ferry cottage, and the sweet Highland lass a nice picture. The boat gone to the preaching, and we stayed all day in the comfortless hovel, comfortless, but the two little lasses did everything with *such* sweetness, and one of them, 14, with such native elegance. O she was a divine creature!

The sight of the boat full of Highland men and women and children, from the preaching, exquisitely fine. We soon reached E. Tarbet – all the while had rain. Never, never let me forget that small herd boy, in his tartan plaid, dim-seen on the hilly field, and long heard ere seen, a melancholy *voice*, calling to his cattle! – nor the beautiful harmony of the heath, the dancing fern, and the ever-moving birches. That of itself enough to make Scotland visitable, its fields of heath (those not subject to yearly burning) giving a sort of feeling of shot silk and ribbon *finery* (in the *apotheosis* of finery).*

On Monday [29 August] we went to Arrochar, formerly a gentleman's house on Lake Long. The view of the Cobbler interesting no doubt, but I was disappointed with the place! Here I left Wordsworth and D. and returned myself to E. Tarbet – slept there.

30 August

Tuesday, am to make my own way alone to Edinburgh. The rain drops on the lake [like] to an army of spirits, or faeries, on a wilderness of white sand – multitude + joyance, motion or a moving.

My words and actions imaged on his mind, distorted and snaky as the boatman's oar reflected in the lake.

The Cross – the Butter Hill – Ben Bean – and Benvaloch: the four mountains opposite the Inverslade Ferry.

Walked to the shore opposite to the ferry, and having waited and shouted and made signals for near an hour in vain, I wandered on. Seeing a boat on the shore, went to the cottage, which I found to be a small slaughter house. Engaged the men to go with me, went and obtained my watch, returned. I gave the man 2s and he said I must drink a glass of whisky with him, and carried me up the mouth of a river called Inveydougle and there I found a distillery all under and among foliage, which with its hogs et cetera sufficient picturesque – tho' as offensive to my sense of smelling, is perhaps melancholy in its moral relation. Passed on, the mountain close by my side, high and green with ferns, grasses, and young trees. Trees scattered here and there, and often a handsome full grown birch on the edge of the top of a naked precipice. Crossed little bridges, where streams came down over black rocks, with many views of that species of scenery which is always so interesting, where naked rocks stand above each other, some perpendicular and smooth and grey, from a yard high to twenty fathom with green *ledges* interspersed, some so narrow that a single sheep goes cautiously, some so

*When Coleridge speaks of heath, he of course means heather.

broad that a small flock might graze there, or an industrious Chinese raise a crop of corn. Holly trees wedging the solid rock, large birch tree filling up the hollow of the arch of the bridge. Passed by bays and promontories, some wooded, some craggy and heath-rich, some cultivated, often a boat heaving in the secure bay. Now the road ascending a hill led me to the last reach of Loch Lomond, which resembles a majestic river, distinguished from it by the ledger-like lines of foams, and its own lakish *sound* of water. The head is crowned by three ridges of mountains, the highest not very high, but bare and black and of very various outline; and such as in rainy or misty weather would be sublime. In this reach too is one of those *terraces* before described, and there is another between this and the ferry. The road up and down another hill, on my descent I see to the left a large single rock, far away from the foot of the mountain, in a green plot by itself. A little stream winds almost around it, overhung with alder bushes. It is cowl'd with heath, all its sides bare. The amplest side, viz, that facing the road, is 25 strides in length, and I suppose at least 40 feet high. It is 60 strides round and in shape it resembles the gavel end of a house. This is called, I find, the Bull Stone [now called Pulpit Rock]. 'Cry to the guid man to come up, the gentleman wants to *crack* wi' 'im.' Two bulls fighting said to have thrown down the stone. The river is a fine one and one side of it an O shaped pond (Falloch – i.e. White Lake) of 200 yards or so, in length, and one all wooded hill standing by itself close by its bank, which I mention because half a mile on it forms a beautiful feature in a fine river view, as you look backward down toward Loch Lomond, upon Ben Lomond and the ridges of hills intervening.

I stop at a farm house, and meet the kindest reception. From E. Tarbet 7 + 9 miles up the lake and up Glenfalloch but three farms. One farmer has within a very trifle one whole parish, a farm of £1100 per annum, in this *wild* country. Preaching four times a year at the great Bull Stone, by the desire of the inhabitants: this is one among the many proofs that natural objects do *impress* the minds of the inhabitants who are familiarized to them, tho' they do not use epithets of delight or admiration. A cloud broke on the hill a little above Garbel, the name of the dram house where I stopt, broke in the day time, and swept away two whole villages, all but one strong slate house, which however it filled with stones and gutted of its furniture. The houses came floating down, standing upright, and the poultry, and cats on the house tops, mewing, clucking, crowing, and beds floated by with dogs yowling on them. The people all away. Here I determined to go to Glen Coe. My landlord asked me 8s for pony and lad for twelve miles! – Good people nevertheless. Comment on this.

31 August

Had a wretched night and with an aching head, eye, face, ear, tooth, left Garbel Wednesday morning. Pursued my way up Glenfalloch toward Tyndrum, the glen narrowing, the river becoming more and more wild and rocky, running and roaming among alders and coppice woods, the hills landlocking the glen with less than half a mile interspace, the hills not very high, but much broken, and their wildness a ragged wildness. I now passed over a bridge with a stream dashing down over rocks, and under table rock on which the foam of Monday's storm was lying yet. This I learnt was Fiona Glen or the Glen of Fingal. Met with three good Highlanders, two understood and talked Gaelic, the third, an intelligent man, spoke low Scottish only. I went with him into a field to my right, and visited a noble waterfall – during rain it must be a most noble one. The trees are old, and *army*, one on each side. It is one great *apron* with an oval pool at the bottom, but above it you look up through a rocky stream with trees and bushes, and the fall itself is marked by two *great cauldrons* delved out in the black rock, down which it falls – into which cauldrons it boils and rebounds. This is on the river of *Glenfalloch*, which word signifies the *Hidden Glen*. I talked much with the Scotchman – the oppressions of the landlord – and he used these beautiful words: 'It kills one's affections for one's country, the hardships of life, coming by change, and wi' injustice.'

The hills on each side of me are low, for I myself am on very high ground. They are almost cragless, an intermixture of beds of purple heath, slumbring in its beauty, and beds of green fern, always alive and fluttering. But to my right the hill breaks, and lets in upon the view a triangular mountain of fine outline. And in the break a little stream with glimmering waterbreaks and cowering alders. Wild sheep-folds in the hills, but before me Ben More or the Huge Mountain, one of the highest in the Highlands, shaped like a haystack, which dallies with the clouds, that now touch, now hide, now leave it.

Among the beauties of the Highlands in August and September let me not forget the fumitory with its white flower on the hovels and barns and the potatoe fields with white blossoms, appearing to my eye the loveliest and richest flower of gardens.

About two miles from the Glen of Fingal, Glenfalloch – how altered its character altogether. I had been lost in reverie and on awaking found myself with low hilly ridges to my left, for the road itself was now very high indeed. But behind me, before me, and close by my right (just over a narrow bottom in which were a cluster'd cottage, and near it one slate house) high, separating mountains, pyramids, cones, ridges, which one

Glencoe from the West

might stride across, some running straight on, some curving into arcs of circles, and forming basons and hollows. A break of an inverted triangle shape, and a naked sugar loaf looks in from a distant country. A vast multitude of sheep, alas! the very first time I ever looked at sheep with melancholy and indignant feelings!*

Waited an hour and a half for a dish of tea, the most civil promises all the while, at Inverooran. This a fair specimen of Highland Manners.

Took shelter under a bridge in a tremendous storm on a rock by the side of the stream that overflowed it – till this, I expect swoln by the rains, forced him once again into the storm . . .

I come to a double road, one to Shirley, the other to Tyndrum, and for about a mile the moors and hills are less interesting, but soon regain their former size. Dined at Tyndrum and walked a brisk pace under the inspiration of a bottle of Burton ale, from Tyndrum to Inverooran. A fine road though a perfectly houseless moorland, the mountains on each side, behind, before, most noble – though green. I seemed to think that these high green mountains, so furrowed, delved, and wrinkled with torrents, are still wilder than craggy mountains. The mountains were all detached, a great beauty! One I shall never forget, in shape resembling a schoolboy's top, or rather presenting to the eye two sides of a spherical triangle. As I looked back, on my left, at the extremity of this side of the triangle, a curving wall of green highland, and over it from the distance a mountain. At the extremity of the other side another mountain from the distance, but of wild and fantastic outline. The mountain itself, the spheric triangle, so very vast, so high, so worn and marked. The same road to Inverooran, the same to Kingshouse, eighteen miles of beautiful road, such as you may see in noblemen's pleasure grounds, through a wide wide moor, with rocky rivers, mountains of all shapes, scarr'd and lay'd open, but none craggy. The rain all the way, except now and then a blow off that discovered all the forms of the mountains and that I had lost nothing else. Add to these large moorland pools with bushy islets – and *one goat* – and you have the whole, I saw from Tyndrum and Inverooran to Kingshouse. *The whole Road from E. Tarbet to Ballachulish!*

1 September
I have walked from Inverooran to Kingshouse.† Nothing, they tell me, will grow here, it is so high. They have tried it. They burn peat and turf here,

---

*A reference to the Highland Clearances, when people were removed from the land to make way for sheep.
†On the old drovers' road to Inverness.

but have no bellows. The weather so misty and rainy that I have small heart to visit Glencoe this afternoon.

This Kingshouse, from the rancid moorland peat, smells like a dirty macquerel with bilge-water. Nine miles every way from all dwelling. Vile troop of drovers, with fiddle and dancing, and drinking, kept it up all night, one clamour like a crew of pirates that 'house on the wild sea with wild usages'. When they broke up, one of the household had the modesty to open my bedroom door, and bring me in a drover for a bedfellow, and I might have been forced to get up, if the drover had not had some sense and good manners.

2 September
Friday morning. A.m., when at length I shall have procured a bit of break-fast, to go to Glencoe and thence whither? – Eighty-four miles to Inverness. Half past nine left that devoted Kingshouse, and in less than a mile entered Glencoe, the white mists (white with interspaces of diluted black) floating away from the mountains, and thinning off along their breasts – gathering again – again thinning – all in motion – giving phantoms of motion even to the hills. The first hill, the Helm Crag and Sentry of the Glen, on my right, rises up into a naked sharp [spike], craggy in the rude shape of a church and steeple, then flows down in a green curve to the moorland stream at its feet. O, the green shining spots on the hills through the openings and rents of the mist. O, those other rich white mists seen through the thinning of the nearer mist! and blue sky, here and there, in the *low* heaven! Near the top of this Sentry hill, one figure of a saint kneeling, very wild and distinct.

In my road from Tyndrum, a large number of young trees in the valley below me, by the burn, but they seemed as if they had no business there, no abiding place at least, as if they were met there, on a moorland *fair-day*. So too in Glencoe, on the mountain walls, for so they are, brown-green with moss, bright green with stream-hiding grass, and pinky in streaks where the rain-rills flowed or are flowing – here too I glimpsed trees here and there, but they looked like apparitions.

The first six miles of Glencoe a winding glen, on my right a bulgy rifted continuous mountain, but the mists lay heavy and thick on its top, and the rifts and caverns were dark as darkness. To my left the lower and grassy half of the mountains was continuous, save only that they were rifted, often to the foundation, but the rifts in general were narrow – though a few wide enough to contain furious waterfalls. The higher and craggy half rose up into separate mountains, turrets, steeples, sugarloaves, and often bulls' brows, brows savager than those of urus or byson. One *cone*, of great height, was connected with a rude triangle-shaped mountain, of equal height, by a semicircular bason, or wall of rock in behind. After two hours' walk I came in sight of a cottage, two or three green enclosures, so green within stone walls, and a lake. About a furlong before I reached it, an enormous *facing* of mountain. The highest had almost one-third of the whole height of the mountain – a perfectly perpendicular smooth precipice with a huge cavity in a cylinder. This whole mountain more like Grasmere or Crummock than anything I have hitherto seen, 'tis the noblest too that I have seen. It is ledge and precipice as I have elsewhere described, only no bushes or trees, and only that the precipices are separate from each other seemingly not by their own protrusion but by channels of delving storms [streams?] – some traversing the mountain, but by far the greater number running straight down. At its feet are two sets of housage with their inclosures, and a small dead tarn out of which rushes a madcap of a river.

The next mountain to it, with a torrent between, is green and ragged with trees, but at the summit of the interspace, somewhat retiring, is a most remarkable naked rock resembling a house with two gavel ends fronting you, the one nearest (here I was rather alarmed by a Highland bull, who tore up the ground etc.) *Grasmere* pointed, the other next the green mountain, round and resembling a porch. Now straight before me within a slingthrow, the vale is closed by a green mountain, and I am to commence a new reach of the Glen.

This new reach brought in view another lake at its termination. It pleased me much. The surface of the mountain close by my right hand is playful, and its craggy half is bulgy and brown with moss and pinky with screes. Close by my left hand the arch of the vale is crowded with nine sugar-loaf green hills. . . An ocean of mist (there retiring) behind the *Grasmere* and its greener neighbor with her ten rain channels floating down it (though now no water – I speak only of the imaginary motion of its curvatures) like ten pink ribbons.

. . . I stood, turned round, and [surveyed] the view that had been *upon* my back, as it were. So finely do the mountains on my left – as I *now* stand – and *Grasmere* close up the reach, so tight, so narrow. For *Grasmere* seems now to run across the vale, it and its pink-ribbon'd neighbour of equal height. . . In this reach oats, potatoes (O that one tiny strange hovel of boughs of trees, and its tiny plantation of potatoes) and alder bushes innumerable! it is a sweet reach, no doubt.

So the country growing more and more cultivated, I came down on Loch Leven, a sea lake, with a green hill at its head, and a house under it, with *Mr Olive's very own garden walls* [?] on the side of the hill. On the side of the lake what seemed many houses after the solitude of the last thirty miles. The hills woody – at the foot of the lake, or what seems so, high mountains with one deep gap or valley, through which, I guess, the road goes. The road is here a fine one again. In Glencoe the torrents had torn it up.

Three peat islands, in file, near the opposite shore of the lake, an uninteresting ruin of a chapel on the largest. The smell of the sea water refreshing to me and the long rul'd lines of foam always a thing to look on. Pass a slate quarry, with a brig close under it. . .

Dined at the Ferry House at Ballachulish. . . After having crossed the ferry, walked on, on a delightful road, high hills on my right most richly wooded, all wood save where huge rocks with heath flowers, burst out of the hill. Trees too on my left, with the sea dashing its spray among their leaves. So for a mile and a half, or more, when I turned, looked back, and saw O what a sight! – the two Mountains running in and forming an obtuse V and they, and the mountains in between and behind them covered with illumined clouds, and so very yellowly and richly lighted up by the sunbeams stealing down from under the clouds. O this does indeed surpass Porlock – O that the hovels looked comfortable. Sea truly, the roar and the waves and feeling are of the sea, but far as my eye can reach, it is all embosomed, and all the mountains separate, how various in their forms. (The curiosity attributed to the Americans incident to all rude and thin-scattered people.) Glen running up by my right, a furlong in length. The red cloudlike edging in one straight line on the distant shore. Here just as I came in sight of a nice house, sheltered from the sea by trees, which I thought I should pass – my road turns off, and O Sorrow! I quit it! My blessing go with it and all its deep murmurs! In a dell with hills on each side, and in a mile regained the sight of the sea, crossing the bridge of a river creeping under alder bushes on both banks.

The road again by the sea – a narrow lake – the mountains its other bank, have their tops in one even line of lead-color'd cloud. They are deeply gullied, straight down and aslant. Here I saw a field of potatoes, within an inclosure of turf, waving like fern, a stone wall seaward, the sea not a foot from the stone wall.

The road now continues by the sea lake side. Mountains on the opposite shore, rocks and woods, or woody rocks, by my right hand, and sometimes over my head. Now darkness came on and I saw only that I was in the same scenery – so on *briskly* till within a mile and a half of Fort William, when I unfortunately drank. Instant fatigue and pains in my thighs. Arrive at Fort William – Mr Monro's – to Mr Livingstone's – hysterical weeping – etc. etc.

3 September

Spent Saturday having my stockings and shirt washed, and writing. On Saturday night threatened with another attack of gout in my stomach, and frightened into diverting by a violent stimulus, which kept me half-awake the whole night.

This is the moment to insert two letters which Coleridge posted to his wife in Fort William. The details of his seizure in the second letter point to this being a symptom of opium withdrawal.

To Sara Coleridge   *Fort William, 2 September 1803*

I write from the Ferry of Ballater [Ballachulish] . . . We slept in a hay-loft, that is, Wordsworth, I, and a young man who came in at the Trossachs and joined us. Dorothy had a bed in the hovel, which was varnished *so rich* with peat smoke an apartment of highly polished [oak] would have been poor to it – it would have wanted the metallic lustre of the smoke-varnished rafters. This was [the pleasantest] evening I had spent since my tour; for Wordsworth's hypochondriacal feelings keep him silent and self-centred. The next day it still was rain and rain; the ferry-boat was out for the preaching, and we stayed all day in the ferry wet to the skin. Oh, such a wretched hovel! But two Highland lassies, who kept house in the absence of the ferryman and his wife, were very kind, and one of them was beautiful as a vision, and put both Dorothy and me in mind of the Highland girl in William's 'Peter Bell'. We returned to E. Tarbet, I with the rheumatism in my head. And now William proposed to me to leave them and make my way on foot to Loch Katrine, the Trossachs, whence it is only twenty miles to Stirling, where the coach runs through to Edinburgh. He and Dorothy resolved to fight it out. I eagerly caught at the proposal; for the *sitting* in an open carriage in the rain is death to me, and somehow or other I had not been quite comfortable. So on Monday I accompanied them to Arrochar, on purpose to see the Cobbler which had impressed me so much in Mr Wilkinson's drawings; and there I parted with them, having previously sent on all my things to Edinburgh by a Glasgow carrier who happened to be at E. Tarbet. The worst thing was the money. They took twenty-nine guineas, and I six – all our remaining cash.

I returned to E. Tarbet; slept there that night; the next day walked to the very head of Loch Lomond to Glen Falloch, where I slept at a cottage-inn, two degrees below John Stanley's (but the good people were very kind), meaning from hence to go over the mountains to the head of Loch Katrine again; but hearing from the gude man of the house that it was forty miles to

Glencoe (of which I had formed an idea from Wilkinson's drawings), and having found myself so happy alone (such blessing is there in perfect liberty!) I walked off. I have walked forty-five miles since then, and, except during the last mile, I am sure I may say I have not met with ten houses. For eighteen miles there are but two habitations! and all that way I met no sheep, no cattle, only one goat! All through moorlands with huge mountains, some craggy and bare, but the most green, with deep pinky channels worn by torrents. Glencoe interested me, but rather disappointed me. There was no *superincumbency* of crag, and the crags not so bare or precipitous as I had expected.

I am now going to cross the ferry for Fort William, for I have resolved to eke out my cash by all sorts of self-denial, and to walk along the *whole line of the Forts*. I am unfortunately shoeless; there is no town where I can get a pair, and I have no money to spare to buy them, so I expect to enter Perth barefooted. I burnt my shoes in drying them at the boatman's hovel on Loch Katrine, and I have by this means hurt my heel. Likewise my left leg is a little inflamed, and the rheumatism in the right of my head afflicts me sorely when I begin to grow warm in my bed, chiefly my right eye, ear, cheek, and the three teeth; but, nevertheless, I am enjoying myself, having Nature with solitude and liberty – the liberty natural and solitary, the solitude natural and free! But you must contrive somehow or other to borrow ten pounds, or, if that cannot be, five pounds, for me, and send it without delay, directed to me at the Post Office, Perth.

To Sara Coleridge   *Fort William, 3 September 1803*

I learnt at the ferry that it would be safer to take my letter with me to this place, as the same post took it, and did not go off till early on Sunday morning. I walked on very briskly, when now night came on. My road lay all the way by a great sea lake, rocks or woods, or rocks among woods close by my right hand, great mountains across the sea on my left. And now I had walked 28 miles in the course of the day, when being thirsty I drank repeatedly in the palm of my hand. Thinking of writing to Sir G. Beaumont,* I was saying to myself – this using one hand instead of a cup has one disadvantage that one literally does not know when one has had enough, and we leave off not because the thirst is quench'd but because we are tired of stooping. Soon after (in less than a furlong) a pain and intense sense of fatigue fell upon me, especially within my thighs, and great torture in my

*See p.251.

bad toe. However I dragged myself along; but when I reached the town, I was forced to lean on the man that shewed me my inn (to which I had been recommended by a Dr Hay Drummond who met me at Kingshouse, and *created* an acquaintance in the most farcical manner imaginable). Mrs Munro, the landlady, had no room at all – and I could not stand – however she sent a boy with me to another little inn, which I entered – and sitting down . . . [*bottom of page of letter cut here*] an affair altogether of the body, not of the mind – that I had, it was true, a torturing pain in all my limbs, but that this had nothing to do with my tears which were hysterical and proceeded from the stomach.

Just as I had said this, a kind old man came in to me, who had crossed the ferry with me, and being on horseback had been here half an hour before me. I had had some chat with him in the boat, told him of the gout in my stomach, and that this tour was an experiment for exercise, etc. 'I never saw a man,' says he, 'walk so well or so briskly as this young Gentleman did – and indeed he must have done so, for I rode as hard as I could, and yet have not been in much more than half an hour – or three quarters.' I told him with faltering voice that I should have been in half an hour sooner, but that the last mile and a half I could scarcely drag my limbs along: and that the fatigue had come upon me all at once. 'WHOO! WHOO! WHOO!' says the old man, 'you drank water by the road-side then?' I said, yes! 'And you have gout in the stomach – indeed, but you are in *peril*.' By this time they had gotten me a dish of tea; but before I could touch it, my bowels were seized violently, and there . . . [*bottom of page of letter cut here*] gallon of nasty water, and so went to bed. Had a bason of hot tea brought up to me – slept very soon, and more soundly than I have done since I have been in Scotland.

I find myself a little stiffish, this morning. Twenty miles was perhaps too much for one day, yet I am positive, I should not have felt it, but for that unfortunate drench of water! I might have gone on; but I wished to have a shirt and stockings washed. I have but *one* pair of stockings and they were so clotted and full of holes that it was a misery to *sit* with them on. So I have sent them, and sit with none. I had determined to buy a pair of shoes whatever befell me, in the way of money distresses; but there are none in the town ready made – so I shall be obliged to go as far as Inverness with these – perhaps to Perth. I speak in the simplest earnest when I say, that I expect I shall be forced to throw them away before I get to Inverness, and to walk barefoot. My bad great toe, on my left foot, is a sore annoyance to me.

4 September
Sunday Morning, a little after eight. After a hearty breakfast, my whole

charges only 5s 10d for six meals and two gills of whisky and my bed, I walk off, first for Glen Nevis, then to return all the way, and begin anew my road to Fort Augustus. It is a lovely morning, but will it continue? I passed a church yard close by the road, fended from the sea by a natural wall of rock, went *up* two of my steps, and sate down on a flat grave-stone, and wrote this. Peace and Blessing be with us all! With thee, my Sara!

Passed a cottage, not only the roof but all the walls overgrown like a hill with weeds and grass. Why not a crop of peas on the roof and sallad on the walls? The Day continues glorious. Enter Glen Nevis, a broadish valley with a broad shallow river, single trees, alders and sycamores, planted thick without interspace along its banks. Ben Nevis to my left, its height entirely lost to me, but its sides are nobly torrent-rifted. A belt of ragged wood athwart it, half way, the *apparent* ascent – above the woods grey crags stained with yellow green, eight great rifts, each no doubt forming tremendous precipices to look down into. The mountain at the head of this reach of the Glen shoots out in ridges from a lower wall of mountain. . . The river Nevis is a poor likeness of our Greta.

I had scarcely written the words when the river improved most surprisingly, huge masses of pinky rock forming its side and narrowing its channel and lo! as I turn with its turn an enormous single rock, higher than the high banks, in the very middle of the river, filling up one half of the whole channel, leaving a quarter on each side (the river is on my left hand). On the quarter under the further bank it flows deep and as calm as the pool of a waterfall can do. For two or three yards beyond the rock on that side, seen under boughs of birch trees, arching from the bank to the birch bushes and heath on the rock, a fine fall. On the other side, close under me as I shall pass it, the river flows rough and shallow over stones, the bank naked, but fine young birch trees on the rock two yards from the top, all along its whole side. So it *appeared*, but as I moved on ten or twenty yards, I found that there were but three trees, two growing out of the cleft and as it seemed one root. Here too I found a break in the bank, where another stream flows into the Nevis, a large stream. The break *so exactly* corresponds in size to the rock, that one cannot help thinking, that some dread torrent at the first bursting forth of this stream must have shouldered away the opposing bank, and pushed it in its madness just up the stream.

I cross this stream by a bridge half of rock, half of an alder tree, whose one bough curves over the rock over which the clear water, so clear its very foam seems scarce to lose its transparency, resembles undrest lights [lungs] so exactly in color (and curvature) that the likeness must excuse the ungainliness. I come to the great rock. Now I could easily get on it, by the

William Wordsworth

trees that grow on this bank and bend over to it, so that the end of their boughs hang over it. There are three trees on the rock all birches, and then just where these leave off, three on the bank, two birches and one ash; this occasioned the delusion. But the ash is farther from the stone, a thing for itself, hangs over a pool of water, in a bason of its own, from rain or flood. Divided by a great stone from the grand fall of water, its root and bason is in the same line with the head of the fall. For there are two falls, one on each side the rock, the further broad, this narrow and higher. The huge stones above this fall, one adhering to the bank, a middle stone, and the prolongation of the rock. The water of this fall runs in two gutters one each side this middle ridge of stone. I must get from one to the other, and so on the rock to see the other waterfall, and the black jagged precipitous wall of its pool.

The broader fall among the sublimest I have ever seen. It divides itself, I might say, it distinguishes itself into three falls. The one nearest the great rock shoots out and leaves a large cavern underneath where a man might stand and, but for the *dashing in under* of the other part of the fall, shelter himself from a storm under the ceiling of foam. The two other parts are divided only at the very head by a tall pink rock. The one nearest the shoot drives aslant the third which falls down in an opposite direction, and though they touch, they preserve their individuality, the slanter covering all but the higher part of the third. The pink rocks seen every now and then at the bottom through the white foam, most *lovely*! . . .

First the green gavel, then, far lower than, but exactly like it in shape, a slender rocky gavel, then higher perhaps even than the green gavel this sharper and more perfect gavel, then behind that a ridge having two sister cones! This is to my right – to my left the river, and the *ledge-precipicy* side of the proboscis of the elephant, with savage trees, all straight, and by that extreme straightness harmonizing with the perpendicularity of the little precipices, of which the great precipice is made up. Before me two huts, and beyond them two ridges of savage mountain, though not without trees.

The Head of Glen Nevis how simple for a painter, and in how many words and how laboriously, in what dim similitudes and slow and dragging circumlocutions must I give it – so give it that they who knew the place best would least recognize it in my description. . .

So having mounted a little and seen that there was not probably anything more to be noticed, I turned back. Now my mind being as it were leisurely and off the stretch, with what delight did I look at a floatage of shadows on the water, made by the wavelets of the stream, with what delight that most exquisite net at the bottom of the sandy, pebbly river, all whose loops are wires of sunshine, gold finer than silk. Beside yon stone the breeze seems to have blown them into a heap, a rich mass of light, light spreading from the loop holes into the interstices. O we turn from novelties and rarities to old delights and simple beauty!

On the whole I can scarcely say that Glen Nevis is worth all the fatigue of travelling through it, as you must return the same way every step. The mountains, both Ben Nevis and those Helvellyn-shaped ones by and near the green gavel, are far better and more impressively seen on the road to Fort Augustus. In the Glen itself, from its narrowness, the mountains *needs* look very low.

On the main road again, passed the black castle, to my left. A huge patch of snow low down on the baldness of Ben Nevis; dreary moorlands, with distant mountains, but naught impressive except those close to my right, Ben Nevis to wit.

Highbridge [Spean Bridge] – refused tea – Highland inhospitality explained. The desolation dreamlike of the fine road, of the ghost-like 'High Bridge' and its two arches and a half, the mountain ridges so backlike, odd and void of connection or harmonizing principle. The mountains in perhaps eight main lines, all pushing toward the bridge bank but each so savage, and broken. . . O it is indeed a High Bridge. What can Sappho's Leap have been beyond this? The building of the bridge mixes so indistinguishably with the schistous slanting strata, that form the banks of the river. The sunshine half on the bank, the lower half shadow, with so marked a line and the noise of the rapid above, for under the bridge and for 200 yards above the river is calm, wrinkly indeed, in watery puckers and folds, with detachments of broken foam between the *so already split slate*. O for words to explain how slate and limestone lie! Verily it is a savage dreamlike, unlively place, and the river on the left hand of the bridge – after it has passed its savage black and grey slate banks – wild and mean, where a man falling would break his neck without dignity. Then it is fine to see the moorland river melt away in metallic scoria [slag]. Much as I have been among mountains, still this is new.

A moorland with two mute flocks of sheep in sight, and one or more in *sound, guarded round* by mountains, not walled, the mountains are too separate and individual. Before me, on my road to Fort Augustus, it is indeed more of *one mass*, delved, rifted, channel'd, wrinkled, and with a dipping, leaping, tipsy outline; but behind me, and to my left as I turn to look behind, I count 29 great lines of motion or direction, the 14, 15, 16 so semicircled and hollowed, that I might have made 30 out of the 3 – all indeed subdivisible enough! . . . A File of sheep among heath, perfect ribboning – it is an *intuition*.

The moor now tossed up and about into hills, and these hills inclosed, with corn, or potatoes in blossom. All this to my left – and a lake beyond, and a peep of another, and five heads of mountains with a continuous ridge before them, close in the whole. But what a joyous sight of cows and calves, a lowing browsing multitude, with milking lasses chattering Erse [strictly, Irish Gaelic]. Church and twenty or more scattered hovels on the cultivated hill, that climbs half way up the black mountain Brays of Lochaber. Between the lake and the peep of the lake a mountain of very various, but all superficial and gentle segments, runs down in between almost as gently as a man would lie on a bed, so imperceptibly declining from an horizontal line into a slope. Those who hold it undignified to illustrate Nature by Art – how little would the truly dignified say so – how else can we bring the forms of Nature within our voluntary memory! The first business is to subjugate them to our intellect and voluntary memory, then comes their dignity by sensation of magnitude, forms and passions connected therewith.

Arrived at Letir Finlay, 9 o'clock, all in bed. They got up – scarce any fire in; however made me a dish of tea and I went to *bed*. Two blankets and a little fern and yet many fleas! Slept however till ten next morning. No more tea in the house – three eggs beat up, two glasses of whisky, sugar, and two-thirds of a pint of boiling water I found an excellent substitute.

5 September

Left this house of poverty (the apartments large and sufficiently commodious) Monday 11 o'clock, for Fort Augustus. Loch Lochy very like the narrowest, and barest parts of Ullswater, a lake, in short, among bleak hills. The first two miles from Letir Finlay the road torn up and covered by flood torrents of stones from the stream. . .

I come to Loch Oich, a more chearful lake with some comfortable-looking mansions on it, and opposite a tongue of land on the left bank of the lake (suppose you sailing up to Fort Augustus) a very fine ruin of a castle among trees, upon a precipitous rock-bank, but the mountains, now mere hills and scurfy with trees and bushes. Went into a hovel at the foot of Loch Oich, and drank a cup of whisky and hot water, the gout rising: four stout men purely lazy! the women at work. In about a mile from this, on a savage piece of uncultivated ground on the other side of the wall on the left hand of the road (to wit, as I face Fort Augustus), eight miserable huts, a neighbourhood! the best of which would have disgraced a beaver, or republic of termites. Out of their low slanting doors come with a [? dip] five tall men, wearing on their backs and limbs cloathes-masks of the present century! A little way on, another cluster of turf huts with peat roofs, wretched as the

Glen Nevis

former, on the right hand of the road – four huts. Do not forget the little black dancing master at Highbridge.

Fort Augustus, 4 o'clock, afternoon. Very unwell and could eat only the broth at dinner. A most interesting view from the back door of the inn: to the left the river, and beyond it a cluster of wood, the bridge or ridge of rock intercepting the lake, heads of high mountains behind each other seen over the ridge. On my right orchard gardens with one cottage in one of them, a smooth large field. The Fort Augustus, an ample and handsome mass of building, the lake, and its noble mountain right-hand bank.

6 September

Tuesday Morning, 11 o'clock. Left Fort Augustus, having breakfasted with the Governor, ascended a very steep, high hill, found myself in thwarting coombes with brook and birch woods. On a second ascent found a sixpence, the first in my life.

Pass a tarn, almost surrounded by five bare-knobby hills, with four islands in it, covered with bushes and heather. Continue ascending, the road on the breast, and above the breast, and on the summit of the heathland hill, a wild tarn under bulgy grey rocks in the bottom on my right. Over the hill a most extensive area of heath and moorland crowded to the right and left and not empty in the middle, of grey stony hills with purple patches, two tarns in sight.

Have passed through Strathherick, a broken country, granite rock, and birch trees in among them and in one place a beautiful round island of heath in a circle of granite rocks. This to my right hand and as the road leaves it, it climbs a small height through fine birch trees, the lower halves of the stems split longitudinally in thick rough scales; now a deep bason of fine cultivated land is below me as I descend. I look down in and upon it through a grove of birch trees, one large corn-field walled by a mountain of granite carpeted with moss and heath on the ledges only of its precipices.

The road turns down into it like a winding staircase, and I face what was before at my back and see at the head of this bottom a most lovely hill of birches, a rich wood! – overhanging a brook, the bare points of granite mountain towering over the rich wood.

The road passes through the bottom, climbs again – still birches amid granite rocks, and on the summit of this ascent I regain Loch Ness and its mountain wall. A stream brawling through a *convulsed* channel on my left in a deep cleft of the hill on which my road is, the deep wide cleft dividing from the birch and granite mountain that forms a part of the left bank of Loch Ness. In this deep wide cleft, I suppose, I am to find the fall of Foyers.

Some fifty yards on the descent of the hill I come to a part of the wall built higher and the higher interspace bounded by two gate heads. From thence look down, a prodigious depth! and see a fine narrow fall at the bottom. A volume of smoke the foam seems, or like the softest plumage of the eagle or ostrich. Determined not to go without a guide, for I sadly fear that I shall be disappointed – so went down through woods to a river side, beautifully gliding smooth and broad into Loch Ness, to a house which I supposed the General's Hut, but which was indeed the house of a gentleman – of a vera great gentleman, as a child told me, yan Mr Fraser. And I wound up through a wood to the General's Hut where I was received with sufficient and increasing civility.*

7 September
Dined on lean mutton, and good tea, and supt on sewens [sea-trout] and roasted potatoes, had a miserable screamy night, and after breakfast Wednesday morning, walked back about a mile. Entering by the two pillars, wound down to the green beak of a slender promontory and afterwards still lower. Though the feeling of disappointment lingered awhile, the fall at length grew into sublimity and its own dimensions. On my first calculation I made it not exceed 110 feet, and the whole height of the chasm 220 – but it grew upon me, and my feelings at least coincided at length with Stoddart's account. The plumage of the fall, the puffs of smoke in every direction from the bed of plumy foam at the bottom, the restless network of waves on its pool; the vase-like shape of the fracture out of which it comes, as if one side of a huge vase had been chipped out, and this stream flowed out at the rim. You see up into the vase, and its rim is wreathed with delicate birches. The water atoms driving away the myriads of midges, now driven away by a puff of wind. The fall and pool are in a noble inverted chamber 300 feet high, with a long winding antechamber, only a very few trees in the chamber itself – the enormous walls mossed or bare. . . Four trees I shall never forget: the hazel bent down and half uprooted with its broad canopying head over a flock of mossy stones – under this I sate; two birch trees, one not very far below the summit of the precipice, bent like a bow, with its slender stem, over the channel of the stream; above this a straight fir, noble and lovely in its singleness. Another birch and a Scotch fir above the pool thrust out

*General Wade built a network of roads in the Highlands after the 1715 Jacobite rebellion. His working office, in 1732, when constructing the road down the southeast side of Loch Ness, from Inverness to Fort Augustus, later became an inn. Dr Johnson stayed there on his Highland tour. It no longer exists.

straight like an arm from an oak, a strange perplexity and twisting of head and boughs. Then the stones, and trees, and uprooted trees, and half uprooted, and roots of trees – one set of these formed half a cavern, and a huge root an arched doorway to it. Altogether it is no doubt a glorious scene.*

Hen, nervously blown forwards, tumbling topsy turvy, in the strong wind. General's Hut.

A room, a wooden bureau locked up, a sea[?] board on it under shelter of birchen boughs, three tables, eleven chairs. 'The Surrender of the Island of Malta to General Pigot', published by Thomson, 'The Farm House on Fire', just over the fire place, 'An Exact Draught of the City of Jerusalem', by C. Thomson (these three fill up nearly the fire-place side of the wall). On the other side, under birch boughs, the 'Storming of Seringpatam' and on the side opposite the fire a large map of Europe, a stuffed roebuck, a week old, lying over Tartary, the Dominions of Russia in Asia, and the Caspian. Close by them on the same side a wild duck, and a sargeant's cap, scarf and cartouch bag – the birchen boughs with their moveless twigs and leaves hanging down in between the rafters – and the wind moaning above them.

Over the lower wall of the chasm you see the lake, its high mountain bank. . . Pleasing sort of terrace walk with an enormous descent below it. That descent, so covered with wood as still to see the red soil, and yet nowhere not to see the woods – and the road climbing up along its breast even to the summit of the cultivated hills, into which this mountain bank descends. Fields of lovely cultivation are seen crowning, as with a bald friar's top, the woody descent to the lake. The road from the General's Hut goes between birch trees.

That sweet delicate birch with its tri-prong root, and the other twisty little creature near it. O Christ, it maddens me that I am not a painter or that painters are not I! The *chapped bark* of the lower part of the trunk, the bark like a rhinoceros rolled in mud and exposed to the tropic heat. The second fall [like] to sheep forced through water, and vaulting over each other, throwing off the pearly streams from their heavy fleeces.

About three-quarters of a mile from the General's Hut, divided from the lake by a birch coppice and a cornfield, two burnt down huts bearing every mark as if the owners had burnt them in heart's-spite-joy before their emigration.

*The Falls of Foyers are no more. They were first harnessed by the British Aluminium Company in the 1890s and more recently by the Scottish Hydro-Electric Board.

A horse, two birchen poles with five cross rafters with twists of hazel and rope, enclosing a few sheaves of oats, the poles dragging along the ground, their ends merely flattened. This I stopped and examined by the burial ground of Stratherich, 40 strides long, 35 broad – a grave dugged, two spades in it, the bank of earth, thighbone and shin by it. 'Tis a wild burial place – contrast it with St Clement's in the Strand. Twice I walked round it, and stripped the seeds from a large dock which I will plant at home in its memory.

Still goes the straight road: birches, and the ascending hill on my right, birches and the descending hill and lake on my left. O never, never let me forget the beautiful birch stems, like silver tarnished, rising out of the *chapped 'Elephantiasis'* bark of the six lowermost feet of the trunk. O the endless endless lines of motion of the trees here.

Now to my right hand over a thin coppice of birch is a wall, a rampart-wall, of granite, birches growing along its ledges or terraces, and a rampart, more bulgy, before me, and over the lake on my left the segment of a rainbow on the hills. So on to a bridge high over a rocky stream overhung with birch and one other large tree unknown to me, where the road turns touchingly close to the bulgy rampart; and here over a field of rocks over the stream a huge mountain like a castle wall, the lower half birch, the higher bare grey precipice with a thwart smear of reddish clay. Here I do not see the lake, but the road ascends to it. Let me not forget the Ode to my Shadow.

The left hand the lake and its now half copsy, half cultivated bank; the right, birchen hills, more or less thick, now straight, now bulging, now concave, an embracement; heath, fern, stones white with lichens, birches of all shapes and twisture, and white clouds of many shapes in the blue sky above. Salvator Rosa had the conifers and chestnut: I would study the birch, it should be my only tree.

A break in the mountain bank of the Loch Ness, the interspace green and yellow, but mostly yellow, with cultivated ground. At its foot washed by the loch, on a rock-ground of its own, a mass of building, tower, castle, I know not what [Urquhart Castle]. Beyond this the bank of the lake loses its cultivation, bulgy, and knobby rocks, with patches of wood; the other bank, on which my right hand rests, rocks as before, and trees, O in what wild twistures, starting out of the rocks, which their roots split as with a wedge. After this my road, maintaining its character in all other respects, loses its birches and has hazels instead, with ash trees intermixed.

Let me not, in the intense vividness of the remembrance, forget to note down the bridging rock, cut off alas! from the great fall by the beaked promontory, on which were four cauldrons, and a small one to boot. One at the head of a second fall, the depth of my stick, reflected all the scene in a mirror – Gracious God. The fourth on the side of the fall, larger and deeper than all the others together, its low water in unceasing waves and agitation from the fall *vibrating* its rocky sides. All four had the appearance of the tooth-sockets of some mammoth among mammoths, fox + mammoth.

Now approaching the end of the loch, many juniper trees on each side of my road. The mountain across the lake, one single farm excepted, naked, clay scars, with grey-blue slate screes; then a break and a dip, just like the former, all cultivated land. The mountain rising again loses its slate and is all clay scar and patch, in several places from top to bottom. A wooded hill-ridge runs across the lake, and I suppose, terminates it. A pleasant 100 yards – a fir grove on my right, the lake, a mass of molten silver, on my left – its own lacustrial sounds and the fir grove its own! Long may they thus sound together!

8 September

Left Inverness in a return post chaise, with a mad drunk post boy whom I was soon obliged to quit, though the mad blackguard was not so well disposed to quit me. I was every way unfortunate – dancing with Indian yells to a late hour at the new inn in Inverness. However, owing perhaps to the camphor and ether, what sleep I did get was quiet – O anything for quiet sleep.

Six miles from Inverness, the country rude moorland, after this the wildest of all wild moorlands, cloven and tossed up into hills of all shapes and sizes, all of sharp lines, the greater number having whole sides stripped of their heath, bare screes of white clay and rubbishy pebbles. After this, dreariness itself with one patch of cultivation, and across the road a village of strange peat hovels. The road ascending, on my left a high hill, the pearly white clay staring through the purple heath, and ever so straight before me. But to my right in a wide and distant semi-circle, a glorious circumvallation of mountains, ridges smooth and billowy, sugar loaves, triangles, pyramids, and whatever other misted shapes these mountain masses put on to the distant eye. The ninth milestone locks me in compleatly with high heath-hills, a few Scotch firs – the hill often black – and the whole surface tossed about, rising, dipping, bulging and sinking. Eleventh milestone, a water [ornamental lake?] and handsome house, Moy Hall, to my left, both under a hill scurvily planted with mineral-green Scotch firs. Hovel on my right and enclosed field; in one field potatoes, barley, oats, and a square plot of wheat; a copse of birches on the other side of the road. Bridges with turf and sod rims, two or more every mile, over half viewless streams or none. A good deal of low cowring juniper with its fruit of various years, purple and green. Beyond the twelfth milestone a square furlong of perfect level, through which the road runs: oats on each side, no enclosures, but it is enclosed naturally by low hill-*banks*. A public house here, a bell outside of the window ringing in the wind, its shadow on the glass quarries [diamond panes].

A stone throw before the sixteenth mile stone a village of hovels of turf, some quite green; one a spinning wheel reaching above the eaves, but the roof as high again as the eaves. Seventeenth milestone past half a mile, my eyes at last get out of their long prison of heathland moor, and I gain a view of distant mountains. After the eighteenth milestone the high hill to the left of the road is cleft – a rent to the ground, even as Foyers, only not so high. But what a difference, even from the materials: dirt and dusty grass! and rocks and trees! Both above and below me the largest quantity of junipers growing together, that I ever saw, the whole hillside from top to the very bottom, save where the road runs, covered with it, as thick as ever Somerset-shire hills with furze. From the twentieth the country changed, mountain and more cultivation. Observed a lazy boy pasturing a miserable rope-legged horse!

Cross a high bridge over the river [?Slugan]. A pretty wooded bank, long field, and then a hill-bank of birches – seen till my road comes among firs, and at last through a *noble* firwood. Remember that bough caught up by the wind, forced over the fork of the tree, and there growing, its elbows on the side split and naked! O what work the winds make with these branches! and yet what noble creatures! Compare them with the stifled ones (in favor of Wordsworth's Theory).* The darkness came on. I walked through a birch grove and so on to Aviemore.

9 September

Left it, Friday morning, 10 o'clock. A dreary country, seeming drearier for cultivation – at length gain a view of mountains before me. Once more imprisoned. A little before the thirty-seventh mile, a very pleasant bottom, bridge shouldering a woody hill, stream winding away prettily under a woody bank. Regain a view of mountains with a noble outline; they seem bare from their bases. The whole country is very wild. The meagre oat-harvest, I thought *they were weeding* – low oats, so meagre! – and the harvesters so lazy and joyless. The fields all common and the only mock

*Wordsworth thought larches were stifled in regular plantations.

inclosure bleak walls of rocks. Thirty-ninth mile, a huge house to my right, Mr Macpherson's. Fortieth, a new or new-making village, Kingussie, and a fine ruin of a castle to the left. And so to Pitmaine, the first place where *whisky* was not – and rum commenced. Forty-one miles from Inverness at Glentruim Craig, girls shiv'ring, two under a cloak. Hay and shearing at the same time, peas, few and hard, but this is the season. Met a girl carrying a lighted peat to make a fire in the hay and harvest field, three miles, at least, from Pitmaine.

The *wildest* of all countries (NB I might have gone twenty miles nearer, had I been earlier and the day fine). It is not only that the distant mountains before me, all named 'du' black, are of the wildest shapes (one of them a bridge tumbling topsy turvy, called mountain Croupean), all dark, of a hundred shapes, and no shape of grandeur, none combining – it is not only this, but the whole land through which the road lies, is cloven and cut into a vast room left by drunkards: short tables, and high tables, and side tables, and cushions in confusion – and the hundred forms that can be brought into no analogy. In short, I who adore Nature, was kept *grinning* at the scene – and the faces of the Highlanders like faces on wooden sticks.

To be sure, the gardens at Pitmaine worthy of note. A bank, a sloping down bottom, a semi-ellipse of trees, form the only inclosure; and many trees in the garden itself. Beyond it a perfect level, cultivated land, perhaps a mile broad, and then wild banks swelling up into hills, those into mountains. Four miles from Pitmaine a house. Arches that form a rainbow, on sundown on the ridge; a crag behind the rainbow and a solemn sound in the foreground that bids 'Listen!'

10 September
A wild and desolate moorland, with moorfowl, on the Dalwhynny; a good bed, and left it Saturday morning 9 o'clock. Moors, streaks and soils of green upon the purple hills. Poles along the roadside as from F. Augustus. . .

From this point, Coleridge's description of the remainder of his walk to Perth becomes something of a catalogue of moor, hill, and increasing signs of cultivation. So far he had been following the route of the present A9, but he left it at Dalnacardoch in Glen Garry to strike south, passing the west end of Loch Tummel and the east end of Loch Tay, before going down Glen Quaich to Amulree, then Methven. When he reached Edinburgh, he learned from a letter that Robert Southey's daughter Margaret, born in 1802, had died.

There are, however, a number of fragments at the end of the tour description.

Loch Tay, Perthshire

Men noticed in the history of the Dark Ages, as single hovels are in the map of the north of Scotland.

Whenever her eye turned, gladness came, like spots of sunshine on green moorland hills, creating a new field in the waste. Spots of sunshine seen through floating mists, or thinning showers.

I feel as if I were here to wander on the winds, a blessed ghost, till my beloved came to me, [then to] go back with her and seek my children.

To Sara Coleridge   *Perth and Edinburgh, 11 and 12 September 1803*

I was writing to you from Fort Augustus when the Governor and his wise Police Constable seized me and my letter. Since then I have written to nobody. On my return, if God grant! we will take the Map of Scotland, and by help of my pocket book I will travel my route over again, from place to place. It has been an instructive though melancholy tour. At Fort Augustus I got a pair of shoes. The day before I had walked thirty-six miles, twenty the worst in conception, and up a mountain, so that in point of effort it could not be less than forty-six miles. The shoes were all to pieces, and three of my toes were skinless, and I had a very promising hole in my heel. Since the new shoes I have walked on briskly – from thirty to thirty-five miles a day, day after day – and three days I lived wholly on oat cake, barley bannock, butter, and the poorest of all poor skim-milk cheeses, and still I had horrors at night! I mention all this to shew you, that I have strength somewhere, and at the same time, how deeply this disease must have rooted itself.

I wrote you my last letter, overclouded by despondency – say rather, in a total eclipse of all hope and joy – and as all things propagate their like, you must not wonder, that misery is a misery-maker. But do you try, and I will try; and peace may come at last, and love with it. I have not heard of Wordsworth; nor he of me. He will be wondering what can have become of me. I have only read the first letter, and that part of Southey's, containing the £10 note, which relates to himself, for they have stunned me. I am afraid of hysterics, unless a fit of vomiting which I feel coming on, should as I hope it will, turn it off. I must write no more: it is now 10 o'clock and I go off in the Mail at four in the Morning. It went against the grain to pay 18 shillings for what I could have made an easy day's walk of: and but for my eagerness to be with dear Southey, I should certainly have walked from Edinburgh home. O Sara! dear Sara! – *try* for all good things in the spirit of unsuspecting love, for miseries gather upon us. I shall take this letter with me to Edinburgh and leave a space to announce my safe arrival, if so it please God. Good night, my sweet children!

Monday Morning, 12 o'clock
I am safe in Edinburgh and now going to seek out news about the Words-worths and my cloathes. I do not expect to stay here above this day. Dear Southey's letter had the precise effect of intoxication by an overdose of some narcotic drug – weeping – vomiting – wakefulness the whole night, in a sort

of stupid sensuality of itching from my head to my toes, all night. I had drunken only one pint of weak porter the whole day. This morning I have felt the soberness of grief. God bless you all, and S. T. Coleridge.

To Robert Southey   *Edinburgh, 11 September 1803*

I arrived here half an hour ago, and have only read your letters – scarce read them. O dear friend! it is idle to talk of what I feel. I am stunned at present by this beginning to write, making a beginning of living feeling within me. Whatever comfort I can be to you I will. I have no aversions, no dislikes that interfere with you – whatever is necessary or proper for you becomes *ipso facto* agreeable to me. I will not stay a day in Edinburgh, or only one to hunt out my clothes. I cannot chitchat with Scotchmen while you are at Keswick, childless! Bless you, my dear Southey! I will knit myself far closer to you than I have hitherto done, and my children shall be yours till it please God to send you another.

I have been a wild journey, taken up for a spy and clapped into Fort Augustus, and I am afraid they may have frightened poor Sara by sending her off a scrap of a letter I was writing to her. I have walked 263 miles in eight days, so I must have strength somewhere, but my spirits are dreadful, owing entirely to the horrors of every night – I truly dread to sleep. It is no shadow with me, but substantial misery foot-thick, that makes me sit by my bedside of a morning and cry. I have abandoned all opiates, except ether be one. . . And when you see me drink a glass of spirit-and-water, except by prescription of a physician, you shall despise me, but still I cannot get quiet rest. [*Coleridge's terrifying poem 'The Pains of Sleep' follows, of which the second verse is given here:*]

> But yester-night I pray'd aloud
> In anguish and in agony,
> Awaking from the fiendish crowd
> Of shapes and thoughts that tortur'd me!
> Desire with loathing strangely mixt,
> On wild or hateful objects fixt.
> Sense of revenge, the powerless will,
> Still baffled and consuming still;
> Sense of intolerable wrong,
> And men whom I despis'd made strong!

Vain glorious threats, unmanly vaunting,
Bad men my boasts and fury taunting;
Rage, sensual passion, mad'ning Brawl,
And shame and terror over all!
Deeds to be hid that were not hid,
Which all confus'd I might not know,
Whether I suffer'd or I did:
For all was Horror, Guilt, and Woe,
My own or others' still the same,
Life-stifling Fear, soul-stifling Shame!

I do not know how I came to scribble down these verses to you – my heart was aching, my head all confused – but they are, doggerel as they may be, a true portrait of my nights. What to do, I am at a loss; for it is hard thus to be withered, having the faculties and attainments which I have. We will soon meet, and I will do all I can to console poor Edith. O dear, dear Southey! my head is sadly confused. After a rapid walk of thirty-three miles your letters have had the effect of perfect intoxication in my head and eyes. Change! change! change! O God of Eternity! When shall we be at rest in thee?

To Robert Southey   *Edinburgh, 13 September 1803*

I wrote you a strange letter, I fear. But, in truth, yours affected my wretched stomach, and my head, in such a way that I wrote mechanically in the *wake* of the first vivid idea. No conveyance left or leaves this place for Carlisle earlier than tomorrow morning, for which I have taken my place. If the coachman do not turn Panaceist, and cure all my ills by breaking my neck, I shall be at Carlisle on Wednesday, midnight. . .

What a wonderful city Edinburgh is! What alternation of height and depth! A city looked at in the polish'd back of a Brobdingnag spoon held lengthways, so enormously *stretched-up* are the houses! When I first looked down on it, as the coach drove up on the higher street, I cannot express what I felt – such a section of wasps' nests striking you with a sort of bastard sublimity from the enormity and infinity of its littleness – the infinity swelling out the mind, the enormity striking it with wonder. I think I have seen an old plate of Montserrat that struck me with the same feeling, and I am sure I have seen huge quarries of lime and free stone in which the shafts or strata stood perpendicularly instead of horizontally with the same high

Edinburgh

thin slices and corresponding interstices. I climbed last night to the crags just below Arthur's Seat – itself a rude triangle-shaped-base cliff, and looked down on the whole city and firth – the sun then setting behind the magnificent rock, crested by the castle. The firth was full of ships, and I counted fifty-four heads of mountains, of which at least forty-four were cones or pyramids. The smoke was rising from ten thousand houses, each smoke from some one family. It was an affecting sight to me! I stood gazing at the setting sun, so tranquil to a passing look, and so restless and vibrating to one who looked stedfast; and then, all at once, turning my eyes down upon the city, it and all its smokes and figures became all at once dipped in the brightest blue-purple: such a sight that I almost grieved when my eyes recovered their natural tone! Meantime, Arthur's Crag, close behind me, was in dark blood-like crimson, and the sharp-shooters were behind exercising minutely, and had chosen that place on account of the fine thunder echo which, indeed, it would be scarcely possible for the ear to distinguish from thunder. The passing a day or two, quite unknown, in a strange city, does a man's heart good. He rises 'a sadder and a wiser man'.

Walter Scott is at Lasswade, five or six miles from Edinburgh. His house in Edinburgh is divinely situated. It looks up a street, a new magnificent street, full upon the rock and the castle, with its zigzag walls like painters' lightning – the other way down upon cultivated fields, a fine expanse of water, either a lake or not to be distinguished from one, and low pleasing hills beyond – the country well wooded and cheerful. 'I' faith,' I exclaimed, 'the monks formerly, but the poets now, know where to fix their habitations.'

There are about four things worth going into Scotland for, to one who has been in Cumberland and Westmoreland: first, the views of all the islands at the foot of Loch Lomond from the top of the highest island called Inch Devanna; secondly, the Trossachs at the foot of Loch Katrine; third, the chamber and antechamber of the Falls of Foyers (the fall itself is very fine, and so, after rain, is White-Water Dash, seven miles below Keswick and very like it); and how little difference a height makes, you know as well as I. No fall of itself, perhaps, can be worth going a long journey to see, to him who has seen any fall of water, but the pool and whole rent of the mountain is truly magnificent. Fourthly and lastly, the City of Edinburgh. Perhaps I might add Glencoe. It is at all events a good make-weight and very well worth going to see, if a man be a Tory and hate the memory of William the Third, which I am very willing to do; for the more of these fellows dead and living one hates, the less spleen and gall there remains for those with whom one is likely to have anything to do in real life. . .

I am tolerably well, meaning the day. My last night was not such a noisy night of horrors as three nights out of four are with me. O God! when a man blesses the loud screams of agony that awake him night after night, night after night, and when a man's repeated night screams have made him a nuisance in his own house, it is better to die than to live. I have a joy in life that passeth all understanding; but it is not in its present Epiphany and Incarnation. Bodily torture! All who have been with me can bear witness that I can bear it like an Indian. It is constitutional with me to sit still, and look earnestly upon it and ask it what it is? Yea, often and often, the seeds of Rabelaisism germinating in me, I have laughed aloud at my own poor metaphysical soul. But these burrs by day of the will and the reason, these total eclipses by night! Oh, it is hard to bear them. I am complaining bitterly to others, I should be administrating comfort; but even this is one way of comfort. There are states of mind in which even distraction is still a diversion; we must none of us *brood*; we are not made to be brooders.

From Table Talk, *24 June 1827*
When I first looked on the Falls of Clyde, I was unable to find a word to express my feelings. At last, a man, a stranger to me, who arrived about the same time, said 'How majestic!' It was the precise term, and I turned round and was saying, 'Thank you, Sir! that *is* the exact word for it', when he added *eodem flatu* [in the same breath], 'Yes! how very *pretty!*'

From Dorothy Wordsworth's Recollections
Coleridge, who is always good-natured enough to enter into conversation with anybody whom he meets in his way, began to talk with the gentleman, who observed that it was a 'majestic waterfall'. Coleridge was delighted with the accuracy of the epithet, particularly as he had been settling in his own mind the precise meaning of the words grand, majestic, sublime, etc., and had discussed the subject with William at some length the day before. 'Yes, sir', says Coleridge, 'it *is* a majestic waterfall.' 'Sublime and beautiful', replied his friend. Poor Coleridge could make no answer and, not very desirous to continue the conversation, came to us and related the story, laughing heartily.

From Table Talk, *26 September 1830*
The intervals between the fine things in Scotland are very dreary, whereas in Cumberland and Westmoreland, there is a cabinet of beauties.

A waterfall near Keswick by Sir George Beaumont. Coleridge told Beaumont 'It will give a lasting interest to the drawing of the waterfall, that I first saw it (in the summer of 1803) through tears. I was indeed unwell and sadly nervous; and I . . . found a bodily relief in weeping, and yielding to it.' This was just before the Scottish trip designed to rid Coleridge of his addiction.

September 1803
There have been times when looking up beneath the sheltring trees, I could invest every leaf with awe.

29 September
Thursday morning, 10 o'clock, with Southey left Greta Hall, through the turnpike, over Calvert's Bridge, through the wood, by the sweet Housage of Wesco with its ivy and outhouse, through Threlkeld, up Saddleback, over Blenkarthur having the horse road a great deal to our right, to Saddleback Tarn. I had quite forgotten the fearfully sublime precipice and striding edge on its farther or northern side, and the colours of this little tarn: blood-crimson, and then sea-green, etc., etc., and so go on in sections, now calms, now ruffled spaces. Nowhere where more beautiful can you see the breeze-race, blowing a rich blue like the peacock's neck over the tarn, till where it comes near the blood-crimson, and then it turns the most beautiful purple.

. . . Caldbeck Howk [Scoop], Vista Brook – waterfall down the Pulpit – covered with foam waves that beat against the buttress of the natural bridge. The pool and the natural bridge with two arches of unequal sizes, with an enormous middle buttress and the bridge finely wooded. The stream through the larger arch falls down after a twist or two in a noble waterfall under a pendent mass of ivy, itself under a ceiling of lime trees. Through the lesser arch, on the left hand as you look down the stream, it pours into and fills up a round cauldron ten feet in diameter, its wall like the wall of an open tower. Close by it, the two parlours. Descend to the bed of the river [where there is] a second pool still more beautiful and wide and green and deep, and as sweetly over-canopied by limes and ashes, the limes absolutely showering their yellow leaves.*

*Compare this with the description of the same place in the Notebook entry for 11 October 1800 on page 101.

30 September

On a ledge on the side of the rock on the right of this second pool, as you look up the stream and directly above the pool – in high water it would scarcely leave your soles unwetted – [is] the best view of the whole under part of this scenery. On the left-most of the swinging ivy, a mass of rock, the water gushing out from under, like a furious gush of blood from a plethoric artery, fighting with the mossy middle buttress of this sub-bridge. Another stream rushes in the same manner through the lefter arch, and [there is] one quiet fillet falling adown, without contact, the mossy rock, often intercepted by the shooting of this or that waterfall. In the centre [there is] a round tower of rock, fifty feet high from the bed of the river, with an Indian chief's lofty dancing coronet of limes and hazels. To the right of this, a beautiful opening, with a round faery cauldron below it, whose wall forms the connection between this turret and the second turret, equal in height and much larger in diameter, and so wreathed as the other. Under this on the right-most [are] the parlours; and above my head where I stand the cathedral seats.

The water was so low that I saw the whole anatomy of the place, especially those *gushing* waterfalls, which in full water are hidden by the fall of water over their bridge or cavern roof. Nothing can be conceived more beautiful than the left-most of these gushes, the higher half far within in a [square] of cavern and then rushing over on the right of its little cavern flooring. . .

The deluge of stones from Carrock: no stones immediately under the mountain and but few on the left of the road, but on the right several acres wholly covered with stones of hugest size.

On our return from Caldbeck it seemed to threaten rain, one shower came, Southey was weary and already homesick. So we turned off at the fifth milestone, passed by the bald Overwater, that might be made so lovely, dined at a Quaker Statesman's where for the first time I ate sugar-sop, a composition of flour, cream, butter and sugar.

O what a clean happy house, and the good folks how solicitously hospitable! The servant maid, a fine lass who talked and looked on in equality, went out and shewed us the way and positively and obstinately refused all money. Her master and mistress were Quakers, but she, she said, and most of the people thereabout, were Protestants. So too at Isaac Tod's at Grisdale, where we stopped at quarter past three to get a dish of tea.* Both master

*Isaac Tod lived at Mungrisdale, east of Bowscale Fell and Saddleback, so this incident must have been on the way to Caldbeck.

and mistress were out, but the old servant, a poor crazy matterless body, bestirred herself to do what she could. But a neighbour woman, well-drest and well spoken, came in, bustled about, made the tea for us, brought a bottle of spirits from her own house, where she had left a visitor, and warmly pressed us to go home with her, and take beds at her house, which was a quarter of a mile off. In short, it is a universal virtue: one house may be more comfortable, more neat than another, but the hospitality and cheerful eagerness to entertain strangers, without the least thought of re-muneration or endurance of it when offered, is universal.

The view of the Vale on the Skiddaw side of Bassenthwaite is so divine, that one wonders how it can be equalled, and yet equalled it is by the other side of the Lake, by the lovely vale displayed to you by the break of the Hartop [Barf] and Wythop fells and Hay Hill with those two sweet little hills on the edge of the water. We returned about 5 o'clock in the afternoon.

October
The wild rose the lightest bright yellow; next to that, one shade deeper, the common ash. [Then] the birch, which is golden, [then] the mountain ash, a shade deeper than the birch.

Aromatic smell of the poplar, especially in the fall of the leaf.

St John's Vale, O the lights, the watery white sun-sections, like a moonlight – indeed the whole walk is enchantment.

The tree or sea-weed like appearance on the side of the mountain all white with snow, made by little bits of snow loosened. Introduce that and the stones leaping, rabbit-like, down, in my Sopha of Sods.*

19 October
Slanting pillars of light, like ladders up to Heaven, their base always a field of vivid green sunshine. Tomorrow my Birth Day, thirty-one years of age! O me! My very heart dies! This year has been one painful dream. I have done nothing! . . .

The general Fast Day, and all hearts anxious concerning the invasion. A grey day, windy, the vale, like a place in Faery, with the autumnal colours, the orange, the red-brown, the crimson, the light yellow, the yet lingering green, beeches and birches as [if] they were blossoming fire and gold! The sun in slanting pillars, or illuminated small parcels of mists, or single spots of softest greyish light, now racing, now slowly gliding, now stationary. The

*See the footnote on p.104.

mountains cloudy, the Lake has been a mirror so very clear that the water became almost invisible. Now it rolls in white breakers, like a sea, and the wind snatches up the water and drifts it like snow. Now the rain storm pelts against my study window!

O Sara, Sara why am I not happy! Why have I not an unencumbered heart! These beloved books still before me, this noble room, the very centre to which a whole world of beauty converges, the deep reservoir into which all these streams and currents of lovely Forms flow. My own mind so populous, so active, so full of noble schemes, so capable of realizing them; this heart so loving, so filled with noble affections. O Asra! Wherefore am I not happy! Why for years have I not enjoyed one pure and sincere pleasure! One full joy! One genuine delight that rings sharp to the beat of the finger! But still have said to the poetic feeling when it has awak'd in the heart – Go!

St John's Vale: 'the whole walk is
enchantment' (p.229)

– come tomorrow. All cracked and dull with base alloy . . .

Storm all night, the wind scourging and lashing the rain, with the pauses
of self-wearying violence, that returns to its work as if maddened by the
necessity of the pause. I, half-dozing, list'ning to the same, not without
solicitations of the poetic feeling . . .

October
In clear water over an uneven channel, as in the Greta behind my house, a
huge *boa convolvulus*, an enormous adder – at other times the waving sword
of fire of the Cherub over Paradise.

On St Herbert's Island [in Derwentwater] I saw a large spider with most
beautiful legs floating in the air on his back by a single thread which he was

spinning out, and still as he spun, heaving in the air, as if the air beneath were a pavement elastic to his strokes. From the top of a very high tree he had spun his line, at length reached the bottom, tied his thread round a piece of grass, and re-ascended, to spin another. A net to hang as a fisherman's sea net hangs in the sun and wind, to dry.

21 October

A drisling rain, heavy masses of shapeless vapour upon the mountains (O the perpetual forms of Borrowdale). Yet it is no unbroken tale of dull sadness. Slanting pillars travel across the Lake, at long intervals. The vaporous mass whitens, in large stains of light. On the lakeward ridge of that huge armchair, of Lodore, fell a gleam of softest light, that brought out the rich hues of the late autumn. The woody Castle Crag between me and Lodore is a rich flower-garden of colours: the brightest yellows with the deepest crimsons, and the infinite shades of brown and green, the *infinite* diversity of which blends the whole, so that the brighter colours seem as *colours* upon a ground, not coloured things.

Little wool-packs of white bright vapour rest on different summits and declivities. The vale is narrowed by the mist and cloud, yet through the wall of mist you can see into a bason of sunny light in Borrowdale. The birds are singing in the tender rain, as if it were the rain of April and the decaying foliage were flowers and blossoms. The pillar of smoke from the chimney rises up in the mist, and is just distinguishable from it. The mountain forms in the Gorge of Borrowdale consubstantiate with the mist and cloud even as the pillared smoke, a shade deeper and a determinate form. (Cleared up, the last thin fleeces on the bathed fells.)

23 October

To Grasmere yesterday, I returned today. O Thirlmere! let me somehow or other celebrate the world in thy mirror. Conceive all possible varieties of Form: fields, trees, naked or ferny crags, ravines behaired with birches, cottages, smoking chimneys, dazzling *wet places* of small rock-precipices (dazzling castle windows in the reflection) – all these within a divine outline in a mirror of three miles distinct vision! The distance closed in by the reflection of Raven Crag, which by every bemisting of the mirror by gentle motion became a perfect vast castle tower, the corners rounded and pillared or fluted. Each corner ending in (received into) a round pillar, round save that slice off by which it lies flat on (and connects) the two sides. All this in bright lightest yellow, yellow-green, green, crimson, and orange! The single birch trees hung like tresses of seaweed, the cliffs like organ pipes! When a little breath of air spread a delicious network over the Lake, all these colours seemed then to float on, like the reflections of the rising or setting sun.

24 October

I walked with Southey and Hazlitt through Borrowdale into Watendlath, and so home to a late dinner. Of course it was to me a mere walk; for I must be alone, if either my imagination or heart are to be excited or enriched. Yet even so I worshipped with deep feeling the grand outline and perpetual Forms that are the guardians of Borrowdale, and the presiding majesty, yea, the very soul of Keswick. The birches were in all their pride of gold and orange. The lake was very full of foam, the late great flood having not yet wholly retired. I thought still more than before that if the lake had pushed up into Borrowdale, as far as the Bowder Stone, and if Borrowdale were still better wooded, it would be distinguished from the Trossachs chiefly by its continuity of massiveness. Though there is one vast crag to the left, as you go up Borrowdale, complete Trossachs, all the dislocation and multitude of outjuttings and precipices – but this had only the *Tale* of wood, no more! On the whole, and as a whole, it is superior to the Trossachs, the view of the vale of Keswick being greatly superior to the banks of Loch Katrine, and the lovely round vale of Borrowdale with its exquisite combination of nigh and distant mountains so incomparably finer than the vale and Loch Achray.

I ascended in a wrong place, but it led me to some glorious fantastic rocks – the mitre, the huge pyramid, and Peak Fantastic, with a lower rock to the right of it. Between which two, in a narrow defile I went, having in this toilsome climb two most singular and noble views of the lake and vale of Keswick. A whole flight of small birds flung themselves down in a gale of wind into Borrowdale like a *shoot* of stones. Each bird seemed to dart onward by projection, and to descend by its own lifelessness and weight. What was the name of that most vivid of all vivid green mosses by the side of the falling water, as we clomb down into Watendlath? That red moss too, and that blood-red fungus? The lake of Watendlath has hitherto always appeared of inferior impressiveness to me. It is so bare and pondish and swampy; the mountains at its head would be better in a picture than they look in nature, for the forms and combinations are fine, but they want something or other in colour and distance to make them *Satisfiers*. Neither do the crags on each side of us as we go by the riverside till we have passed the bridge impress me so deeply as they seem to have done many. But from the Bridge and all the rest of the way down to Baragh [Barrow] House, O

'O Thirlmere!' (p.232)

what is there on Earth that can better deserve the name of Divine? There should be some mark, some cross or heap of stones to direct the traveller to turn off to his left, fifteen or twenty yards through the coppice, about a hundred yards or so before he comes to the road-view of the Lake of Keswick. Twenty yards through this open coppice brings him suddenly to the edge of a finely wooded precipice, with Lodore, the bridge, the road seen in three different distances, so very beautiful – the Lake of Keswick and Bassenthwaite. The height, from the extreme steepness and direct plumb-down look into the Lake, seems vast. The breezes rush in pencil brushes

over it. You look down on everything and everything spreads in consequence, broad and long and vast! This is – I have no hesitation in saying it –
the best, every way the best and most impressive view in all the Lake
Country – why not in all the island?

Bowder Stone, the Stone under Dumbarton Rock, and the Bull Stone in
the foot of Glenfalloch – the three great stones of the island. Of these,
Bowder is the least, by far. How could Wordsworth think otherwise?

Go and build up a pile of three [stones] by that coppice. Measure the
strides from the bridge where the water rushes down a rock in no mean
cataract if the rains shall have swollen the river, and the bridge itself hides a
small cataract . . . Write a poem, thus beginning – 'From the Bridge' etc.
Repeat such a song, of Milton, or Homer – how many lines, I must find out,
may be recited during a moderate healthy man's walk from the bridge
thither . . . There turn in and then describe the scene. O surely I might
make a noble poem of all my youth nay *of all my life*. One section on plants
and flowers, my passion for them, always deadened by their learned names.
Yet ever to note those that have and may hereafter affect me.

25 October
The moon setting over the mountain pale. The sky very dim and marbled,
or water-stained as blue marine canopy. In the blue interspaces the stars all
dim and lustreless. Until I looked steadily at them, *one* only of all the stars
twinkled. The water between me and it, and the few house roofs are bright.
The water is the only sound. The moon is more than half a moon. It sank to
a rude [segment], then to a crescent, its bow stiff and imperfect. Still
keeping this shape, it thinned and thinned and thinned, till *once* it became a
star, at its vanishing. But immediately after sent up a *throb* of light in its
former shape and dimension. And so for several seconds it throbbed and
heaved, a soft boiling up or restlessness of fluid in carrying.

Now all is alike through the vale, the vast ellipse of mountain suffused
with dim hoariness, and the sky where white and where blue, still dim. Save
only that the whole range of mountains behind which the moon sate,
namely from Bonitas [Heavitas] under Grisedale Pike to Rowling End
under Causey Pike, are blacker and more definite than the rest, the white
cloud-stains, or cloud-inlays, brighter, the blue more genuinely blue. It
wants fifteen minutes of one o'clock [a.m.].

27 October
Forty minutes past one o'clock. A perfect calm. Now and then a breeze
shakes the heads of the two poplars and disturbs the murmurs of the

moonlit Greta that, in almost a direct line from the moon to me, is all silver – motion and wrinkle and light. Under the arch of the bridge a wave ever and anon leaps up in light. The evergreens are bright under my window. The moon now hangs midway over Cowdale [Coledale] Halse. In a line, and resting on each of the divergent legs of its triangle, a fish-head-shaped cloud, the whole area of the triangle blue sky. But above the cloud and in the interspaces between it and the moon, little cloudlets, scarcely larger than large stars.

Wrinkles [on the Greta], long roundish floating braids of hair, making single hairs distinguishable as they wanton on some regular breeze. Black smooth space of shade, silver mirror, gleaming of moonlit reeds beyond. As the moon sets the water from silver becomes a rich yellow. Sadly do I need to have my imagination enriched with appropriate images for shapes – read architecture and ichthyology.

The moon sets fifteen minutes past two, just behind the point between Grisedale Pike and Cowdale Halse. As it entered the fish's head (the body and tail stretch atop the mountains down to Bassenthwaite), the moon was so barred and cross-barred, over its whole face, as I never before saw. And I observed that it became quite a shapeless, or perhaps unshapely, lump in consequence. (The Greta now only a grey gleamer!) But before the moon reached the hill, there was a space of blue, only half its own length, and so it emerged, an half in brightness. So it sank, in thinner and thinner strips of light, till just at the last it had a strong likeness of a sheep on the mountain, head and all! No soft ebullience of light after its setting; but the space above the clouds looked bluer and gladder, as before. The moon will be at its full Saturday or Sunday night.

28 October

Oct. 27, I sate for my picture. Heard from Southey the Institution of the Jesuits, during which some interesting idea occurred to me, and has escaped. I made out, however, the whole business of the Origin of Evil satisfactorily to my own mind, and forced Hazlitt to confess that the metaphysical argument reduced itself to this: [2½ pages of argument follow].

This I wrote on Friday morning [28th], forty minutes past three o'clock. The sky covered in one cloud, that yet lies in dark and light shades, and though one smooth cloud, by the dark colour it appears to be *steppy*. A sad night. Went to bed after tea and in about two hours absolutely summoned the whole household to me by my screams, from all the chambers. And I continued screaming even after Mrs Coleridge was sitting and speaking to me! O me! O me!

Noon. Walked with Southey up the Greta, to the Theatre of Wood with the *Cowl* of green field on its top, opposite the Sopha of Sods, for the last time unless the woodmen let other leaves come out next Spring before they begin their devastation.

29 October

Sat. morn. Three o'clock. The moon hangs high over Greta, and the bridge, on the first step of her descent and three hours at least from the mountain behind which she is to sink. Nearly full, not a cloud in Heaven, the sky deep sable blue, the stars many and white in the height of the sky, but above, around and beneath the moon, not a star; she is starless as the sun. Yet there is no gleam, much less silver whiteness, on the lake: simply it is easily seen. Even the Greta strait in an oblique line is not silver-bright or anywhere brilliant; but rather the gleam of some baser composition imitating silver. It is the grey brightness like the colour of an ash grove in keenest December moonlight. The mountains are dark, low, all compact together, quiet, silent, asleep. The white houses are bright throughout the vale, and the evergreens in the garden. The only sound is the murmur of the Greta, perpetual Voice of the Vale.

31 October

The full moon glided behind a black cloud, and what then? and who cared? It was past 7 o'clock in the morning. There is a small cloud in the East, not larger than the moon and ten times brighter than she! So passes Night and all her favours vanish in our minds, ungrateful!

Between seven and eight the sun rises behind Helvellyn, white, glowing like a globe of iron in white heat, restless and as it stands just one finger's breadth above the mountain, [going] round rapidly, like a wheel that circumvolves so rapidly that you see the motion only, not the turns. The moon full, now right opposite hanging directly above Barugh [Barrow] . . . has hid self in a cloud, that a few minutes ago was *brassy bright*, how far brighter than the moon that entered it, but now is pale and wan before the rising intensity.

See! The cloud parts, the moon comes out and fills the interspaces, just touching the cloud above and below and of the same colour with the cloud. How sharp lined the shadows are on Skiddaw, a cloud creeping and never getting away, in shape and size like a tortoise, on its summit. A little below the sharp shadow cuts it off, a section from the mountain. On the opposite mountains, Grisedale etc., the shadows are loose and treelike. The sun (I turned again to it) itself is overpowered in the great bason of tempestuous light, of glowing whiteness, which it has circumfused. I looked steadily, I recovered the sun, still looked, till all that glowing whiteness became a beautiful crimson, then turned round to the pale moon and it became all at once a rich purple to my eye. The church, the vale – all purple. Now as I sit by the lime heap to write it down, a spot of the size of a shilling, of the richest and most delicate yellow, has followed my pencil all down the white paper, fainter and faint and yet it is still under it even now, only very faint.

The moon will set on the Bassenthwaite side of Barugh. I have been looking again at the sun. Again, after the pink and the purple, this yellow spot has come. O how very rich! and lo! I give it to the moon and still more to all the sky above and below it. Only there it is chrysolite, yellow green; on the paper it is topaz. How long the yellow green lasts: I looked at the moon more than five minutes, and it continued in all its strength, a yellow green parallelogram.

The moon set at the lowest part of Wythop, just behind Sir F. Vane's three-cornered *shave* out of the wood [Smithy Green]. As it approached near the mountain, it was with the utmost straining of the eye that I could discern it and before it reached the mountain, it vanished completely by its own dimness. Only I could know it by a dim difference of tint in the sky where it was.

2 November

Wednesday morning, twenty minutes past two o'clock. The voice of the Greta, and the cock crowing. The voice seems to grow, like a flower, on or about the water beyond the bridge, while the cock crowing is nowhere particular: it is any place I imagine and do not distinctly see. A most remarkable sky! The moon, now waned to a perfect ostrich's egg, hangs over our house almost; only so much beyond it, garden-ward, that I can see it, holding my head out of the smaller study window. The sky is covered with whitish dingy *cloudage*, thin dingiest scud close under the moon, and one side of it moving, all else moveless. But there are two great breaks of blue sky – the one, stretching over our house and away toward Castlerigg, is speckled and blotched with white cloud; the other hangs over the road, in the shape of a [elongated lozenge] I do not know what to call. This is unspeckled, all blue, three stars in it; more in the former break, all un-moving. The water leaden white, even as the grey gleam of water is in latest twilight. Now while I have been writing this and gazing between whiles (it is forty minutes past two) the break over the road is swallowed up, and the stars gone; the break over the house is narrowed into a rude circle and on the edge of its circumference one very bright star. See! already the white

William Hazlitt

mass thinning at its edge *fights* with its brilliance. See! it has bedimmed it. And now it is gone and the moon is gone. The cock-crowing too has ceased. The Greta sounds on, for ever. But I hear only the ticking of my watch, in the pen-place of my writing desk, and the far lower note of the noise of the fire. Perpetual, yet seeming uncertain, it is the low voice of quiet change, of Destruction doing its work by little and little.

'Fancy in Nubibus' or *'The Poet in the Clouds'*

> Oh, it is pleasant, with a heart at ease,
> Just after sunset, or by moonlight skies,
> To make the shifting clouds be what you please,
> Or let the easily persuaded eyes
> Own each quaint likeness issuing from the mould
> Of a friend's fancy; or with head bent low
> And cheek aslant see rivers flow of gold
> 'Twixt crimson banks; and then, a traveller, go
> From mount to mount through Cloudland, gorgeous land!

5 November

From half past six to eight o'clock, bonfires in the town. General Peche's white house resplendent, but on Swinside and Latrigg the whinns set on fire. Swinside represented a city – Bath approached at night, and when the fire grew duller, a street in London. I almost fancied the house doors and shop windows, each under its own lamp. But Latrigg scarcely permitted us to look at Swinside. Women and children and the little infant Sara, we all gazed at Latrigg, so great and so intense the conflagration, that I could read a part of a letter a few yards from our front door. The sky, low hung with rainy clouds that actually drizzled over Latrigg and even all over our house, reflected the fire in a bright salmon colour, while the vale and the church inclusive was of that most interesting light, which often lies on the fields in the very earliest dawn of a Winter morning – or at midnight under a setting half moon!

6 November

Walked with Southey to Braithwaite. Interesting lagune in the river not far from Mr Smith's at How. Weeds forming three beautiful clouds in the water among weeds of distinct vegetable character. An appearance of down, jelly, and cloud combined – most like the cloud of precipitation in some chemical decomposition. The colour olive-green. Indisposed in my bowels. Observe that this feeling of bowel-uncomfortableness etc., is combined with *Fear*, with *tender* thoughts, tender and serious recollections; and if I were with one whom my soul loved, it would rather increase than decrease my happiness. I had a violent motion (in the field under an oak by a fence with the brook on the other side). About three minutes after, having got over a petty fence from the field into the turnpike road, I found myself quite a coward, till the thought awakened and scouted the feeling. The rest of the walk I was deeply impressed by the faith, that my illness would not materially diminish my happiness if I were Housemate with Love.

9 November

Forty-five minutes past six. The town with lighted windows and noise of *clogged* passengers in the streets, sound of unseen river. Mountains scarcely perceivable except by eyes long used to them, and supported by the images of memory flowing in on the impulses of immediate impression. The sky black cloud, two or three dim untwinkling stars, like full stops on damp paper, and large stains and spreads of sullen white, like a tunic of white wool seen here and there through a torn and tattered cloak of black. Whence do these stains of white proceed, all over the sky so long after sunset and, from their indifference of place in the sky, seemingly unaffected by the West?

10 November

Half past two o'clock [a.m.]. Awoke after long struggles and with faint screaming from a persecuting dream . . . Drizzle. The sky uncouthly marbled with white vapours and large black clouds, their surface of a fine woolly grain: but in the height and key-stone of the arch a round space of sky with dim watery stars, like a friar's crown . . .

A quarter after seven [p.m.]. The sky covered with stars; the wind up; right opposite my window . . . an enormous black cloud exactly in the shape of an egg. This, the only cloud in the sky, impressed me with a daemoniacal grandeur. O for a change in the weather!

11 November

The barometer for the last three days portentously low, and I not only frenzied with rheumatic tortures, now in the right jaw, teeth, face, eye, forehead, and now in the left, but wandering about unable to sit or lie, and miserable when in motion, from a *stifling asthmatic* flatulence. This latter calamity, and all like it, seem to be *in* one, to be *the state* of one's sum total; while the former tortures seem like cruel enemies out of us and attacking and tormenting us. I almost think, I should prefer the stone to asthma.

The gorge of Watendlath

13 November

Sunday morning, half past two. The sky in upon Grisedale Pike and onward to Wythop fells floored with *flat* smooth dark or dingy clouds, elsewhere starry. The seven stars and all the rest in the height of the heaven bedimmed, those on the descent bright and frosty. The river has a loud voice, self-biographer of today's rains and thunder showers. The owls are silent – they have been very musical. All weathers on Saturday the 12th: storm and frost, sunshine, rain, hail, thunder, lightning and what not! I, God be praised! though sleepless, am marvellously better, and take it for granted that the barometer has risen.

20 November

O after what a day of distempered sleeps – out of which I woke, all sense of time and circumstance utterly lost – of fever, rheumatic pain and loads of stomach-sickness, I get up. Am calm, like one lownded.

As I lifted up the sash and looked out at the sky, the first minute I thought it all dark, a starless sky. The wind, all the summer swell lost and the winter hollowness and whistle not yet come, mixed its sea-like solemn roars with the rustle from the yet remaining half-dry leaves on all the trees. But I looked again at the sky, and there were many stars, so dim and *dingy* that they might have put into Paracelsus's* fancy his whim of the *astra tenebricosa* [dark stars], that radiated cold and darkness, with hollow rays, tube-like as hairs, ensheathing the rays of light and heat, and so producing cold and darkness.

Morning: cold rain in the valley, which is snow upon the mountains.

21 November

. . . What is a mountain else but a great flat picture – trees, houses, crags, beasts, etc. – placed by Nature on an easel? . . . It fills the mind with *distinct* images without any painful effort to acquire them and joins therefore all the requisites of pleasure: ease, sufficiency, and vividness . . .

The view of an extensive plain, all cultivated, from a high mountain, would be merely an amusing object – a curiosity, a map, a picture, a model – were it not for the imposingness of the situation from which we view it, the feelings possibly worked on by the air, etc. Hence the advantage of sea, and lake in these views: they take off the littleness and picturishness, the camera obscura effect.

*Swiss physician and philosopher, died 1541.

. . . From the distance in mountain countries being so distinct, you have a continual inducement to look forward to the distance, whereas in flat countries you look just before you or on each side of you, at the turn in the road or the flowers in the hedge. Now there certainly is an intellectual movement connected with looking forward, a feeling of hope, a stirring and inquietude of fancy. To look down upon, to comprehend, to be above, to look forward to, are all metaphors that shew in the original feeling a resemblance to the moral meaning christened hereafter. . .

23 November
I went to the window, to empty my urine-pot, and wondered at the simple grandeur of the view. 1. Darkness only, and not utter black undistin-guishableness 2. The grey-blue steely glimmer of the Greta, and the lake 3. The black yet form-preserving mountains 4. The sky, moon-whitened there, cloud-blackened here, and yet, with all its gloominess and sullenness, forming a contrast with the simplicity of the landscape beneath.

29 November
Carpets of weeds or chopped reeds, which the waves on the shore lift and belly up without breaking, as an under-door wind lifts up a loose carpet.

The beggar and her children asleep on the *dry* torrent, by a slender ash which had been sheltered by a huge rock in the middle of the stream. That ash [persists] in Autumn, Spring, and Winter fury, shaken all its leaves by the water-blast, and its very trunk by the stray cataractlings, that just touch and lave its roots. But now they are all asleep, on the dry stones, lulled by the noise of the water that crept unseen under the dusty stones.

The torrent opposite to the Cherry Tree, out of Harrop Tarn, and a few hundred yards lakeward from the Rock of Seats and Thrones with mossy cushions: this torrent, I have repeatedly observed, is *the loudest* in the whole Country.*

December
To analyse the pleasure received from gates, in corners of fields, at twilight. *Vide* Wordsworth, 'Evening Walk': 'The sound of closing gate across the water borne'.

Three and nearly four days' work for a stout woman, a stout girl, and a feeble old woman: one stone of wool, for which they get £0 2s 10d. Spinning

*Dobb Ghyll, flowing into the south-west end of Thirlmere. The Cherry Tree was an inn, submerged when the level of the lake was raised.

Coleridge in 1804

The Bowder Stone in Borrowdale

from seven in the morning to nine at night, of course using coal and candle, they can do it in three days. But then they have to reel it and carry it to Collarth Bridge [Colwith in Langdale], at least five miles. O women are hardly off!

The common fern fades into an orange, the stone fern into a *rich* brown.

December
When in a state of pleasureable and balmy quietness I feel my cheek and temple on the nicely made up pillow in *caelibre toro meo* [my single bed] – the fire-gleam on my dear books that fill up one whole side from ceiling to floor

of my tall study – and winds, perhaps, are driving the rain, or whistling in the frost, at my blessed window, whence I see Borrowdale, the Lake, Newlands – wood, water, mountains, omniform beauty – O then as I first sink on the pillow, [it is] as if sleep had a material *realm*, as if I was entering that region and realized Faery Land of sleep – O then what visions have I had, what dreams. The Bark, the Sea, all the shapes and sounds and adventures made up of the Stuff of Sleep and Dreams, and yet my Reason at the Rudder. O what visions (breasts), as if my cheek and temple were lying on me gale o' mast on [transliterated Greek: large breasted] – Seele meines Lebens! [soul of my life] and I sink down the waters, through seas and seas – yet warm, yet a Spirit.

31 December

Visited Green Head Gill with W. Wordsworth. . . Butterlip How with its patches of hair, its mole-tufts, on its shaven green head, under the rough mountains. . .

Chopt-hay looking *olla* of all the vegetation of a wild mountain: moss, buds, stiff grass, etc., perfectly chopt lying upon the unmelted snow by the brink of the steep sike [stream], in a beautiful network in the lower part, carpeting the higher.

The eye – let it be a spectrum in my feverous brain! The connection by intakes* of the smooth bowling-green vale with the steep mountain, and of the sides of the mountain with its craggy castle-ruin-like top. Road between walls, the lake [Grasmere] with three walls rising each above the other, the bridge with two arches, the smoke a perfect pillar, the whole river from the force to the quiet lake, on this blessed calming day. Sitting on the very sheepfold, dear William read to me his divine poem, 'Michael'.†

The two apparition-birch-trees, close together, abreast, with the *chocolate mist* of winter branches and tresses around and above the silver body, by the side of the steep steep noisy syke, with two sheep-tracks enclosing an irregular oval area – picture of a robe round a spirit.

The waterfall at the head of the vale, white, steadfast, silent from distance – the river belonging to it, smooth, full, silent – the lake into which it empties also silent – yet the noise of waters everywhere. Something distant, something near, 'tis far off, and yet everywhere. The pillar of smoke, the

*Stone walled hillside fields 'taken' from the moorland.
†The poem ends

'. . . the remains
Of the unfinished sheepfold may be seen
Beside the boisterous brook of Greenhead Ghyll.'

smooth winter fields, the *indistinct* shadows in the lake are all eloquent of silence.

January 1804
The spring, or well-spring, under the rock; bowl on it brown, flesh-like, or jelly-flesh. Oakleaves a sober silver gray on their backs. Soothing sound of drops, and the breezy sun-shadows thereby on the pale green house-leeky [stonecrop] weeds that cloathed the one steep bank.

Remember to describe water (apparition – tadpoles) pulsating, really gliding down, under ice. Water – black, under ice – silver.

4 January
In the highest and outermost of Grasmere Wordsworth read to me the second part of his divine Self-biography [the *Prelude*].

A boy sucking an icicle with what affectionate remembrance of a lollipop.

Horsedung echoing to the merry foot-traveller on a frosty morning.

5 January
Snow on the ground snatched up by the wind that, full of frosty particles, seemed to rush from the valley up the mountain. It galloped transversely from the middlemost of the mountains to their very top and along their summits, like a vast ghost cavalry scouring a country. Item, I distinctly and repeatedly saw the wind raise up from the mountain a true genuine cloud of snow, that rose high (seemingly to the eye, but not really, as high as the highest clouds). It sailed along, a true genuine large white cloud with all the form and varied outline of a cloud. This in several instances dropped again, snow at second hand, and often in the sun resembled a shower of diamond spearlets.

6 January
I observed the beautiful effects of *drifted snow* upon the mountains: the divine tone of colour from the top of the mountain downward, from the powderiness and grass, a rich olive green warmed with a little brown and in this way harmonious and combined by insensible gradation with the white. The drifting took away all the monotony of snow; and the whole vale of Grasmere seen from the Terrace Wall in Easedale, called Lankrigg, was as varied, perhaps more so, than even in the pomp of Autumn. . .

On returning we prolonged our walk on to Rydal, saw two quite per- pendicular black rocks, smooth as steep, windowed with ice, resembling cylinders of cut and bulbous glass frozen together into one rough plate. Under this glided in pulses the innumerable tadpoles, like one's nervous creepings down one's limbs, back and thighs.

9 January
Monday morning, in the dark with my eyes shut, a loud thaw wind. Derwent asleep in the other bed, God love little dear Heart, and Dorothy in the parlour, O dear Dorothy – and O dear Sara Hutchinson.

Shadows in snow weather on the Lake I have observed indistinct, just like Derwent's face when the wanton has veiled it in the thin white window curtain in a pretty strong light, the white calico strained tight to his face.

11 January
Thaw. Half the lake bright, the other half breezey-dull, the snow-zebraed mountain in the *reflection*, all *bright*. The gap between Seat Sandal and Fairfield a beautiful upright blue *triangle* in the water with, as I thought, six or seven slips of clouds most beautifully coloured and as beautifully disposed. I looked at the gap itself and could not perceive any corresponding clouds. Noticed it to William, who immediately discovered and made me perceive that they were not clouds, but flakes of ice on the hither shore close by.

14 January
Left Grasmere, Saturday noon, on foot. Arrived at Kendal after a sweltring walk through heavy hot air and the latter half of the journey through drizzle, at 5 o'clock in the evening – nineteen [sixteen] miles in five hours, and I rested once to lunch.

Images of calmness on Rydal Lake; fresh delves in the slate quarry I *mistook* for smoke in the reflection. An islet stone, at the bottom of the Lake, the reflection so bright as to be heaved up out of the water. The stone and its reflection looked so compleatly one, that Wordsworth remained for more than five minutes trying to explain why that stone had no reflection, and at last found it out by me. The shore, and green field, a hill bank below that stone, with trees and rock, forming one brilliant picture without was such, that look at the reflection and you annihilated the water. It is all one piece of bright land. Just half wink your eyes and look at the land, it is then *all* under water, or with that glossy unreality which a prospect has, when seen through smoke.

Epilogue

COLERIDGE KEPT HIS FRESHNESS OF OBSERVATION ON THE VOYAGE out to Malta, recording with the glittering eye of his own Ancient Mariner shipboard life, a call at Gibraltar, and the moods of the sea. Once in Malta, that small stony island, the opportunities for such description were less and he turned in upon himself and his books. An occasional lifting of the spirits allowed him to revel in the new flora and fauna:

'Lizards glide across the sunny walk like shooting stars, green, grey, speckled. Exquisite grace in motion, all the delicacy of the serpent and a certain dignity from even just the increasing erectness of it to its hind paws. Dragon-flies purple and – most common – a deep crimson. Not so long in the *sheath* as our finest ones in England. Butterflies, glorious ones, but their flight unwieldy. I could catch them with ease. The lizard's motion, and the dragonfly's – both darting and angular, yet how different. The dragonfly's always and naturally angular, the lizard's only by choice. This is Friday, July 13th [1804] at St Antonio's. Yesterday and today I seem to *live*. O Sara! – yes I could be happy here with *you*! Let me write to her today. Lizard, green with bright gold spots all over – firmness of its *stand-like* feet, when the *life* of the *threddy* toes makes them both seem and be so firm, so solid, yet so very, very supple. One pretty fellow whom I had fascinated by stopping and gazing at him as he lay in a thick network of sun and shade . . . looked up half-watching, half-imploring. At length, taking advantage of a brisk breeze that made all the network dance and toss, he darted off as if an Angel of Nature had spoken in the breeze, "Go, I'll take care, he shall not hurt you." I should like, if I could know what they eat, or if they eat bread, to tame one.'

He noticed that the pinks which people grew in Malta and Sicily were 'never propped up, but are suffered to hang down and are put in pots, etc., on balconies and walls, so as to give them play and room.'

In the autumn of 1804, when he was touring Sicily, there were moments when the pages of the Notebooks became filled once more with landscape and nature: 'a green frog sticking to a stalk like an old bigot at his prayers – his hands up and his under-jaw membrane trembling . . .' But when he left Malta for Italy a year later the changes of scene made little impact, or little that he chose to record, though he did set down one horrid incident in March 1806:

'To remember the fellow in the market at Rome, twisting the necks of near 200 goldfinches, one after another, leaving them fluttering and gasping, he meantime chit-chatting with a neighbour stallman, throwing his head about, and sometimes using the neck-twisting gesture in help of his oratory – either twisting them phlegmatically, his hands near his belly – sometimes violently, both hands thrown out from him; but never intermitting it.'

There was to be no renewal of Coleridge the scenic and natural observer on his return to England in August 1806, but luckily, in October 1807, when in the West Country, he showed a flash of his former self, which allows this final image to be one of delight rather than disgust:

'Yesterday I saw seven or eight water wagtails following a feeding horse in the pasture, fluttering about and hopping close by his hooves, under his belly, and even so as often to tickle his nostrils with their pert tails. The horse shortens the grass and they get the insects.'

The salient facts of Coleridge's life from 1804 are set out to complete the record given in the earlier linking passages. He acted as Secretary to the High Commissioner of Malta until September 1805, then wintered in Naples before moving on to Rome and Florence. His intention to live by journalism and lecturing when back in London did not survive Wordsworth's pressing invitation to stay at a house of Sir George Beaumont's at Coleorton in Leicestershire, especially since Sara Hutchinson was to be there too. (Beaumont was a patron of the painters Girtin and Constable, as well as of Coleridge and Wordsworth.) Coleridge left Coleorton frustrated, in June 1807, and returned to his West Country haunts and friends. In January 1808 he started giving a course of lectures at the Royal Institution in London and this method of reaching an audience played a large part in his life thereafter. His plans for launching a new journal, *The Friend*, were interrupted by another invitation from Wordsworth, this time to join his family and Sara Hutchinson at Allen Bank in Grasmere. Coleridge managed to issue a regular run of *The Friend* from September 1809 to March 1810 in spite of the difficulties of production and distribution from the Lakes. Sara Hutchinson acted as his assistant and nurse, but no more. Eventually she left, exhausted by the demands made on her. Increasing debts closed *The Friend* and Coleridge went to London. Shortly after, he and Wordsworth quarrelled as a result of some of Wordsworth's criticisms of his behaviour being repeated to him by an indiscreet friend.

Coleridge became chief writer for Daniel Stuart's new paper *The Courier* and gave the first of a series of ground-breaking lectures on Shakespeare. In 1813 a reworked version of his play, first written in 1797, was a success at Drury Lane, with a change of name from *Osirio* to *Remorse*. But all the time his addiction and fits of depression were worsening. The nadir was reached at Bath in December 1813 when he nearly killed himself with an overdose. For the first time he admitted his addiction, and started receiving proper medical supervision for it.

In 1815 he revived and began writing the *Biographia Literaria*: Biographical Sketches of my Literary Life and Opinions. In 1816 he moved to the household of Dr James Gillman in Highgate where he was to live for the rest of his life. In May 1816 *Christabel and Other Poems*, which included 'Kubla Khan', was published by John Murray, at the urging of Lord Byron. His collected poems, under the title *Sybilline Leaves*, and the *Biographia Literaria* appeared in 1817. A revised and enlarged edition of *The Friend* was published in three volumes in 1818. For his last decade, he was enthroned as the Sage of Highgate, where the best and brightest came to sit at his feet and be bathed in the unceasing flow of his discourse. *Aids to Reflection* appeared in 1824 and was to have a profound influence on the Christian Socialist movement within the Church of England. He occasionally met Sara Hutchinson socially in London, and was visited by his wife and their daughter. Their son Hartley, alas, became a victim of opium himself. In 1828 Coleridge went on a short tour to Germany with Wordsworth and his daughter Dora. His last book appeared in 1830, *On the Constitution of Church and State*, with its concept of the 'Clerisy' – the literati, the cultivated among the professional classes – as the vital element within a country. Coleridge died of a heart attack in July 1834.

Index